JESUS AND

'Gospel' initially referred to oral proclamation concerning Jesus Christ, but was later used to refer to four written accounts of the life of Jesus. How did this happen? Here, distinguished scholar Graham Stanton uses new evidence and fresh perspectives to tackle this controversial question. He insists that in the early post-Easter period, the Gospel of Jesus Christ was heard against the backdrop of a rival set of 'gospels' concerning the Roman emperors. In later chapters Stanton examines the earliest criticisms of Jesus and of claims concerning his resurrection. Finally, he discusses the early Christian addiction to the codex (book) format as opposed to the ubiquitous roll, and undermines the view that early copies of the gospels were viewed as downmarket handbooks of an inward-looking sect. With half the material previously unpublished and the rest carefully gathered from sources difficult to access, this is a timely study with broad appeal.

Graham Stanton is Lady Margaret's Professor of Divinity, University of Cambridge, and a Fellow of Fitzwilliam College. His publications include *Gospel Truth? New Light on Jesus and the Gospels* (1995), *A Gospel for a New People: Studies in Matthew* (1992), *The Gospels and Jesus* (1989: revised and expanded 2002) and *Jesus of Nazareth in New Testament Preaching* (1974).

JESUS AND GOSPEL

GRAHAM N. STANTON

CAMBRIDGE
UNIVERSITY PRESS

PUBLISHED BY THE PRESS SYNDICATE OF THE UNIVERSITY OF CAMBRIDGE
The Pitt Building, Trumpington Street, Cambridge, United Kingdom

CAMBRIDGE UNIVERSITY PRESS
The Edinburgh Building, Cambridge, CB2 2RU, UK
40 West 20th Street, New York, NY 10011-4211, USA
477 Williamstown Road, Port Melbourne, VIC 3207, Australia
Ruiz de Alarcón 13, 28014 Madrid, Spain
Dock House, The Waterfront, Cape Town 8001, South Africa

http://www.cambridge.org

First published 2004

Printed in the United Kingdom at the University Press, Cambridge

Typeface Adobe Garamond 11/12.5 pt   *System* LATEX 2$_\varepsilon$ [TB]

A catalogue record for this book is available from the British Library

ISBN 0 521 81032 9 hardback
ISBN 0 521 00802 6 paperback

Dedicated to Professor C. F. D. Moule

Contents

Preface

The completion of a book is a time for stock-taking. Why have I written on this topic, and not another? How have I managed to complete it, given the ever-growing demands teaching and administrative duties make on the time of an academic?

The topics explored in this book are at the very centre of the concerns of anyone interested in earliest Christianity and, indeed, in Christian theology. I have tried to approach them from fresh angles and, where possible, in the light of new evidence. So I have spread my net more widely than is often the case. The questions discussed have captured my interest for a variety of reasons. In some cases I think that I have found new paths through well-traversed territory. In others, I have become dissatisfied with the standard answers.

Chapter 2, 'Jesus and Gospel', is a considerably extended version of the Inaugural Lecture I gave as Lady Margaret's Professor of Divinity in the University of Cambridge on 27 April 2000. In my introductory remarks I referred to the debt I owe to my two predecessors in the Cambridge Chair, Professors C. F. D. Moule and Morna Hooker, who were both present.

An earlier version of Chapter 5, 'The Law of Christ and the Gospel', was one of eighteen seminar papers given as part of the celebrations of 500th anniversary of the establishment of the Lady Margaret's Professorship in 1502. The seminar papers attempted to encourage dialogue between Biblical scholars and theologians; they have now been published as *Reading Texts, Seeking Wisdom: Scripture and Theology*, ed. David F. Ford and Graham Stanton (London: SCM, 2003). Two lectures on the history of the Professorship were given as the centrepiece of the celebrations; they are included in Patrick Collinson, Richard Rex, and Graham Stanton, *Lady Margaret Beaufort and her Professors of Divinity at Cambridge* (Cambridge: Cambridge University Press, 2003).

Several of the other chapters are revised and extended versions of invited lectures or seminar papers. The original settings have been diverse:

universities and colleges in New Zealand, Australia, Singapore, Canada, the USA, Finland, France, and the Netherlands, as well as in the United Kingdom. I am grateful for the initial invitations and the warm hospitality received. Discussion following the lectures and seminars has often been encouraging. Sometimes new lines of inquiry have been suggested, and now and again I have been forced to abandon false trails.

How have I managed to complete this book? I could not have done so without the keen interest of my colleagues in Cambridge and earlier at King's College London. They have given me far more support and advice than they are aware of. They have known when not to ask about progress, and have often found ways of helping me to find time to press ahead. Only a small number of my many doctoral students have been working with me in the general field discussed in this book. But their enthusiasm for our discipline, their lively questions, and their own promising scholarly work have been a constant delight. My wife's support has been unflagging; I hope that I have not taken it for granted.

This book is dedicated to Professor C. F. D. Moule, the supervisor of my doctoral research nearly forty years ago. His example of scholarly rigour and his unswerving Christian commitment have meant more to me than I can express. At ninety-five, he writes astute reviews for learned journals, and by correspondence continues a ministry of encouragement to his many friends, former colleagues and students.

Abbreviations

ANRW	*Aufstieg und Niedergang der römischen Welt*, ed. H. Temporini and W. Haase (Berlin, 1972–).
BDAG	*A Greek–English Lexicon of the New Testament and Other Early Christian Literature*, 3rd edn. revised and ed. F. W. Danker (Chicago and London: University of Chicago Press, 2000).
BJRL	*Bulletin of the John Rylands Library University of Manchester*
CBQ	*Catholic Biblical Quarterly*
CTQ	*Concordia Theological Quarterly*
E. tr.	English translation
EKK	Evangelisch-katholischer Kommentar zum NT
ETL	*Ephemerides theologicae lovanienses*
ExT	*Expository Times*
FS	*Festschrift*
ICC	International Critical Commentary
JBL	*Journal of Biblical Literature*
JSNT	*Journal for the Study of the New Testament*
JTS	*Journal of Theological Studies*
LCL	Loeb Classical Library (Cambridge, Mass.: Harvard University Press)
NovT	*Novum Testamentum*
NTS	*New Testament Studies*
REB	Revised English Bible (1989)
RSR	*Religious Studies Review*
SC	*Second Century*
SJT	*Scottish Journal of Theology*
ST	*Studia Theologica*
TB	*Tyndale Bulletin*

TDNT	*Theological Dictionary of the New Testament* (Grand Rapids: Eerdmans, E. tr., 1964–76)
TS	*Theological Studies*
Vig. Chr.	*Vigiliae Christianae*
WUNT	Wissenschaftliche Untersuchungen zum Neuen Testament
ZPE	*Zeitschrift für Papyrologie und Epigraphik*

CHAPTER I

Introduction

The main lines of inquiry pursued in this book are nearly all foreshadowed in the lengthy, wide-ranging Chapter 2, 'Jesus and Gospel'. Here I explore the origin and the varied meanings of the 'gospel' word group all the way from its use by Jesus to refer to his own proclamation to its use as the title of a 'book' containing an account of the words and deeds of Jesus.

Although the term 'gospel' is as prominent in Christian vocabulary today as it ever has been, there have been very few detailed studies in English of the word group. It is difficult to account for the silence. Part of the answer may lie in the onslaught James Barr launched in 1961 against the then fashionable word studies.[1] Only a fool would try to turn the clock back and ignore Barr's strictures. But I am not alone in thinking that it is now time to reconsider some of the most important theological terms developed by the earliest followers of Jesus. Of course, full attention must be given both to the whole semantic field of which a given word group is part and to the varied social and religious contexts in which it is used. I shall argue that, when that is done, we find that, in the decade or so immediately after Easter, followers of Jesus developed language patterns which differed sharply from 'street' usage in both the Jewish and the Graeco-Roman worlds. Some of the terms which shaped early Christian theology were forged in 'rivalry' with contemporary language patterns. Scriptural themes and distinctive Christian convictions played their part, but so too did dialogue with current usage on the streets of east Mediterranean cities.

German scholars have been less coy about discussing the 'gospel' word group. No doubt their interest has been encouraged by the prominence of the terminology in the Lutheran tradition. Gerhard Friedrich's important article εὐαγγέλιον, first published in 1935 in the *Theologisches Wörterbuch zum Neuen Testament*, drew on his teacher Julius Schniewind's influential

---

[1] James Barr, *The Semantics of Biblical Language* (London: SCM, 1961).

study, *Euangelion*.[2] Friedrich's article is not immune from some of the criticisms raised by James Barr, but it includes mountains of invaluable background material. I shall also refer to the major studies by Peter Stuhlmacher
(1968), Georg Strecker (1975), and Hubert Frankemölle (1994), sometimes
in disagreement, and in the later sections of my chapter I shall follow paths
none of these scholars has pursued.[3]

I shall suggest a quite specific setting in which Paul, his co-workers, and
his predecessors first began to use 'gospel' in ways at odds with current
usage. I shall insist that, although the imperial cult was not *the source* of
early Christian use of the word group, it was *the background* against which
distinctively Christian usage was forged and first heard. Christians claimed
that God's once for all good news about Christ was to be differentiated from
Providence's repeatable good news about the birth, accession, or return to
health of Roman emperors.

In the opening section of Chapter 2 I draw attention to the gap which is
opening up between the varied ways Christians use the 'gospel' word group
today and current secular usage. Sociolinguists have observed at first hand
the ways religious, political, ethnic, and other social groups develop their
own 'insider' terminology, often by adapting the vocabulary of 'outsiders'.
So too in the first century. The first followers of Jesus developed their own
'in-house' language patterns, partly on the basis of Scripture, partly in
the light of their distinctive Christian convictions, but partly by way of
modifying contemporary 'street' language. I hope that this study of one
small part of the 'social dialect' of earliest Christianity will encourage similar studies, for this phenomenon seems to have escaped close attention
until now.

There is a further reason for focussing on the gospel word group. The
term 'gospel' is being used in some scholarly circles to provide legitimation
for particular views about the importance and authority of Q, the collection
of about 240 sayings of Jesus shared by Matthew and Luke. Q is now

---

[2] G. Friedrich's article εὐαγγέλιον was translated in G. Kittel, ed., *Theological Dictionary of the New Testament*, Vol. II (Grand Rapids: Eerdmans, E. tr. 1964), pp. 707–37. See also J. Schniewind, *Euangelion. Ursprung und erste Gestalt des Begriffs Evangelium*, Vols. I–II (Gütersloh, 1927/31).

[3] P. Stuhlmacher, *Das paulinische Evangelium* (Göttingen: Vandenhoeck & Ruprecht, 1968); G. Strecker, 'Das Evangelium Jesu Christi', in G. Strecker, ed., *Jesus Christus in Historie und Theologie, FS H. Conzelmann* (Tübingen: Mohr, 1975), pp. 503–48; H. Frankemölle, *Evangelium. Begriff und Gattung*, 2nd edn (Stuttgart: Katholisches Bibelwerk, 1994). Frankemölle's book includes a helpful and very full discussion of earlier literature.

3

referred to by some as a 'gospel',[4] or as the 'lost gospel',[5] in order to signal
that this hypothetical source is as important both for the historian and for
the theologian as the canonical gospels, Matthew, Mark, Luke, and John.

There is historical precedent for referring to Q as a 'gospel', for in the
second century some sets of diverse traditions concerning the life and teaching of Jesus were referred to as 'gospels'. But that precedent is beside the
point.[6] In most references today to Q as a 'gospel', a different agenda is
at work. Modern portrayals of Jesus as a wisdom teacher on the basis of
an alleged original and largely historically reliable layer of Q traditions are
being offered as 'good news' to the post-modern world. What better way
of legitimating such views than by dubbing Q traditions 'gospel'?[7]

So too with the exaggerated historical and theological claims made by
some on behalf of the Gospel of Thomas. In its present form it is a fourth-
century gnostic collection of sayings in Coptic attributed to Jesus. It is
now being referred to by some as 'the fifth gospel' in order to shore up
claims that its earlier layers provide access to a Jesus more congenial today
than the Jesus portrayed by New Testament writers as God's good news for
humankind.[8]

So in spite of the second-century precedent for referring to diverse collections of Jesus traditions as 'gospels', the assumption in some circles that
Q and Thomas are 'gospel' for humankind today is to be repudiated. The
primary reason for that is theological, not historical. Q and Thomas (and
several other apocryphal gospels) do contain valuable historical traditions,
but they do not proclaim the Gospel of Jesus Christ as witnessed to by Paul,
by Mark, and by other early Christians later deemed to belong to the circle

[4] For a history of the use of 'gospel' for Q since 1988, see J. S. Kloppenborg Verbin, *Excavating Q: The History and Setting of the Sayings Gospel Q* (Edinburgh: T. & T. Clark, 2000), p. 398 n. 63. See, for example, R. A. Piper, ed., *The Gospel Behind the Gospels: Current Studies on Q* (Leiden: Brill, 1995); J. M. Robinson, P. Hoffmann, and J. S. Kloppenborg, eds., *The Sayings Gospel Q in Greek and in English* (Minneapolis: Fortress, 2002).
[5] M. Borg et al., eds., *The Lost Gospel Q: The Original Sayings of Jesus* (Berkeley, Calif.: Ulysses, 1996).
[6] F. Neirynck, a doyen Q specialist, still refuses to refer to Q as a 'gospel' on the grounds that it is a hypothetical source; he prefers 'the Sayings Source Q'. See 'The Reconstruction of Q', in A. Lindemann, ed., *The Sayings Source Q and the Historical Jesus* (Leuven: Peeters, 2001), p. 57.
[7] In effect this is conceded by Kloppenborg Verbin, *Excavating Q*, pp. 398–408. See also, for example, R. W. Funk, *Honest to Jesus: Jesus for a New Millennium* (New York: HarperCollins, 1996); R. W. Funk, ed., *The Gospel of Jesus according to the Jesus Seminar* (Sonoma, Calif.: Polebridge, 1999).
[8] S. J. Patterson and J. M. Robinson, *The Fifth Gospel Comes of Age* (Harrisburg: Trinity Press, 1998); Cf. N.T. Wright, 'Five Gospels but No Gospel', in B. Chilton and C. A. Evans, eds., *Authenticating the Activities of Jesus* (Leiden: Brill, 1999), pp. 83–120.

of apostles and their followers. When is a gospel not 'Gospel'? When it is a set of Jesus traditions out of kilter with the faith of the church. In essence, this was Irenaeus' answer at the end of the second century. I believe that it still has theological validity today.

By now it will be apparent that consideration of the gospel word group raises a whole set of historical and theological issues of perennial interest. Towards the end of Chapter 2 (in 2.9) a particularly fascinating question is discussed. When was 'gospel' first used to refer to a writing made up of narratives about Jesus rather than to oral proclamation or its content? My own answer is that the evangelist Matthew was the first to do so.

Once this new development in early Christian usage of the gospel word group had taken place, further questions crowded in. How many 'gospel books' did the church possess? Why did the second-century church eventually decide to fly in the teeth of critics who claimed that retention of four inconsistent accounts of the life and teaching of Jesus undermined the credibility of Christianity? What were the factors which led to Irenaeus' classic answer, 'one Gospel in fourfold form'? Chapter 3 discusses the emergence of the fourfold Gospel by drawing on many strands of evidence. The final section of this chapter changes gear from historical to theological issues, for acceptance of the fourfold Gospel carries with it several theological implications.

Chapter 4 explores in detail one of the topics touched on in the previous chapter. What status did Justin Martyr attach to the Jesus traditions and the gospels he referred to in the middle of the second century? To what extent does Irenaeus three decades or so later mark a break with Justin? I emphasize more strongly than most scholars the importance of *written* Jesus traditions for both Justin and Irenaeus.

In Chapter 5, the final chapter of Part I, I am still concerned with 'Jesus and Gospel', but from a very different angle. I take as my starting point Paul's enigmatic phrase 'the law of Christ' (Gal. 6.2). I insist that for Paul this 'law' is part of the Gospel he proclaimed, and not merely a slogan used to refer to ethical teaching linked only loosely, if at all, to his major theological concerns. I sketch the main ways this phrase and its cousins were understood in early Christianity and in some parts of the later tradition. Paul's phrase needs considerable unpacking if it is to be of service to the Christian Gospel today. When Paul's understanding of 'the law of Christ' is complemented by the varied themes associated with this phrase and its cousins up to the time of Justin Martyr, it can still enrich current theological reflection. I remain a great admirer of the apostle Paul, but in this particular case 'earliest' is not necessarily best. A canonical perspective helps, but some of the most significant steps in interpretation of 'the law of Christ' were taken in the second century.

In Chapters 6 and 7, the two chapters in Part II, I consider the earliest sets of objections raised to the actions and teaching of Jesus, and to Christian claims concerning his resurrection. The approach will seem to some to be somewhat off-beat, and so it is. However, opponents of a political or religious leader often see more clearly than followers what is at stake. So it is entirely reasonable to search for polemical traditions. The quest is not easy, for most of the anti-Jesus traditions have been preserved 'against the grain' within early Christian writings.

Contemporary opponents of Jesus perceived him to be a disruptive threat to social and religious order. His proclamation of God's kingly rule and its implications was rightly seen to be radical. For some, his teaching and actions were so radical that they had to be undermined by an alternative explanation of their source. Jesus, it was claimed in his lifetime, was a demon-possessed magician, and probably also a demon-possessed false prophet. Readers who are *au fait* with the flood of recent literature on the so-called historical Jesus will recognize that this is a conclusion which runs against the tide. But I do not repent: I believe that it is well founded.

There is an intriguing parallel with one of the key points made in Chapter 2. From very early in the post-Easter period, proclamation of the Gospel of Jesus Christ was heard against the backdrop of a rival set of 'gospels' concerning the Roman emperors. The key question was this: whose gospel? Providence's provision of the emperor as saviour and benefactor, or God's provision of Jesus Christ as redeemer and life-giver? Already in the lifetime of Jesus there were rival answers on offer to the question: who is this Jesus of Nazareth? For some he was in league with Beelzebul, for others he was proclaiming in word and action God's good news to the poor as a messianic prophet. Both before and after Easter, followers of Jesus rested their claims concerning him on their convictions concerning God, and the relationship of Jesus to God.

The two chapters in Part III are, both, concerned with the earliest surviving written traditions concerning Jesus Christ. Even though the earliest papyri of the gospels are all quite fragmentary, they are of special interest, for they are the earliest material evidence we have for Christianity.

In the past five years more very fragmentary papyri in the codex format have become available. They confront us with the pressing questions which are tackled in Chapters 8 and 9. Why are the earliest fragments of Christian writings all in the unfashionable codex format? And do those early papyri tell us anything about the status and use of the writings in the Christian communities which preserved them?

Chapter 8 asks why early Christians were addicted to the codex. I tackle this question in some detail, and partly in the light of new evidence. I differentiate three stages in early Christian use of the codex. My stage 3 concerns c. AD 300, the point at which Christian scribes' addiction to the codex may have first influenced non-Christian scribes. My stage 2 discusses the variety of pragmatic factors which *sustained* early Christian addiction to the codex. I then turn to stage 1, the initial precocious use of the codex by scribes copying Christian writings.

My own insistence that in very earliest Christianity there was an almost seamless transition from 'notebook' to 'codex' will seem blindingly obvious to some, but in fact this explanation differs markedly from the 'big bang' theories on offer at present. If use of the codex was an extension of the use of notebooks, then there are important corollaries: notebooks were used by the very first followers of Jesus for excerpts from Scripture, for drafts and copies of letters, and perhaps even for the transmission of some Jesus traditions.

Chapter 9 claims that the recently published papyri of the gospels undermine the often-repeated view that, in contrast to Jewish copies of Scripture, early copies of the gospels were the 'workaday', 'utilitarian', 'downmarket' handbooks of an inward-looking sect. The earliest surviving papyri of the gospels confirm that, by the later decades of the second century, if not earlier, the latter's literary qualities and their authoritative status for the life and faith of the church were widely recognized.

In this book I frequently try to build up a cumulative case on the basis of as many strands of evidence as possible. Too much current New Testament research is confined within ever smaller circles. Whenever the pot of familiar questions is stirred repeatedly without the addition of new ingredients, the resulting fare is both bland and predictable.

In nearly every chapter I have worked backwards from later, clearer evidence and formulations to earlier, often partly hidden roots. Of course, anachronism lurks at every corner, but disciplined use of this approach can open up sorely needed fresh perspectives.

The origins of most books are complex. This one is no exception. Chapters 2, 8, and 9 make up over half the book; only a handful of paragraphs in these chapters have been published before. Chapters 3–7 are revised and in some cases extended versions of earlier publications. Details of the original publications are given at appropriate points in the notes.

PART I

Jesus and Gospel

CHAPTER 2

Jesus and Gospel

The subject of this chapter is the origin and early Christian use of the noun 'gospel', the verb 'to proclaim good news' (or, 'to gospel'), and a set of near-synonyms.[1] Given its importance in earliest Christianity and for Christian theology more generally, discussion of this topic has not been as extensive as one might have expected.[2] On several key points opinion has been keenly divided and no consensus has emerged. I shall revisit some of the disputed issues and hope to advance discussion by offering several fresh considerations. In particular, I shall focus on the function of the word group in the religious and social setting of the earliest Christian communities.

2.1 'GOSPEL' IN CURRENT USAGE

In the sixteenth century the term 'gospel' featured frequently in the language repertoire of Erasmus and the Reformers. Erasmus often referred to 'the gospel philosophy'. In his 'Prologue to the New Testament' (1525) the translator William Tyndale included an astute summary of 'gospel':

Euagelio (that we cal gospel) is a greke worde,
and signyfyth good, mery, glad and joyfull tydings,
that maketh a mannes hert glad,
and maketh him synge, daunce and leepe for ioye.[3]

In that tumultuous century the term 'the gospel' often functioned as a shorthand way of referring to the Reformers and their distinctive views.

---

[1] This chapter is a considerably extended version of my Inaugural Lecture as Lady Margaret's Professor of Divinity in the University of Cambridge, given on 27 April 2000.

[2] There have been several major studies in German; details were given above, p. 2 nn 2–3. The word group has attracted curiously little attention from English-speaking scholars, though a notable exception is the Australian ancient historian G. H. R. Horsley's discussion, 'The "Good News" of a Wedding', in *New Documents Illustrating Early Christianity*, Vol. III (Macquarie University: The Ancient History Documentary Research Centre, 1983), pp. 10–15. See also A. J. Spallek, 'The Origin and Meaning of Εὐαγγέλιον in the Pauline Corpus', *CTQ* 57 (1993) 177–90.

[3] I owe this reference to R. I. Deibert, *Mark* (Louisville: Kentucky, 1999), p. 6.

For example, in 1547 John Hooper noted in a letter that, if the emperor (Charles V) should be defeated in war, King Henry VIII would adopt 'the gospel of Christ'. 'Should *the gospel* [i.e. the German Lutheran princes of the Schmalkdic League] sustain disaster, then he will preserve his ungodly masses.'[4] In section 2.8 of this chapter we shall see that in the first century the term 'Gospel' functioned similarly, as a shorthand term and as an identity marker.

In recent decades 'gospel' has been commandeered with increasing frequency by all colours and shades of Christians. Not long ago I discovered a church in Canada which calls itself not simply 'The Full Gospel Church', a tag I knew, but 'The Four Square Gospel Church'. I have noticed that Pope John Paul II likes the word 'gospel'.[5] In order to be ecumenically and theologically correct today, 'gospel' has to be sprinkled liberally in all manner of theological and ecclesiastical statements. Authors of popular Christian books also like to include the term in their book titles.[6]

In current Christian use 'gospel' is a shorthand term whose content is construed in different ways. Although the term sends out varying signals according to context, there are usually some lines of continuity with the early Christians' insistence that 'the Gospel' (τὸ εὐαγγέλιον) is God's good news concerning the life, death, and resurrection of Jesus Christ.

In sharp contrast, however, the noun is used today in common parlance very differently. In 'street' language it has one primary sense: 'gospel truth' is a statement on which one can rely absolutely. A recent article in a UK national newspaper about new developments in lie detectors carried this caption: 'Do you tell porkies or gospel truth?' Not long ago our builder gave me a timetable for planned alterations to our home and said, 'Graham, don't take this as gospel truth!'

There is a curious irony about current use of 'gospel' or 'gospel truth' to refer to a statement on which one can rely completely. In 'street' language today the phrase is a secularized version of Paul's use of the phrase 'the truth of the gospel' in Gal. 2.5 and 14. Current usage is miles away from

---

[4] See Diarmaid MacCulloch, *Tudor Church Militant: Edward VI and the Protestant Reformation* (London: Allen Lane, the Penguin Press, 1999), p. 58.

[5] For example: Pope John Paul II, *Fides et Ratio* (1998). 'The Gospel is not opposed to any culture . . . Cultures are not only not diminished by this encounter; rather, they are prompted to open themselves to the newness of the Gospel's truth and to be stirred by this truth to develop in new ways.'

[6] My colleague Dr Julius Lipner has drawn my attention to a fascinating and very different use of 'gospel' in a book title: *The Gospel of Sri Ramakrishna*, translated and edited by Swami Nikhilandanda (New York: Ramakrishna-Vivekanda Center, 1942). Sri Ramakrishna is one of the best-known modern Hindu holy men. Dr Lipner notes that here 'gospel' is clearly a loan-word from Christianity as it impinged on Indian culture in nineteenth-century Bengal.

Paul's rich and profoundly theological understanding of the phrase.[7] There is now a considerable gap between Christian and secular use of 'gospel'.

Secular use of 'gospel' is gradually becoming more common. If that were to continue, in some countries the distinctive Christian use of the word group would be overshadowed by secular use and thus become part of the 'in-house' language of somewhat marginalized minority groups of Christians. 'Gospel' would then be a 'sociolect', to use the term now favoured by sociolinguists.[8] I shall suggest in section 2.8 that the word group functioned in precisely this way in the first century.

2.2 PLOTTING THE PATH

In this lengthy chapter my main points will be developed along the following lines. In the next section I shall claim that, although Jesus used the verb 'to proclaim God's good news' and was strongly influenced in his own messianic self-understanding by Isa. 61.1-2, he did not use the noun 'gospel'.

I shall then consider several possible explanations for the origin of the word group in the early post-Easter period. The most striking feature of earliest Christian usage is the way 'the Gospel' rapidly became a set phrase whose content could simply be assumed by Paul and his co-workers without the need for further explanation. I shall suggest that use of the noun probably first emerged in Greek-speaking Christian circles as a radical 'Christianizing' of both the limited Biblical and the more extensive contemporary usage. Although we cannot be certain about the precise *origin* of the distinctive ways Christians used the word group, it is clear that they developed in rivalry with the prominent use in the propaganda and ideology of the imperial cult of this word group and *a clutch of associated themes*. The latter point is most important. The rivalry between 'the one Gospel of Jesus Christ' and 'the gospels' of the Caesars encompasses far more than the use of the 'gospel' word group.

In section 2.5 I shall refer to the ways in which ancient historians have made considerable strides in the last two decades or so in advancing our knowledge of the imperial cult in the first century. I shall then discuss some of the more important literary and epigraphical evidence.

---

[7] The Revd Barbara Moss has suggested to me that current secular use of 'gospel truth' may derive from the custom of swearing on the Bible in a law court to tell 'the truth, the whole truth, and nothing but the truth'.

[8] Sociolinguists now differentiate between an 'idiolect' and a 'sociolect'. The former is an individual's idiosyncratic pattern of language, while the latter is pattern of language specific to a group – it may include new coinage of vocabulary or specialized use of 'normal' terms. See section 2.8 below.

In section 2.6 I shall cautiously suggest that Paul's initial proclamation and his subsequent letter to the Galatian churches may have been heard against the backdrop of the all-pervasive religious and social influence of the imperial cult in the Roman colonies of Pisidian Antioch, Iconium, and Lystra. I shall then refer more briefly in section 2.7 to the possibility that this may also have been the case in Thessalonica and Philippi. In section 2.8 the function of the word group as a shorthand term and as part of an early Christian 'sociolect' or social dialect will be considered.

One of the most surprising developments in early Christian use of the noun 'gospel' took place towards the end of the first century, or early in the second. In Paul's day, and for at least a decade later, 'gospel' was used by Christians in the singular to refer solely to oral proclamation. A century later (c. AD 160) Justin Martyr referred to written accounts of the life and teaching of Jesus as 'gospels'. At some earlier point 'oral gospel' became 'written gospel', and 'gospel' became 'gospels'. When was the noun 'gospel' first used to refer to a writing? I shall argue in section 2.9 that the evangelist Matthew first took this momentous step – not the evangelist Mark, and not Marcion. In Chapter 3 I shall discuss the emergence of the fourfold Gospel in the second century, and in Chapter 4 the first use of 'gospels' by Justin Martyr.

In the conclusions in section 2.10 I shall refer to an aspect of the sharp question which has haunted New Testament scholarship for the last 200 years: how much continuity is there between the proclamation of good news by the prophet from Nazareth and post-Easter proclamation of Jesus as God's good news? Is there a measure of continuity in the use of the 'gospel' word group and related terms before and after Easter?

There is a further preliminary point to mention before we go any further. I shall focus primarily on one word group, though strictly speaking I should discuss the whole semantic field of words and phrases used in early Christian writings to refer to the heralding of God's good news concerning Jesus Christ: e.g. 'the word' (ὁ λόγος; τὸ ῥῆμα), 'proclamation' (τὸ κήρυγμα), 'the message' (ἡ ἀκοή, e.g. Gal. 3.5) and ἡ ἀγγελία (I John 1.5),[9] witness (τὸ μαρτύριον), and 'the faith' (ἡ πίστις, Gal. 1.23). Of these terms, ὁ λόγος, 'the word', is the most significant for my present purposes. As we shall see, it is used by Paul, Mark, Matthew, Luke, and the authors of Hebrews and Revelation almost synonymously with τὸ εὐαγγέλιον, 'the Gospel'.

---

[9] R. E. Brown translates ἡ ἀγγελία as 'the gospel' and suggests that it may be the technical Johannine equivalent of τὸ εὐαγγέλιον. He also claims that, when the Johannine believers spoke about the content of what we call the Gospel of John, they may have referred to it as the *angelia* (ἡ ἀγγελία). *The Epistles of John*, Anchor Bible (Garden City: Doubleday, 1982), p. 193.

2.3 JESUS' USE OF THE 'GOSPEL' WORD GROUP

Discussion of Jesus' use of the word group must start with its use in the Old Testament, for the importance of Scripture for Jesus himself cannot be exaggerated. There are only six examples of the Hebrew noun 'Gospel' (*b^{e}sorah*). In two cases (II Sam. 4.10; 18.22) the noun means 'the reward for good news'; in four passages it refers to the 'good news' of deliverance from the enemy (II Sam. 18.20, 25, 27; II Kgs. 7.9). In all six passages theological or religious overtones are conspicuous by their absence – and this is a surprise to most Christians nurtured on the term 'gospel'.

In five of the passages just listed, the Septuagint renders the Hebrew noun *b^{e}sorah* as ἡ εὐαγγελία, a word not found in the NT. The noun τὸ εὐαγγέλιον, which is so important in early Christian writings, is found only once in the LXX, and then in the plural in II Sam 4.10.[10] Here David states that he restrained and then killed the man who had told him that Saul was dead and thought that he was thereby bearing good news (εὐαγγελιζόμενος). 'This was how I had to reward him for bringing good news' (ᾧ ἔδει με δοῦναι εὐαγγέλια). The plural (τὰ εὐαγγέλια) is not found in the NT at all. So, rather unexpectedly, neither the Hebrew text nor the LXX is the direct source of the NT use of the noun τὸ εὐαγγέλιον.

With the verbal forms, however, matters are very different. They are found in a number of OT passages with the general sense 'to announce', and in some they are accompanied by a clear theological note. At Ps. 40.10 and 68.11 the good news proclaimed concerns an act of Yahweh's. At Deutero-Isaiah 40.9; 52.7; 60.6 and 61.1 and the related Ps. 96.2-3 (Ps. 95.2-3 LXX) there is a strong eschatological and universal note: the victory and kingly rule of Yahweh is proclaimed as good news by his messenger-prophet.[11]

These passages form the backdrop to numerous NT passages, and in particular to several Jesus traditions. We need not doubt that Jesus saw his words and deeds as fulfilment of the opening verses of Isaiah 61. 'He has sent me to announce good news to the poor, i.e. to gospel the poor . . . to comfort all who mourn.' Indeed, I believe that this passage was the most important part of Scripture for Jesus' own self-understanding: not Isaiah 53 with its references to the so-called suffering servant, but Isaiah 61.[12]

---

[10] See further Stuhlmacher, *Das paulinische Evangelium*, pp. 155–6. He notes two further examples in variants, 2 Sam. 18.27 and 2 Sam. 18.31 (LXX = 2 Kings), but accepts that the LXX contains no examples of theological usage of εὐαγγέλιον.

[11] The differences between the Hebrew and the LXX repay close attention, but they do not affect the general point being made here.

[12] See C. M. Tuckett, 'Scripture and Q', in C. M. Tuckett, ed., *The Scriptures in the Gospels* (Leuven: University Press, 1997), pp. 20–6.

The evangelist Luke certainly took this view. He opens his account of the ministry of Jesus with that dramatic scene set in the synagogue in Nazareth. Jesus stands up and reads the lesson, and is handed the scroll of the prophet Isaiah. He opens the scroll and reads,

The spirit of the Lord is upon me
because he has anointed me to announce good news to the poor (εὐαγγελίζεσθαι
  πτωχοῖς),
to proclaim release for prisoners
and recovery of sight for the blind;
to let the broken victims go free,
to proclaim the year of the Lord's favour.

Jesus rolled up the scroll, gave it back to the attendant, and sat down. Luke adds, 'all eyes in the synagogue were fixed on him'. Then Jesus addresses those present: 'Today, this scripture has been fulfilled in your hearing' (Luke 4.16-21).

Now, in its present form this passage has undoubtedly been shaped by Luke as a dramatic opening to his account of the ministry of Jesus, a scene which is programmatic for his two volumes: many of Luke's distinctive themes are foreshadowed in these verses. Nonetheless, the core of this passage goes back to Jesus. I shall mention only two reasons for taking this view. First, the two other passages in which Jesus refers to Isaiah 61 (to which we shall turn in a moment) have even stronger claims to historicity; the core of this passage coheres with them. Secondly, not even Luke makes Christological capital out of this passage. It is often overlooked that only in the scenes which follow in chapter 4 is Jesus said (and then only by demons) to be the Holy One of God (4.34), the Son of God, the Messiah (4.41). But in the Nazareth synagogue scene Luke's Jesus makes no more than an indirect claim that he himself is the anointed prophet sent by God to announce good news to the poor. The reticence of Jesus to claim that he himself is *the content* of the good news (and not merely its proclaimer) is all of a piece with the evidence elsewhere: this passage has not been deeply impregnated with post-Easter Christology.

Isaiah 61 also plays an important role in the wording and themes of the opening Beatitudes, both in Matthew and in Luke. 'Blessed are you who are poor, for yours is the kingdom of God' might almost be paraphrased as, 'God is announcing good tidings of salvation to the poor', for 'blessed' (μακάριος) echoes LXX usage, where it expresses the happiness which is the result of God-given salvation.[13] The authenticity of the opening Beatitudes and their close link with Isaiah 61 are generally agreed upon.[14]

Matthew opens the first of his five carefully constructed presentations of the teaching of Jesus with the Beatitudes. In fact, I think it is very probable that the evangelist Matthew extended the echoes of Isaiah 61 already present in the tradition which came to him. So in Matthew's Gospel, as well as in Luke's programmatic scene in the synagogue in Nazareth, Isaiah 61 is prominent in the very first words spoken by Jesus. Quite independently, and I think quite correctly, both evangelists discerned the importance of this passage for Jesus himself.

I turn now to an important Q passage which I shall discuss in more detail: the reply of Jesus to John the Baptist's inquiry. The wording of Matt. 11.2-6 and the parallel passage in Luke 7.19, 22-3 are almost identical, so that the underlying Q tradition can be set out without difficulty.

When John heard (in prison), he sent word by his disciples saying, 'Are you the
  one who is to come, or are we to expect someone else?'
And Jesus answered them, 'Go and tell John what you have seen and heard:
The blind recover their sight, the lame walk,
lepers are cleansed, the deaf hear,
the dead are raised up, and the poor have the good news brought to them.
And blessed is anyone who takes no offence at me.'

Note how the list of the actions of Jesus comes to a climax with 'the dead are raised to life, the poor are brought good news'. With the exception of 'lepers are cleansed', the items in the list are all allusions to phrases in Isa. 29.18; 35.5-6, and 61.1-2. If we were writing out that list, we might be inclined to place 'the dead are raised to life' as the dramatic conclusion. And that is precisely the alteration to the order of the clauses made by a few scribes.[15] But the list reaches its climax with the clear allusion to Isa. 61.1, 'the poor are brought good news', 'the poor are gospelled'. Jesus is claiming that both his actions and his proclamation of God's good news are fulfilment of Scriptural promises.

---

[13] U. Luz, *Das Evangelium nach Matthäus*, EKK I/1, 5th edn (Düsseldorf and Zurich: Benziger, 2002), pp. 276–7, discusses the problems which face the translator of μακάριος and concludes: 'Eine ideale Übersetzung gibt es im Deutschen nicht.' The same is true in English.

[14] The precise relationship of the opening beatitudes to Isa. 61.1-2, 7 is disputed. For a summary of recent scholarship see Luz, *Matthäus*, pp. 271–2. For detailed discussion see F. Neirynck, 'Q6, 20b–21; 7, 22 and Isaiah 61', in C. M. Tuckett, ed., *The Scriptures in the Gospels* (Leuven: University Press, 1997), pp. 27–64.

[15] Y, family 13 and a few other minuscules, the Curetonian Syriac.

One of the fragments of the so-called Messianic Apocalypse discovered in Cave 4 at Qumran and known as 4Q521 provides a significant parallel and sheds fresh light on the interpretation of this Q passage.

1 [for the heav]ens and the earth will listen to **his anointed one**, *2* [and all] that is in them will not turn away from the precepts of the holy ones. *3* Strengthen yourselves, you who are seeking the Lord, in his service! *Blank 4* Will you not in this encounter the Lord, all those who hope in their heart? *5* For the Lord will consider the pious, and call the righteous by name, *6* and his spirit will hover upon the poor, and he will renew the faithful with his strength. *7* For he will honour the pious upon the throne of eternal kingdom, *8* freeing prisoners, giving sight to the blind, straightening out the twis[ted]. *9* And for[e]ver shall I cling to [those who] hope, and in his mercy [. . .] *10* and the fru[it of . . .] . . . not be delayed. *11* And the Lord will perform marvellous acts such as have not existed, just as he sa[id] *12* [for] he will heal the badly wounded and **will make the dead live, he will proclaim good news to the poor** *13* and [. . .] . . . [. . .] he will lead the [. . .] and enrich the hungry. *14* [. . .] and all [. . .] (Frag. 2, col. II)

This is part of the largest of seventeen fragments from the writing first published in 1992.[16] Once again phrases from Isaiah are woven together. In line 12 we find an astonishing parallel with the reply of Jesus to John. 'He will heal the wounded, give life to the dead and preach good news to the poor.' The order is identical: in both passages proclamation of good news to the poor forms the climax of the list of actions to be carried out by God. In both passages allusion to the fulfilment of Isa. 61.1 is unmistakable.

This fragment of 4Q521 opens with an almost certain reference to the Messiah, 'his anointed one'. In the lines which follow it is *God* who cares for the various needy groups, and raises the dead. God does not usually 'preach good news'; this is the task of his herald, messenger, or prophet.[17] The herald or messenger referred to is the Messiah. So Isa. 61.1 is interpreted messianically in this fragment.

There is further support in another Qumran fragment for this interpretation. In lines 15 and 16 of 11Q13 (known earlier as 11Q Melchizedek) Isa. 52.7 is quoted in full. The 'messenger who announces peace, the messenger of good who announces salvation' is 'the one anointed by the spirit'

[16] The translation is taken from *The Dead Sea Scrolls: Study Edition*, edited and translated by Florentino García Martínez and Eibert J. C. Tigchelaar, Vol. II (Brill: Leiden, 1998), p. 1045. The Hebrew text is printed on the facing page, and a bibliography is included. I have supplied the bold type.
[17] John J. Collins, *The Scepter and the Star* (New York: Doubleday, 1995), pp. 116–23. For discussion of more recent literature and support for the view taken here, see J. J. Collins, 'Jesus, Messianism and the Dead Sea Scrolls', in J. H. Charlesworth, H. Lichtenberger, and G. S. Oegema, eds., *Qumran – Messianism: Studies on the Messianic Expectations in the Dead Sea Scrolls* (Tübingen: Mohr–Siebeck, 1998), pp. 100–19, esp. 112–16; C. A. Evans, 'Jesus and the Dead Sea Scrolls', in P. W. Flint and J. C. Vanderkam, eds., *The Dead Sea Scrolls after Fifty Years* (Leiden: Brill, 1999), pp. 585–8.

about whom it is written (Isa. 61.1-2) that he will proclaim 'comfort to the afflicted'. Although this passage is fragmentary and difficult to interpret in detail, the herald of good tidings of Isa. 52.7 is closely linked with Isa. 61.1 and is identified as '*the* anointed one', the Messiah.[18]

So we now have clear evidence that, before the time of Jesus, Isa. 61.1, with its reference to the anointed prophet being sent to preach good news to the poor, was understood to refer to a *messianic prophet*. It is highly likely that, when Jesus referred to his own actions and words in terms of this passage (and the related passages in Deutero-Isaiah), he was making an indirect messianic claim. He was not merely a prophet proclaiming God's good news; he was himself part of the good news.

But what about the historicity of John's question to Jesus, and the reply? Two points strongly suggest that these verses are not simply a post-Easter development. John asks, 'Are you the one who is to come, or are we to expect another?' Jesus does not reply directly to this question. His refusal to make overt claims about himself coheres with many other Jesus traditions and is out of kilter with post-Easter tendencies.

Jesus leaves John's disciples, and John himself, to work out the answer to their question. John has heard about the actions and words of Jesus, and asks about their significance. Jesus' probing, teasing method of encouraging his questioners to think through matters for themselves is all of a piece with the parables. In the case of the parables there is general agreement that this indirect method of communication is undoubtedly authentic. So too with this passage.[19]

Note how it ends. 'Blessed are those who take no offence at me.' That saying clearly implies that there were those who did take offence at the actions and words of Jesus. We know from both Christian and Jewish sources that Jesus was seen in his own lifetime to be a false prophet who led Israel astray, a magician whose healings and exorcisms were the result of collaboration with the prince of demons. So this passage raises the question of the relationship of Jesus to God. Was Jesus a messianic prophet fulfilling Isaiah 61 and proclaiming God's good news to the poor? Or was he a false prophet leading Israel astray? Jesus' proclamation of God's good news, his

---

[18] For text and translation, with recent bibliography, see *The Dead Sea Scrolls*, Vol. ii, pp. 1206–9. For earlier discussion and bibliography see G. N. Stanton, 'On the Christology of Q', in B. Lindars and S. S. Smalley, eds., *Christ and Spirit in the New Testament* (Cambridge: Cambridge University Press, 1973), pp. 27–42.

[19] See especially J. Ian H. McDonald, 'Questioning and Discernment in Gospel Discourse: Communicative Strategy in Matthew 11.2-9', in B. Chilton and C. A. Evans, eds., *Authenticating the Words of Jesus* (Leiden: Brill, 1999), pp. 333–62.

gospelling, if you like, was in competition and dialogue with an alternative story.[20]

Isaiah 61 is deeply embedded in the three passages I have referred to briefly. Jesus' proclamation of good news, of evangel, is in accordance with Scripture and is its fulfilment. If we have ears to hear and eyes to see, then it is possible to discern that Jesus himself is part of the proclamation.

But did Jesus use an Aramaic equivalent of the noun 'gospel' (*b^e sorah*)? Here we face a puzzle. I have insisted that Jesus used the verb 'to proclaim good news', but that verb is not used by Mark at all. Mark uses the noun τὸ εὐαγγέλιον in the absolute, five times on the lips of Jesus (1.15; 8.35; 10.29; 13.10; 14.9), but never the verb. The mystery deepens when we note that the noun τὸ εὐαγγέλιον is not found either in Q traditions or in Luke's or in John's Gospels. The bafflement continues when we discover that Matthew omits three of Mark's uses of τὸ εὐαγγέλιον on the lips of Jesus (Mark 1.15; 8.35; 10.29) and expands the other two (cf. Matt. 24.14 and 26.13 and Mark 13.10 and 14.9). In other words, Matthew's redactional hand has so clearly reshaped radically Mark's use of the noun that we cannot look to this gospel for evidence of Jesus' own usage.[21] There is no other evidence in the gospels directly relevant to our question.

So we must focus on the five examples of τὸ εὐαγγέλιον on the lips of Jesus in Mark. The evangelist uses the noun in 1.1 and 1.14 as part of the comments he makes as narrator on the significance of the story he is unfolding. In both cases the noun is qualified: 'the gospel of Jesus Christ' (1.1) and 'the gospel of God' (1.14). The other five times in Mark are all in the absolute, 'the gospel', without any qualifying phrase.

Do these five verses reflect Jesus' own use of the noun, or post-Easter terminology? The phraseology of Mark 8.35 and 10.29 is similar, 'for my sake and for the sake of the gospel'. Since 'for the sake of the gospel' (ἕνεκεν τοῦ εὐαγγελίου) is not found in the parallel passages in Matthew and Luke, it has often been suggested that in neither case was this phrase included in the 'first' edition of Mark used by the later evangelists.[22] Whether or not that was so may be left as an open question, but the phrase is an explanation or interpretation of the preceding phrase, 'for my sake' (ἕνεκεν ἐμοῦ), using post-Easter vocabulary. Jesus refers to himself as *the content* of 'the gospel' – but elsewhere he is very reluctant to refer to himself as the content of his own proclamation. With reference to these two passages, Willi Marxsen sums

[20] See Chapter 6 below.   [21] For fuller discussion see section 2.9 below.
[22] So, for example, G. Friedrich in his influential article εὐαγγέλιον in *TDNT* II, p. 727. W. Marxsen, *Mark the Evangelist* (E. tr. Nashville: Abingdon, 1969), p. 124 considers this 'highly improbable'.

up the evangelist's point: 'Whoever suffers today [i.e. in Mark's day] for the gospel's sake or abandons this world's goods for the gospel's sake does so for the sake of the Lord.'[23] 'For the sake of Jesus Christ' and 'for the sake of the gospel' are all but synonymous expressions. Peter Stuhlmacher suggests, surely correctly, that these two verses 'point to the self-understanding and sense of mission of early Christian missionaries to the Gentiles other than Paul'.[24]

In Mark 13.9 Jesus warns his followers that they will be summoned to appear before governors and rulers 'on my account' (13.9, ἕνεκεν ἐμοῦ). Verse 10 explains that this will happen as 'the gospel is proclaimed to all nations', so a post-Easter setting is envisaged. With minimal alteration to the sense, in verse 10 'the gospel' could be replaced by 'Jesus Christ', and in verse 9 'on my account' could be replaced by 'on account of the gospel'. Hence 13.10 does not refer to Jesus' own proclamation of the Gospel, but to post-Easter proclamation of him as God's good news.

In Mark 14.9 post-Easter proclamation of the Gospel throughout the world is again in view: wherever the Gospel is proclaimed 'in the whole world', the woman's spontaneous act of devotion to Jesus in the house of Simon the leper at Bethany will be told in remembrance of her. So in none of these four passages (8.35; 10.29; 13.10; 14.9) is Jesus' own pre-Easter proclamation of good news clearly in view; in all four verses the evangelist uses post-Easter phraseology.

The only further use of the noun 'gospel' in Mark on the lips of Jesus raises a set of problems. Jesus proclaims, 'Repent, and believe the gospel' (1.15). In the preceding verse the evangelist as narrator states that Jesus had come into Galilee proclaiming 'the gospel *of God*' (τὸ εὐαγγέλιον τοῦ θεοῦ). But in verse 15 on the lips of Jesus (as in the other four verses just discussed), the absolute term is used: '*the gospel*', τὸ εὐαγγέλιον; there are no explanatory additional phrases. Unlike the other passages in which τὸ εὐαγγέλιον occurs, post-Easter proclamation to Gentiles is not envisaged. In this summary of the proclamation of Jesus the ripples of distinctively Christian (and especially Pauline)[25] post-Easter use of the noun in the absolute (i.e. 'the gospel') can be seen.

That judgement has been contested. Some scholars draw attention to the unusual phrase, 'believe in the gospel', πιστεύετε ἐν τῷ εὐαγγελίῳ,

[23] Marxsen, *Mark the Evangelist*, p. 128.
[24] P. Stuhlmacher, 'The Theme: The Gospel and the Gospels', in P. Stuhlmacher, ed., *The Gospel and the Gospels* (Grand Rapids: Eerdmans, 1991), pp. 22–3, and esp. n. 81.
[25] For careful discussion of Paul's influence on Mark, see J. Marcus, 'Mark – Interpreter of Paul', *NTS* 46 (2000) 473–87.

and suggest a Semitic background. They then allow that it may go back to Jesus.[26] However, although this phrase is unusual in Greek, it is not impossible.[27] If it is taken as an authentic phrase used by Jesus, then it stands in splendid isolation, for there is no parallel use of the noun elsewhere in the Jesus traditions. On close analysis, the only part of Mark 1.15 with strong claims to authenticity is 'the kingdom of God has drawn near: repent'.[28]

If, as I have argued, the evangelist has used post-Easter phraseology, τὸ εὐαγγέλιον, in the summary of the proclamation of Jesus in 1.15 and in the other four verses where the phrase is found on the lips of Jesus (8.35; 10.29; 13.10; 14.9); then there is a significant corollary. For the evangelist Mark, 'the gospel preached by the church is identical with the gospel preached by Jesus'.[29]

I have emphasized that Jesus understood his own proclamation and role as a fulfilment of Isa. 61.1-2, with its reference to the anointed one who proclaims God's good news. But, since the noun 'gospel' is not used either in the Hebrew or the LXX in Isa. 61, the origin of τὸ εὐαγγέλιον must be sought elsewhere. Jesus himself used the verb 'to proclaim good news', but not the noun. The five occurrences on the lips of Jesus in Mark are best explained as post-Easter usage.

2.4   THE EARLIEST CHRISTIAN USAGE

I turn now to the post-Easter period, and first of all to Paul. The noun 'gospel' is used sixty times in the Pauline letters, forty-eight times in the undisputed letters. In just over half of those passages, τὸ εὐαγγέλιον is used absolutely, i.e. without any additional explanatory phrase such as 'of God' or 'of Christ'. In the Pauline corpus and in Christian writings up to Justin Martyr in the middle of the second century, the noun is *always used in the singular*. The prominence of the noun in early Christian writings is astonishing, especially given the fact that the noun is used only once in the LXX at II Sam. 4.10 – and then *in the plural*, of the supposed 'good news' which turned out to be 'bad news'. In non-Christian writings, inscriptions

---

[26] For example, P. Stuhlmacher ('The Theme: The Gospel and the Gospels', pp. 20–1) suggests that Mark 1.15, 'with its very striking semitism, πιστεύετε ἐν τῷ εὐαγγελίῳ, believe in the gospel, is best explained (as Schlatter had already observed) as tradition'. J. Marcus, *Mark 1-8*, Anchor Bible 27 (New York: Doubleday, 2000), p. 174, suggests that Mark 1.15 is a baptismal formula, though its gist may go back to the historical Jesus.
[27] See further C. F. D. Moule, *An Idiom-Book of New Testament Greek* (Cambridge: Cambridge University Press, 1960), pp. 80–1, 205.
[28] So too J. P. Meier, *A Marginal Jew*, Vol. II (New York: Doubleday, 1994), pp. 431 and 485.
[29] Morna D. Hooker, *The Gospel according to St Mark* (London: A. & C. Black, 1991), p. 34.

and papyri of this period, the noun is used reasonably frequently, but with only a few possible exceptions to be discussed below, *only in the plural*.

The corresponding verb is less prominent in the Pauline corpus than the noun; it is used in sixteen passages in the undisputed letters, and twenty-one times in all. In six of the sixteen passages noun and verb are juxtaposed (Rom. 10.15-16; I Cor. 9.18; 15.1; II Cor. 11.7; Gal. 1.6-8; 1.11), and in several more the context makes it clear that proclamation of God's good news concerning Christ is in mind. In other words, even where the verb is used, the sense conveyed by the noun is usually not far away.

Statistics are often misleading, and word statistics are no exception. But in the case of the 'gospel' word group, they cry out for explanation. What was the origin of the distinctive Christian usage of this word group? And why was it used so frequently in early Christian circles? There are several possible explanations.

We have already noted that early post-Easter usage of the noun was not influenced by Jesus himself, for he does not appear to have used an Aramaic equivalent. It is possible that some of the followers of Jesus drew on their knowledge of extra-Biblical Jewish traditions in Hebrew or Aramaic in developing the earliest Christian use of the noun. From time to time a hypothesis along these lines has been proposed, but has won no more than minimal support.[30] The main problem concerns the dating of the phrases in Aramaic targums or rabbinic traditions which are claimed as the background of early Christian use of the noun in Greek.[31]

Another possibility is that the distinctively Christian use of the noun was 'coined' on the back of post-Easter use of the verb, with its Biblical roots in the LXX passages noted above. Given that the verb is used in a handful of LXX passages to refer to proclamation of good news concerning Yahweh's action on behalf of his people, at first sight this seems to be a plausible explanation. However, it is not entirely convincing.

The LXX passages which use the verb in a rich theological sense and which might most readily be posited as the *fons et origo* of early Christian usage of the word group are as difficult to find in Paul's letters as a needle in a haystack. The only partial exception is Paul's reference to Isa. 52.7 in Rom. 10.15: 'As scripture says, "How welcome are the feet of the messengers of good news!"' (τῶν εὐαγγελιζομένων ἀγαθά).[32] But the apostle is not

---

[30] For full discussion see Frankemölle, *Evangelium* (above, Chapter 1, n. 3), pp. 76–86.

[31] P. Stuhlmacher suggests cautiously that the Targum on Isa. 53.1 may be relevant, but he does not attempt to date the Targum. *The Gospel and the Gospels*, p. 20 n. 74 and pp. 22–3 n. 22.

[32] The extent of Paul's adaptation of either the Masoretic Hebrew text or the LXX has been much discussed. There now seems to be agreement that Paul is adapting a 'non-standard' Greek text. See

referring to part of Isa. 52.7 in order to underline its fulfilment in the good news concerning the coming of Jesus Christ. Isaiah's announcement concerning the good news of Yahweh's deliverance of his people and his kingship is adapted by Paul in order to underline the irony that not all have responded to the Gospel (Rom. 10.16). Hence Isa. 52.7 is not a strong candidate in our quest for the origin of Christian usage of the 'gospel' word group.

Isa. 61.1-2 is an even less likely candidate, in spite of the fact that, as noted above, it was particularly important for Jesus' own messianic self-understanding. For in Paul's extant writings this passage is not referred to at all. So in our quest for the origin of Christian use of the word group, we must look elsewhere and consider extra-Biblical usage.

2.4.1   *When and where?*

In order to pursue our quest for the origin of early Christian use of the word group, we must seek as much precision as possible concerning the date and geographical location of that development.

In his letters Paul regularly assumes that their recipients are thoroughly familiar with the 'gospel' terminology he and his co-workers used. In several passages he explicitly notes that he had used it in his initial preaching. At I Thess. 1.5 Paul refers to 'the gospel' which he and his co-workers had brought to the city of Thessalonica on his initial visit to that city. There are similar references at Gal. 1.8-9,11 and 4.13 to Paul's initial proclamation in the Galatian churches as 'the gospel'. So, long before Paul wrote to Christians in Thessalonica and to the Galatian churches, the distinctive Christian use of 'the gospel' was well established. But how much earlier?

In our quest for origins we must give priority to Paul's own statements, and also take seriously (but not uncritically) information provided by Luke in Acts.[33] Paul states that God's disclosure of his Son to him, i.e. 'the gospel', and God's call to proclaim good news (ἵνα εὐαγγελίζωμαι) concerning him among the Gentiles took place in, or near, Damascus (Gal. 1.14-17; see also II Cor. 11.32). While Paul is claiming that *the content* of the proclamation

---

especially D.-A. Koch, *Die Schrift als Zeuge des Evangeliums* (Tübingen: Mohr, 1986), pp. 66–9, 81–2, 113–14, 122; C.D. Stanley, *Paul and the Language of Scripture* (Cambridge: Cambridge University Press, 1992), pp. 134–41; Shiu-Lun Shum, *Paul's Use of Isaiah in Romans* (Tübingen: Mohr–Siebeck, 2002).

[33] See especially Rainer Riesner's critical appraisal of attempts to reconstruct the chronology of earliest Christianity, *Paul's Early Period: Chronology, Mission Strategy, Theology* (Grand Rapids: Eerdmans, 1998), pp. 3–32 (first published as *Die Frühzeit des Apostels Paulus* (Tübingen: Mohr, 1994)).

he was called to deliver was disclosed to him on that occasion, that does not necessarily apply to the noun, τὸ εὐαγγέλιον.

Three years later, following a visit to Arabia, Paul went up to Jerusalem and saw Cephas (Peter) before travelling into the regions of Syria and Cilicia for an extended visit, where he 'announced good news concerning the faith' (εὐαγγελίζεται τὴν πίστιν, Gal. 1.21-4). Here 'the faith' is almost synonymous with 'the gospel'. That visit to Syria would naturally have included Antioch, and there, surely, Paul preached to Gentiles in Greek, as well as to Jews. Since there is general scholarly agreement that Paul's conversion or call took place in c. AD 33,[34] Paul's first visit to Jerusalem took place in c. 36/7, with a visit to Antioch almost certainly following shortly afterwards.

Luke gives us more details about this period. In spite of his tendency to be somewhat impressionistic in matters chronological, at least at this point there are no major problems in reconciling Luke's implied chronology with that given by Paul himself. If we accept c. 33 as the probable date of Paul's conversion, it is reasonable to suppose that Greek-speaking Jews from Jerusalem 'scattered because of the persecution that took place over Stephen' (11.19) began their mission in Antioch in 36 or 37. At that point, according to Luke, they began to speak to Gentiles as well (11.20), and 'a great number became believers'. Luke states that 'they told them the good news of the Lord Jesus', using the verbal form (εὐαγγελιζόμενοι), not the noun, as is implied in many modern translations. The dramatic developments in Antioch reached the ears of the church in Jerusalem, so Barnabas was sent from Jerusalem to Antioch. He then went off to Tarsus (in Cilicia), and brought Paul from Tarsus to Antioch (in Syria). Paul and Barnabas lived in fellowship with the church in Antioch for a whole year (Acts 11.22-6). And what was that year? It may well have been AD 39 or 40, just before Claudius became emperor following the murder of Gaius. Luke underlines the significance of the time Paul and Barnabas spent in Antioch by noting that it was there that followers of Jesus were first called 'Christians' (11.26).[35]

So on the basis both of Paul's own letters and of Acts, it is reasonable to suppose that it was among Greek-speaking Jews in Jerusalem, and perhaps especially in Antioch between AD 37 and 40, that the gospel word group was first used in a Christian context as God's 'glad tiding' concerning Christ.

---

[34] Martin Hengel and Anna Maria Schwemer, *Paul between Damascus and Antioch* (London: SCM, 1997), p. 27.
[35] Riesner, *Paul's Early Period*, p. 124, suggests 36/7 or perhaps 39/40 as the probable date.

Why might this particular date and geographical setting be significant? The imperial cult first made a major impact on Jews in this region during the reign of Gaius (Caligula), emperor from AD 37 until he was murdered in 41.[36] Writing very shortly afterwards, the Jewish philosopher Philo tells us that the accession of Gaius was warmly welcomed: indeed, twice in his *De Legatione* the verbal form εὐαγγελίζεσθαι is used (§99 and §231). Gaius is referred to as 'saviour and benefactor, who would pour *new* streams of blessings on Asia and Europe' (ὁ σωτὴρ καὶ εὐεργέτης... πηγὰς νέας ἐπομβρήσειν Ἀσίᾳ τε καὶ Εὐρώπῃ, *De Legatione* §22).

But within a couple of years relations between the emperor and his Jewish subjects in both Alexandria and the whole of Judaea went sour. Philo and Josephus give us different explanations for Gaius' provocation of Jews, but they agree that his promotion of the imperial cult was the central issue (Philo, *De Legatione* §§184-348; Josephus, *Ant.* XVIII.261-309). Gaius was in fact the first Roman emperor to emphasize his own divinity: he had cult statues from Greece shipped to Rome, where their heads were replaced by models of his own.[37] This is a clear case of modelling the emperor on the gods. Augustus had been coy about making such claims of divinity for himself, though he readily accepted 'divine honours' given to him. Following 'ethnic cleansing' of Jews in Alexandria, and heightened tension following an incident in Jamnia, Gaius rashly tried to have a statue of himself erected in the temple in Jerusalem with the words: 'Gaius, the new Zeus made manifest' (Διὸς ἐπιφανοῦς Νέου, *De Legatione* §346).

Gaius instructed the governor of Syria, Petronius, to prepare the huge statue. Petronius, who was based in Antioch, was well aware of Jewish sensitivities. He knew full well that Gaius' instructions had brought the whole of Jewish Palestine and Syria to the verge of war.[38] By deploying canny delaying tactics Petronius managed to stave off the threat of war. It is hard to believe that anyone from the whole area from Jerusalem to Antioch would not have been fully aware of the political and religious crisis in AD 39/40. Gaius was murdered in January 41, before matters came to a head.

Note that date. When Christian Greek-speaking Jews in Jerusalem and/or Antioch were probably first starting to use the noun 'gospel' in the singular to refer both to the act of proclamation of God's glad tiding concerning Jesus Christ and to its content, Gaius ordered his statue to be erected in

---

[36] There had been earlier tensions. Twice a day sacrifices were offered in the temple for the emperor. Pontius Pilate's attempt to introduce troops into Jerusalem with the normal insignia bearing the effigy of the emperor provoked outrage (Josephus, *Bell.* II.169-74; *Ant.* 18.55-9). For detailed discussion see Helen Bond, *Pontius Pilate in History and Interpretation* (Cambridge: Cambridge University Press, 1998), pp. 49–94.

[37] Dio Cassius 59.28; Suetonius, *Caligula* 22.   [38] Hengel and Schwemer, *Paul*, p. 181.

the temple in Jerusalem. He was considered by many of his subjects to be a 'saviour and benefactor'. His accession had been hailed as 'good news', and as marking the dawn of a *new* era, but his antics undermined that acclamation. So, from a very early point indeed, Christian use of the gospel word group may have formed part of a counter-story to the story associated with the imperial cult.[39]

If so, it may be significant that, in the undisputed Pauline letters, neither 'benefactor' nor 'saviour' (with the exception of Phil. 3.20) is used of Jesus Christ. Christians were proclaiming a rival gospel with some terminology and themes shared with imperial gospels. But a line in the sand was drawn at some key points – and avoidance of 'saviour' and 'benefactor' was one such point. As we shall see, another was Christian insistence that there was only *one gospel*, proclamation of God's once-for-all provision of Jesus Christ.

I have offered what I hope is a disciplined and responsible historical reconstruction. However, the case I am advancing does not stand or fall with my suggestions concerning Gaius and the years 39 and 40. My main point is that the earliest Christian use of the phrase τὸ εὐαγγέλιον and indeed of the verb εὐαγγελίζεσθαι seems to have taken place between 37 and 40 in Jerusalem, or perhaps more probably in Antioch. Paul and his co-workers may have taken this step themselves, or it may have been taken by other Greek-speaking followers of Jesus. We cannot be certain.

The preceding paragraphs have opened up the possibility that Christians borrowed the 'gospel' terminology from the imperial cult and filled it with new content. The further evidence in the section that follows also suggests that possibility, but even then it will fall short of proof. We may have to concede that a quest for the *origin* of the distinctive Christian use of the 'gospel' word group may not be able to locate the holy grail. But a far more important point has already emerged. Early Christian use of this word group seems to have developed alongside claims being made on behalf of the Roman emperor. And it is that clue which will be followed up in section 2.5.

2.5 THE GOSPEL OF JESUS CHRIST AND THE GOSPELS OF THE CAESARS

In the last two decades or so our knowledge of the imperial cult has increased enormously. It can no longer be denied, as has happened in the past, that

---

[39] On 'story' in Paul's theology see especially B. Longenecker, ed., *Narrative Dynamics in Paul* (Louisville: Westminster John Knox, 2002).

this is the backdrop against which Christians used the 'gospel' word group in their own distinctive ways and made a number of their other claims concerning Jesus Christ.[40]

Before I sketch out the main advances in recent scholarship, it will be helpful if two near contemporary comments on the imperial cult are quoted. Writing about the cult during Augustus' reign, the historian Nicolaus of Damascus is terse and to the point:

Because mankind addresses him thus (as Sebastos[41]) in accordance with their esti-mation of his honour, they revere him with temples and sacrifices over islands and continents, organized in cities and provinces, matching the greatness of his virtue and repaying his benefactions towards them.[42]

In his lengthy, glowing panegyric on Augustus, Philo includes these comments:

This is he who not only loosed but broke the chains which had shackled and pressed so hard on the habitable world. This is he who exterminated wars . . . He was the first and the greatest and the common benefactor . . . The whole habitable world voted him no less than celestial honours. These are so well attested by temples, gateways, vestibules, porticoes, that every city which contains magnificent works new and old is surpassed in these by the beauty and magnitude of those appropriated to Caesar and particularly in our own Alexandria.[43]

Two points are especially noteworthy in these two passages. Augustus is universally revered, for his accession brought a new era of peace. Sacrifices and the building of temples in his honour are the appropriate response of his subjects to his magnanimous benefactions. Political loyalty lies behind these comments, but there is also a strong note of religious devotion.

Scholarly study of the imperial cult has gathered pace in the last decade or so.[44] The evidence from literary sources, documentary sources (inscriptions and papyri), archaeology, and numismatics is now being sifted with critical

---

[40] See D. Georgi, 'Die Stunde des Evangeliums Jesu und Cäsar', in D. Georgi, M. Moxter, and H.-G. Heimbrock, eds., *Religion und Gestaltung der Zeit* (Kampen: Kok Pharos, 1994), pp. 52–68.

[41] S. R. F. Price notes that 'the Latin "Augustus" was a title, implying divine favour, given to the first emperor, whom we call Augustus, and employed by his successors. "Sebastos" is the Greek equivalent, but has a stronger association with the display of religious reverence (*eusebeia*) to the emperor.' *Rituals and Power: The Roman Imperial Cult in Asia Minor* (Cambridge: Cambridge University Press, 1984), p. 2 n. 1.

[42] I have quoted Price's translation, ibid., p. 1. For the Greek text, see F. Jacoby, *Die Fragmente der griechischen Historiker* (Leiden: Brill, 1923–58), 90 F 125.

[43] I have quoted F. H. Colson's translation of *De Legatione* §§146–50 in *Philo*, LCL, Vol. x.

[44] See especially S. J. Friesen, *Twice Neokoros: Ephesus, Asia and the Cult of the Flavian Imperial Family* (Leiden: Brill, 1993); A. Small, ed., *Subject and Ruler: The Cult of the Ruling Power in Classical Antiquity. Papers presented at a conference held at the University of Alberta on April 13–15th, 1994, to celebrate the 65th anniversary of Duncan Fishwick* (*Journal of Roman Archaeology* Supplementary

rigour and with more careful attention to method than was often the case in the past.[45] Although it would be rash to claim that there is a scholarly consensus, there would be considerable support for the following:

(1) The cult of the ruler, and especially of the emperor, was a central element of ancient religious life. The Heidelberg ancient historian Géza Alföldy goes even further: 'Under the Roman Empire, from the time of Augustus to that of Constantine, the cult of the emperor was, according to the patterns of "religion" (not in a Christian sense but in the sense of Roman religion) the most important type of worship.'[46] It is no longer acceptable to claim that the imperial cult was a Christian invention,[47] or that it was simply an expression of political loyalty.[48]

(2) Many aspects of the imperial cult can be traced back to Hellenistic ruler cults, especially the emphasis on the importance of repaying the debts of benefactions. However, with Augustus and the arrival of Empire there are marked changes. 'The Augustan decrees make explicit and elaborate comparisons between the actions of the emperor and those of the gods.'[49] In the Hellenistic period, ruler cults were usually city cults. These continued in the Roman period, but in addition numerous cults were established by the provincial assemblies.[50]

(3) The cult was not the preserve of the élite. All classes and groups in cities and villages throughout the empire participated.[51] However, evidence from rural areas is sparse.[52]

Series 17 (1996)); A. Brent, *The Imperial Cult and the Development of Church Order* (Leiden: Brill, 1999); I. Gradel, *Emperor Worship and Roman Religion* (Oxford: Clarendon, 2002).

[45] See Paul Zanker, *The Power of Images in the Age of Augustus* (Ann Arbor: University of Michigan Press, 1990), p. 3: 'My interest is . . . in the totality of images that a contemporary world would have experienced . . . not only "works of art", buildings, and poetic imagery, but also religious ritual, clothing, state ceremony, the emperor's conduct and forms of social intercourse.'

[46] G. Alföldy, 'Subject and Ruler, Subjects and Methods: An Attempt at a Conclusion', in Small, *Subject and Ruler*, p. 255. Cf. Price, *Rituals and Power*, p. 130: 'The imperial cult . . . was probably the most important cult in the province of Asia.'

[47] G. Alföldy quotes the now generally rejected view of Kurt Latte (writing in 1958) that the imperial cult was an invention of the church fathers. 'Subject and Ruler', p. 254. See also Zanker, *Power of Images*, p. 299.

[48] See Price, *Rituals and Power*, p. 55, for references to a number of scholars who have defended this view. Note his insistence (p. 71) that 'it is quite wrong to reduce the imperial cult to a pawn in a game of diplomacy . . . It was not dreamed up simply to flatter the emperor.' See also Zanker, *Power of Images*, p. 299.

[49] Price, *Rituals and Power*, p. 55. Contrast Stuhlmacher, *Das paulinische Evangelium*, p. 196: 'Der Kaiserkult gehörte, wenn man einmal so formulieren darf, mehr zur politisch-religiösen Engagement der Vielen.'

[50] Price, *Rituals and Power*, p. 56. So too F. Millar, 'The Impact of Monarchy', in F. Millar and E. Segal, eds., *Caesar Augustus: Seven Aspects* (Oxford: Clarendon, 1984), p. 53.

[51] Alföldy, 'Subject and Ruler', p. 255; Price, *Rituals and Power*, pp. 107–11.

[52] Price, *Rituals and Power*, pp. 91–7.

(4) There was no slackening of interest in the cult under the successors of Augustus; it continued (with numerous variations) until the end of the third century. It is a mistake to suppose that early Christianity did not feel its impact before the time of Domitian.[53] Stephen Mitchell does not exaggerate when he insists that public worship of the emperors was the obstacle which stood in the way of the progress of Christianity, and was the force which would have drawn new adherents back into conformity with the prevailing paganism.[54]

(5) The imperial cult, 'with its festivals, games, performances, processions and public meals, must have been very attractive'.[55] Justin Meggitt notes that the cult seems to have been practised enthusiastically in private as well as in public, though the material demonstrating this has generally been neglected in studies to date and much more work remains to be done.[56]

(6) Ancient historians now insist that careful attention should be given to chronology and to possible changes and developments, as well as to the setting of the imperial cult in local contexts. I shall attempt to do this in the following two sections of this chapter.

I shall now discuss some of the main examples of the use of the 'gospel' word group in the imperial cult. I shall begin with literary evidence from Philo and Josephus before turning to inscriptions.

The Jewish philosopher Philo wrote at the time early Christian use began. Philo does not use the noun at all in his extensive writings, but the verb is found eleven times, usually with a non-religious sense, 'to announce (good) news'.[57] In three passages, however, the context is especially important, for here the language and ideology of the imperial cult are reflected.

At *De Legatione* §18 the recovery from sickness of the Emperor Gaius is announced as good news, for he had at first been regarded as a 'saviour and benefactor' who would 'pour new streams of blessings on Asia and Europe' (§22). Later in the same writing a reference to the speed with which good news should be carried is part of the comparison of Gaius to the god Hermes

---

[53] *Pace* Stuhlmacher, *Das paulinische Evangelium*, p. 197.

[54] S. Mitchell, *Anatolia: Land, Men and Gods in Asia Minor*, Vol. II (Oxford: Oxford University Press, 1993), p. 10.

[55] Alföldy, 'Subject and Ruler', p. 255.

[56] J. J. Meggitt, 'Taking the Emperor's Clothes Seriously: The New Testament and the Roman Emperor', in Christine E. Joynes, ed., *The Quest for Wisdom: Essays in Honour of Philip Budd* (Cambridge: Orchard Academic, 2002), pp. 150–1.

[57] For the details, see P. Borgen, K. Fuglseth, and R. Skarsten, *The Philo Index: A Complete Greek Word Index to the Writings of Philo of Alexandria* (Grand Rapids: Eerdmans; Leiden: Brill, 2000).

(§99). A report of the accession of Gaius is said to be good news for which sacrifices were offered in the temple in Jerusalem (§231–2; see also §356). Philo's polemical and heavily ironical account of the reign of Gaius was written shortly after the emperor died in AD 41, so the possible relevance of these passages to earliest Christian use of the 'gospel' word group will be obvious. We shall return to this point below.

Writing about three decades later, the Jewish historian Josephus uses the verb a dozen times, usually with the sense 'announce', but in some passages the announcement is of 'good news', especially news of a victory. In none of these passages are there any religious connotations. However, for our present purposes, his three uses of the noun are of considerably more interest.

Josephus records that at news of the accession of the new Emperor Vespasian (AD 69) 'every city kept festival for the good news (ἑώρταζεν εὐαγγέλια) and offered sacrifices on his behalf' (*Bell.* IV.618). Similar terminology is used at *Bell.* IV.656: the people in Rome celebrated (ἑώρταζε) with one common festival the accession of Vespasian and the downfall of Vitellius; on reaching Alexandria, Vespasian was greeted with this good news (εὐαγγέλια). The religious overtones are obvious. In both passages εὐαγγέλιον is used in the plural.

The third passage is baffling. Josephus records that some leading citizens of Jerusalem had sent a deputation to the Procurator Florus urging him to bring troops to the troubled city. 'To Florus the news was a wonderful godsend [or, preferably, 'frightening'] (φλώρῳ μὲν οὖν δεινὸν εὐαγγέλιον ἦν). Determined as he was to kindle the war, Florus gave the emissaries no reply' (*Bell.* II.420). Here εὐαγγέλιον is unexpectedly used in the singular, as it is without exception in NT writings, but without an article. However, this passage is very difficult, if not impossible, to construe; two textual variants confirm that early scribes were also as puzzled as we remain.[58]

Gerhard Friedrich's insistence that 'neither in Philo nor in Josephus do we find the same conception of the one who brings glad tidings as in Deutero-Isaiah' is undoubtedly correct.[59] However, their use of our word group in the context of the imperial cult points us towards paths worth

---

[58] I have quoted Thackeray's LCL translation of δεινόν as 'wonderful godsend', but this is most unlikely to be correct, for δεινός in Hellenistic Greek has the opposite sense, 'causing or likely to cause fear' (so BDAG). The phrase may be an oxymoron, 'the terrifying good news'. See Stuhlmacher, *Das paulinische Evangelium*, pp. 169–70 n. 2.

[59] Gerhard Friedrich, art. εὐαγγελίζομαι in *TDNT* III, p. 714.

following further, even though until recently they were considered by many to be blind alleys.[60]

The literary evidence just discussed in Philo and Josephus is complemented by evidence from an increasing number of inscriptions. The most important is still the so-called Priene inscription, the first fragments of which were published in 1899. Adolf Deissmann's discussion of this inscription in his *Licht vom Osten* (1908) led to a flurry of interest in the imperial cult. This book was quickly translated into English as *Light from the Ancient East* (London: Hodder and Stoughton, 1910). It remains a classic, in spite of more recent discoveries and discussions.

Much has happened since Deissmann's day, though little has filtered through to the standard New Testament lexicons and handbooks. Many more fragments of this inscription have been discovered; we now have thirteen in all, from five cities in Asia Minor: Priene, Apamea, Maeonia, Eumenia, and Dorylaeum.[61] This inscription was displayed prominently in Greek and in Latin in many more than these five places, not only in the larger cities, but also in less populated areas. Only the well-known *Res Gestae Divi Augusti*, the emperor's own catalogue of his achievements for the whole Roman Empire, had an even greater impact in the first century AD. Copies of the *Res Gestae* in Latin (and often with a Greek translation or paraphrase) were erected on stone blocks in the cities and towns of Asia Minor, and probably also in Galatia at the instigation of the provincial Assembly or *koinon* c. AD 19.[62]

The usual title, 'Priene inscription', is something of a misnomer. Priene, which is about halfway between Ephesus and Miletus, happened to be the place where the first discovery was made; the fragments found in the other four cities are all less substantial, but that is sheer chance. When the Ephesian elders travelled to meet with Paul at Miletus (Acts 20.15-17), they may well have broken their journey at Priene.

---

[60] Justin Meggitt notes that until recently NT scholars who have taken the figure of the Roman emperor seriously have often found themselves the object of ridicule, and their interest regarded as, at best, somewhat eccentric. 'Taking the Emperor's Clothes Seriously', pp. 143–69.

[61] The most comprehensive critical edition and discussion of all the fragments is Umberto Laffi, 'Le iscrizioni relative all'introduzione nel 9 a.C. del nuovo calendario della Provincia d'Asia', *Studi Classici e Orientali* 16 (1968) 5–98. See also Robert K. Sherk, *Roman Documents from the Greek East: Senatus Consulta and Epistula to the Age of Augustus* (Baltimore: Johns Hopkins, 1969), pp. 328–37 for an edition of the Greek text, notes, bibliography, and brief discussion.

[62] See *Res Gestae Divi Augusti*, ed. P. A. Brunt and J. M. Moore (Oxford: Oxford University Press, 1967). See also S. Mitchell, 'Galatia under Tiberius', *Chiron* 16 (1986) 17–33. I owe the latter reference to T. Witulski, *Die Adressaten des Galaterbriefes. Untersuchungen zur Gemeinde von Antiochia ad Pisidiam* (Göttingen: Vandenhoeck & Ruprecht, 2000), p. 147.

I prefer to refer to this inscription as the Calendar inscription, for it was intended to encourage the replacement of the local lunar calendar with the solar reckoning of the Julian calendar, as used in Rome. Changing the calendar was a sensitive matter in antiquity. A recommendation to 'do as Rome does' had to be handled with tact. So in about 9 BC the Proconsul of Asia, Paulus Fabius Maximus, wrote a letter with his proposals to the Provincial Assembly, the *koinon* responsible for emperor worship at the provincial level. His suggestion is worded in such a way that it virtually amounts to a directive.[63] The Assembly duly responded with two decrees. It formally approved the proposed change, and insisted that Paulus Fabius Maximus should be honoured with a crown for suggesting that the Emperor Augustus should be honoured by starting the new year on his birthday, 23 September. The letter and the decrees were inscribed many times over on huge blocks of stone, which were then set up in cities all over Asia Minor.

Literacy levels were low in Asia Minor, so only a small percentage of the population would have been able to read the lengthy inscription; even fewer would have been able to appreciate the rhetorical flourishes. But most people would have had a view about its message, for some cities did not in fact fall for the rhetoric and failed to adopt the proposed calendar reform.[64]

In this inscription the noun εὐαγγέλιον is used in the plural once; there is almost certainly a second example in a damaged line. The context in which this noun occurs is important. Here is the opening of Paulus Fabius Maximus' letter:

(It is hard to tell) whether the birthday of our most divine Caesar Augustus (ἡ τοῦ θειοτάτου Καίσαρος γενέθλιος ἡμέρα) spells more of joy or benefit, this being a date that we could probably without fear of contradiction equate with the beginning of all things (τῆι τῶν πάντων ἀρχῆι) . . . he restored stability, when everything was collapsing and falling into disarray, and gave a new look to the entire world that would have been most happy to accept its own ruin had not the good and common fortune of all been born, Caesar Augustus. (lines 4-9)

'The restoration of stability', 'a new look to the entire world' – this sounds like a press officer's propaganda on behalf of her political masters. 'The beginning of all things' would have rung bells for the first Christians, for they had a very different understanding of what constituted 'the beginning of all things'. The claim that Augustus was 'most divine' would have caused many Christians to clench their teeth, for they claimed that it was

[63] Sherk, *Roman Documents*, p. 334.   [64] Price, *Rituals and Power*, p. 106.

appropriate to ascribe more than human qualities not to Augustus, but to Jesus Christ.

Now part of the Provincial Assembly's reply:

In her display of concern and generosity on our behalf, Providence (πρόνοια), who orders all our lives, has adorned our lives with the highest good, namely Augustus. Providence has filled Augustus with divine power for the benefit of humanity, and in her beneficence has granted us and those who will come after us [a Saviour] who has made war to cease and who shall put everything [in peaceful order] . . . And Caesar, [when he was manifest], transcended the expectations of [all who had anticipated the good news], not only by surpassing the benefits conferred by his predecessors but by leaving no expectation of surpassing him to those who would come after him, with the result that the birthday of our god signalled the beginning of good news for the world because of him (ἦρξεν δὲ τῶι κόσμωι τῶν δι᾿αὐτον εὐανγελί[ων ἡ γενέθλιος ἡμ]έρα τοῦ θεοῦ) (lines 34–41).[65]

There is an unmistakable whiff of eschatology and of soteriology here. The coming of the divine Augustus as 'good news' had been eagerly expected. He came as saviour and benefactor, bringing benefits for all. He has brought peace and will continue to do so. He was himself 'the good news'. The repetition in the reply to the original letter of the claim that the birthday of Augustus was 'the beginning of all things' is especially striking.

The Calendar inscription is by no means an isolated example of the ways in which Augustus was regarded. A lengthy but poorly preserved decree opens with these words: 'Since Emperor Caesar, son of god, god Sebastos has by his benefactions to all men outdone even the Olympian gods . . .'.[66] It is hard to see how Augustus could have been elevated any higher.

Over two centuries later the accession of a new Roman emperor was still considered to be 'good news'. A papyrus letter written soon after AD 238 begins as follows: 'Since I have become aware of the good news about the proclamation as Caesar (of Gaius Julius Verus Maximus Augustus) . . .' (ἐπεὶ γν[ώ]στ[ης ἐγενόμην τοῦ] εὐανγελ[ίο]υ περὶ τοῦ ἀνηγορεῦσθαι Καίσαρα . . .).[67] His emperor father is described as 'lord, most dear to the gods'. This only non-Christian example of εὐαγγέλιον on papyrus uses the noun in the singular. However, the key word is so damaged that we cannot be completely certain that the singular should be read.

---

[65] I have quoted with minor modifications F. W. Danker's translation, *Benefactor* (St Louis, Miss.: Clayton, 1982), pp. 216–17. The Greek is quoted from U. Laffi's edition, 'Le iscrizioni'.

[66] *I. Olympia* 53, as quoted by Price, *Rituals and Power*, p. 55.

[67] *Sammelbuch griechischer Urkunden aus Aegypten* I (1915) 421.2. I have quoted the text and translation given by Horsley, *New Documents*, Vol. III, p. 12. See also A. Deissmann, *Light from the Ancient East* (London: Hodder and Stoughton, E. tr. 1910), pp. 371–2.

At present this papyrus fragment and the baffling sentence from Josephus, *Bell*. ii.420 quoted above are rare exceptions which prove the rule: in Graeco-Roman writings and documents from the two centuries before, and the three centuries after Christ, 'good news' is nearly always found in the plural. In the small number of examples of εὐαγγέλιον in the singular, the 'secular' setting of 'good news' is clear: there is no trace of religious overtones.[68] In sharp contrast, in Christian writings up to the middle of the second century, the noun is *always* used in the singular. By their choice of the singular, Christians were making a point. In the next section of this chapter we shall consider when, where, and why they first did so.

Equally important for our present purposes is the context in which the word group is often used in non-Christian writings. Although the noun is used in the plural without any religious connotations,[69] the frequent association of the word group with the imperial cult is clear. Examples from the writings of Philo and Josephus in the first century were noted above. The use of the noun in the Calendar inscription is but the tip of an iceberg. G. H. R. Horsley has listed nine further examples of the use in inscriptions of 'good news' in the plural (τὰ εὐαγγέλια). He sums up their contexts as follows: 'The usage of the neuter plural noun is clear: it refers to good news (often emanating from a monarch), such as news of their victories or benefactions; and in particular, the word is employed of the sacrifices celebrated on such an occasion. The occurrences are nearly all Hellenistic in date.'[70] So the roots are even deeper than the imperial cult associated with Augustus and his successors.

2.5.1 Rivalry

It is now time to confront the key question. We have noted that the 'gospel' word group was very prominent in early Christian writings, and that the use of the phrase τὸ εὐαγγέλιον, 'the gospel' in the absolute, is particularly distinctive. The word group was used in non-religious contexts, but far more striking is its use with religious overtones in connection with the imperial cult that was almost all-pervasive in the decades in which Christianity first

---

[68] So too Frankemölle, *Evangelium*, p. 89. Of the references given in BDAG, Ps.-Lucian, *Asinus* 26 and Appian, *Bella Civilia* 3.92 are in the singular.

[69] See Horsley, *New Documents*, Vol. iii, pp. 10–15. Horsley refers (*inter alia*) to Cicero's use of εὐαγγέλια in three of his letters to Atticus: 2.3.1; 2.12.1; 13.40.1.

[70] *New Documents*, Vol. iii, p. 13. In an e-mail dated 21 February 2000, Professor Horsley confirmed that he and his colleagues have located further examples, which will be included in their forthcoming new lexicon of the New Testament with documentary examples.

flourished. So what is the relationship between the uses of the gospel word group in these two very different settings?

Early Christian addiction to the noun in the singular cannot readily be explained either as a development of Scriptural usage or as influenced by Jesus traditions, and even with the verb there is only limited continuity. Wholesale borrowing from the imperial cult is equally implausible, for, as we have seen, Christian use of the noun 'gospel' in the singular is almost without contemporary precedent. Although there are some similarities in terms of concepts and ideology, there are also very significant differences.

In the Graeco-Roman world of Paul's day, 'glad tidings' were associated regularly with the new hope, the dawn of a new era, the 'good news' brought about by the birth, the accession, or the return to health of a Roman emperor. Hence there could be more than one set of 'glad tidings'. For Christians, on the other hand, the Gospel is God's initiative, the good news of God's fulfilment of his plan and his purposes for humankind: its focal point is Jesus Christ, God's Son. At the heart of Paul's theology was the conviction that in the fulness of time God had sent forth his Son for salvation, for redemption, for Jew and Gentile alike (Gal. 4.4-5). The life, death, and resurrection of Jesus was God's 'once for all' disclosure of '*the one glad tiding*'. For Paul, his proclamation of 'good news' was not the 'birthday' of Christ which marked the dawn of the new era, as with Augustus, but the crucifixion and resurrection of Christ. This was God's good news.

I have been emphasizing the backdrop against which Paul's 'gospel' proclamation would have been *heard*. For Paul himself there was another backdrop, Scripture. He tells us so explicitly: the Gospel he gospelled to the Corinthians (here he juxtaposes the noun and the verb) was in accordance with the Scriptures (I Cor. 15.1-5). Paul insists that both the death of Christ 'for our sins' and his raising to life were to be understood against this backdrop. To ask which passages were in Paul's mind when he wrote or dictated these verses may be to ask the wrong question. Paul is concerned with the general correspondence of the main themes of the Gospel with Scripture.

So if – and, for the reasons given, it is a very big 'if' – Paul, his predecessors, and his co-workers 'borrowed' well-established current usage from the all-pervasive imperial cult, they adapted it radically and filled it with distinctively Christian content. And, of course, that content has deep Scriptural roots. One set of religious themes was exchanged for another. Christian proclamation of God's provision of Jesus Christ first sounded out in a world familiar with different 'gospels' (τὰ εὐαγγέλια). Gospel proclamation did not take place in isolation from the social, political, and religious culture of the time: it was regularly heard against the backdrop of the imperial cult.

I do not think that we can be certain about the *origin* of Christian use of the 'gospel' word group. At the end of section 2.4.1 I noted that a quest for the *origin* of the distinctive Christian use of the 'gospel' word group may not be able to locate the holy grail. The further evidence set out in this section has confirmed that caution has to be the order of the day. But what is clear is that there were rival 'gospels'.[71]

What would have been ringing in the ears of those to whom Paul first proclaimed God's good news, and those who listened to his letters read aloud? Not the 'non-religious' usage of the noun in the Greek Bible (and perhaps not even the rich theological use of the verb in Deutero-Isaiah and related passages), but the 'religious' usage of the word group in the imperial cult which pervaded the cities in which Christianity first flourished. As always, Gospel and culture are intertwined, and often somewhat at odds with one another.

'Gospel' may have been adapted from its usage in the plural in the imperial cult. Or it may have been adapted from its secular use, in which it meant simply 'good news' without any religious connotations. But either way it was modified radically, partly in the light of the Biblical usage of the verb, and more particularly on the basis of early Christian convictions concerning God's salvific act through the death and resurrection of Christ.

2.6 'GOSPEL' IN THE GALATIAN CHURCHES

I shall now take Paul's letter to the Galatian churches as a test case. Were Paul's initial missionary proclamation and this letter itself *heard* by the first recipients against the backdrop of the imperial cult? At first sight Galatians seems to be most unpromising territory for such an inquiry. Scholarly discussion has always focussed on a whole cluster of issues arising from Paul's dispute with the agitators whom Paul accused of wanting to pervert the Gospel of Christ (Gal. 1.7). The social setting and the pre-conversion religious beliefs of Gentiles in the Galatian churches have rarely received sustained attention.

On the other hand, the gospel word group is particularly prominent in this letter: together, the noun and the verb are used seven times. Only in I Corinthians is the word group equally prominent – and that letter is about

---

[71] I have chosen 'rival' deliberately. Justin Meggitt, 'Taking the Emperor's Clothes Seriously', uses the phrase 'polemical rivalry', but at least in Paul's day it is difficult to find direct polemic being used on either side.

three times as long as Galatians. The gospel word group seems to have been used by Paul in his initial visit to the Galatian churches (1.7-8; 4.13).[72] And it is reasonable to infer that the agitators also used the noun 'gospel' (1.6-9).

Before we can consider the possible presence of the imperial cult in the vicinity of the Galatian churches, we have to decide where they were located. There has been no shortage of scholarly discussion of this old chestnut. A decade or so ago it was common for writers on Galatians to state their preference without bothering to discuss the merits of the alternative destination.[73] In recent years the whole question has been reopened in the light of fresh considerations offered by ancient historians. In my judgement the tide has turned decisively in favour of Pisidian Antioch, Iconium, Lystra, and Derbe as the location of the churches of Galatia, i.e. cities along the Via Sebaste in the southern part of the Roman province. Antioch, Iconium, and Lystra were Roman colonies.[74] It is no coincidence that Paul also sought out Roman colonies at Philippi and Corinth.

Several fine very detailed studies have led to this emerging consensus. They include three published in German;[75] this is somewhat surprising, as, in the past, German-language scholarship has generally supported the so-called north Galatia or ethnic/territory theory; the Galatian churches were thought to be in Ancyra, Pessinus, and Tavium.[76]

Perhaps the most significant voice in recent discussion has been the ancient historian Stephen Mitchell, whose unrivalled knowledge of the history and culture of Anatolia is now set out in two substantial volumes. Mitchell is adamant: 'there is virtually nothing to be said for the north Galatian theory'.[77] As far as I am aware, there has been no recent thorough defence of the north Galatian theory – and one now seems most unlikely.[78]

---

[72] M. Winger, 'Act One: Paul Arrives in Galatia', *NTS* 48 (2002) 548–67.

[73] For example, H. D. Betz devotes only four paragraphs to this issue in his Hermeneia commentary (Philadelphia: Fortress, 1979). In his Anchor Bible commentary (New York: Doubleday, 1998) J. L. Martyn includes only three paragraphs. Both opt for the 'north Galatia' or 'territory' hypothesis.

[74] For references to the literature, see C. Breytenbach, *Paulus und Barnabas in der Provinz Galatien. Studien zu Apostelgeschichte 13f.; 16, 6; 18, 23 und den Adressaten des Galaterbriefes* (Leiden: Brill, 1996), p. 1 n. 4.

[75] Riesner, *Paul's Early Period* (above, n. 33), esp. pp. 273–9; Breytenbach, *Paulus und Barnabas*; Witulksi, *Die Adressaten des Galaterbriefes*.

[76] If one does opt for the north Galatia theory, there is no shortage of evidence for the imperial cult in Ancyra. The impressive temple of Roma and Augustus was already under construction by the middle years of Augustus' reign. The Latin text of the *Res Gestae* and a Greek paraphrase of it were inscribed on the walls of the temple. In Pessinus, cultic worship of the emperors soon followed. See Mitchell, *Anatolia* (above, n. 54), Vol. I, p. 103.

[77] Ibid., Vol. II, p. 3.

[78] In his *The Book of Acts in its Hellenistic Setting* (Tübingen: Mohr, 1989), p. 307, C. J. Hemer doubted whether it would be possible to make an adequate restatement of the north Galatia theory in a form which attempted to make a balanced and representative use of epigraphical evidence.

So the geographical details and 'local colour' in Luke's account in Acts 13 and 14 of Paul's so-called first missionary journey outside Syria and Palestine may be taken seriously. Here Luke seems to have had access to a reliable source, though one must allow for his own reshaping. Following contact with the proconsul Sergius Paullus in Cyprus (and perhaps his conversion) Paul and his companions sailed from Paphos to Perge and then travelled on to the Roman colony at Pisidian Antioch on the Via Sebaste (Acts 13.4-14).[79] Why did Paul not stay in Pamphylia, in the region of Perge and Attalia, rather than undertake the arduous journey over the Taurus mountains to Pisidian Antioch?

Perhaps Sergius Paullus (who eventually became consul at Rome c. AD 70) persuaded Paul to make his hometown, Pisidian Antioch, his inland base. This theory has won strong support on the grounds that the proconsul had strong family ties in Antioch.[80] Stephen Mitchell is even bold enough to claim that it is 'an elementary inference' that Sergius Paullus advised or encouraged Paul to make the trip up-country to Antioch.[81] If so, then the first people Paul would have met in the Roman colony would have been members of the Roman élite, who would have been well acquainted with the imperial cult.[82] However, as this theory rests on little more than disciplined imagination, we need firm evidence for the prominence of the imperial cult in Pisidian Antioch before we can contemplate reading Galatians against this background.

Pisidian Antioch was founded as a Roman colony in 25 BC, as was Lystra; Iconium followed shortly afterwards. In Paul's day Antioch was the second city of the province of Galatia after Ancyra. Barbara Levick notes that 'Antioch was a model of Rome, not only in its magistracies and priesthoods, its deliberative body of substantial citizens, its *vici* and its seven hills, but in the admixture of non-Italian elements within its walls'. She adds that Antioch was an example of a Roman veteran settlement superimposed upon the original town, 'the result being a composite society, a bewildering and contradictory variety of cultural and social phenomena, and a sharp

---

[79] See especially Breytenbach, *Paulus und Barnabas*; P. Pilhofer, 'Luke's Knowledge of Antioch', in T. Drew Bear, M. Tashalan, and C. M. Thomas, eds., *Actes du Ier Congrès International sur Antioche de Pisidie* (Lyons and Paris: Université Lumière-Lyon 2 and Diffusion de Boccard, 2000), pp. 77–84. D. Campbell notes that Luke's references to Perge and Attalia and Paul's journey inland to Pisidian Antioch on the Via Sebaste are 'spot on'. 'Paul in Pamphylia (Acts 13.13-14a; 14.24b–26): A Critical Note', *NTS* 46 (2000) 595–602.

[80] Mitchell, *Anatolia*, Vol. II, pp. 5–8; Breytenbach, *Paulus und Barnabas*, pp. 38–45.

[81] S. Mitchell and M. Waelkens, eds., *Pisidian Antioch: The Site and its Monuments* (London, Duckworth, 1998), p. 12.

[82] S. Mitchell insists that Paul's earliest mission to Asia Minor 'was not aimed at low-status Anatolian natives, still less at "foolish Galatians", but at the Romanised provincial elite'. Ibid.

cleavage between upper and lower classes'.[83] From Antioch Paul continued
to use the Via Sebaste en route to the Roman colonies of Iconium and
Lystra, before using another road, perhaps at that time unpaved, to Derbe.
He returned by the identical route to Antioch, thence to Perge and Attalia
(Acts 14.6, 8, 20–6).[84]

Paul used Antioch as his base; that makes sense as soon as one looks at
the province's road network. Although archaeological excavation here has
been somewhat haphazard and is far from complete, we now have clear
evidence that the imperial cult was a prominent part of the city's religious
life during Paul's visits. In the very centre of the site stood a large temple
connected with a semicircular rock-cut area. Although attribution of the
temple has been debated ever since W. M. Ramsay's excavations between
1912 and 1914, there is now general agreement that it is an imperial temple
from the time of Augustus or, at the very latest, Tiberius. Stephen Mitchell is
convinced that further stylistic analysis and a fresh reading of an inscription
on the triple-arched propylon (gateway) make it difficult to believe that the
building postdates Augustus's death in AD 14. 'The temple . . . was erected
for the cult of Augustus during his lifetime.'[85]

The inscription is especially important. It has now been reconstructed
from six fragments as follows:

IMP • CAES[ARI • DI]VI • [F•AVGVSTO • PONTI[F]ICI • M[AXIM]O
COS•X[III•TRIB]VN[ICIAE] • POTESTATIS • XXII • [IM]P • XIIII •
P[•P•]

Imp(eratori) Caes(ari) Divi f(ilio) Augusto pontifici maximo co(n)s(uli) XIII
tribuniciae potestatis XXII imp(eratori) XIIII p(ater) p(atriae)

For the emperor Caesar Augustus, son of a god, pontifex maximus, consul for the
13th time, with tribunician power for the 22nd time, imperator for the 14th time,
father of the country.

This reading gives a date of 2/1 BC. 'The propylon, accordingly, was dedicated to the living emperor Augustus, soon after he received the title *pater
patriae* on 5 February 2 BC.'[86] Its decoration confirms the message inherent

[83] Barbara Levick, *Roman Colonies in Southern Asia Minor* (Oxford: Oxford University Press, 1967),
pp. 190–1.
[84] David French, 'Acts and the Roman Roads of Asia Minor', in D. W. J. Gill and C. Gempf, eds., *The
Book of Acts in its Graeco-Roman Setting* (Grand Rapids: Eerdmans, 1994), pp. 49–58.
[85] For detailed discussion see chapter 5, 'The Augustan Imperial Sanctuary', in Mitchell and Waelkens,
Pisidian Antioch. Here p. 167.
[86] For the text and translation see Mitchell and Waelkens, *Pisidian Antioch*, p. 147. The *editio princeps* has
not yet been published. However, in an e-mail dated 24 October 2002 Professor Mitchell confirmed
that in his opinion the provisional text given above is reliable.

in the inscription: it was erected to honour Augustus and commemorate the victories he had achieved and the peace these had brought to the Roman world.[87]

This was also the message conveyed by the *Res Gestae*, Latin fragments of which have been discovered at Antioch.[88] In all probability the full text was inscribed in ten columns on the inner faces of the two central piers of the gateway. It opened as follows: 'The achievements of the divine Augustus, by which he brought the world under the empire of the Roman people . . .' ('Res gestae divi Augusti, quibus orbem terrarum imperio populi Romani subiecet . . .').[89] The *Res Gestae* was published at the time of Augustus' death in AD 14. 'It can be taken as . . . his *apologia* for receiving his crowning honour, state divinity, which he had so modestly (or prudently) rejected throughout his lifetime.'[90] A copy may well have been erected at Antioch soon afterwards.

Thus there is cumulative evidence for the prominence of the imperial cult in Antioch well before Paul's day: the ground plan and decoration of the temple, the decoration of the gateway, and the two inscriptions referred to above. But what about Paul's letter to the Galatian churches? Are there passages in the text which may be references to the impact the imperial cult may have made on the lives of Christians in Antioch? There are two themes which may have been *heard* by Christians as a counter-story to the story conveyed by the all-pervasive imperial cult, and two passages which may possibly refer to that background.

(1) Two of Paul's theological emphases in Galatians may have reminded the Galatians that their convictions concerning Jesus Christ were at odds with the beliefs and practices of the Roman religious and political world in which they lived.

The gospel word group is more prominent in Galatians than in any of Paul's other letters. When Galatian Christians heard this word group thirteen times in the opening sections of the letter, they may well have recalled that in his initial preaching Paul insisted that there was *one* Gospel of Jesus Christ, which was at odds with the 'gospels' associated with the birth, accession, and health of the Roman emperors.

---

[87] Mitchell and Waelkens, *Pisidian Antioch*, p. 164.
[88] My graduate student Mr Justin Hardin has drawn my attention to the fact that no fragments in Greek have yet been discovered in Antioch. I have benefited greatly from discussions with Mr Hardin and from his M. Phil. thesis, 'The Social and Religious Setting of Galatians', Cambridge University, 2002.
[89] See Brunt and Moore, *Res Gestae Divi Augusti*.
[90] Gradel, *Emperor Worship and Roman Religion* (above, n. 44), p. 281.

At the centre of the imperial cult stood the recognition that Augustus was a 'son of god', as were his successors. The inscription referred to in section 2.5 was set in bronze letters on the triple-arched gateway to the imperial temple which dominated the city and the surroundings of Antioch. It would have been a constant reminder of the religious status of the emperors. So Paul's counter-claim that Jesus, not the emperor, is God's Son would have been especially meaningful in that context.

And that is precisely the claim that lies at the heart of the Christology of this letter. In the opening chapter Paul defines 'the gospel' (the noun is used absolutely in 1.11) in terms of *God's* disclosure of Jesus Christ as his Son. In his positive statement about the origin of his gospel at the end of 1.12, Paul insists that he received the gospel 'through a revelation (δι' ἀποκαλύψεως) of Jesus Christ'. This NRSV translation preserves the ambiguity of the Greek, which can be construed either as 'Jesus Christ's disclosure of the gospel' or as 'God's disclosure of Jesus Christ as the content of the gospel'. The latter is preferable, especially in view of Paul's further comments in 1.15-16, which unpack his shorthand term 'the gospel' and emphasize (once again) God's initiative in the revelation or disclosure of his Son.

In his striking opening greeting Paul insists that Christ gave himself for sins (Gal. 1.4), and at the climax of a sustained theological exposition in 2.15-20 Paul claims that the Son of God loved him and gave himself for him (Gal. 2.20). These would have been jarring notes for those accustomed to hear that the emperor as *divi filius*, a son of god, had brought many benefactions to the world, including peace and general well-being. Self-giving love on behalf of others, even to the point of death, was *not* part of the imperial repertoire.

Similarly in what I take to be the theological heart of this letter: 4.1-7. In the fulness of time God sent his Son: this is God's good news concerning Jesus Christ. In the Calendar inscription the beginning of good news for the world is Providence's provision of Augustus as a saviour who has made wars cease. But there the partial parallelism stops abruptly. For in imperial cult ideology there is no note of redemption or of the bestowal of sonship by adoption on those committed to faith in the Son of God.

Now, I am not suggesting that either the content of Paul's gospel or a Son of God Christology was borrowed or even strongly influenced by the language and ideology of the imperial cult. But, in the light of the evidence I have set out, we do well to bear in mind the religious and political world in which Paul's initial proclamation and his letter to the Galatian churches were heard. The Gospel of Jesus Christ and the gospels of the Caesars were rivals.

(2) If the general point just made is accepted, then it is worth considering whether there are passages in Paul's letter to the Galatian churches which may refer to possible pressures to practise the imperial cult. Gal. 4. 8-10 is a candidate.

Formerly, when you did not know God, you were enslaved to beings that by nature are not gods. 9. Now, however, that you have come to know God, or rather be known by God, how can you turn back again to the weak and beggarly elemental spirits (στοιχεῖα)? 10. How can you want to be enslaved to them again? You are observing special days, and months, and seasons, and years.

The consensus reading of this passage, which I have followed in the past, runs as follows.[91] Before they became Christians, the Galatians were enslaved to 'beings that by nature are not gods', i.e. to idols (cf. I Cor. 8.5 and 12.2). So they must have been Gentiles. Now as believers they have come to know, i.e. to experience, God's Spirit (cf. 3.1-5 and 4.6). But what are the special 'days, and months, and seasons, and years' which the Galatians now want to observe closely, even as Christians? I have assumed that the influence of the agitators may be detected here. They have been encouraging Galatian Christians to observe the Jewish sabbath ('days') and festivals ('seasons'). Observance of 'months' probably refers to observance of the new moon which marked the beginning of each month. Precisely what is meant by 'years' is uncertain.

However, there is an alternative reading which merits consideration. H. D. Betz notes that the cultic activities described in verse 10, 'observing special days, and months, and seasons, and years', are not typical of Judaism (including Jewish Christianity). He might have added that, unlike Col. 2.16, this verse does not refer explicitly to Jewish observance of sabbaths, new moons, or festivals. Betz insists that 'the description is typical and part of a literary topos well-known in antiquity. It portrays the Galatians as conforming to the religious character of the δεισιδαίμων ("religiously scrupulous" or even "superstitious").'[92] However, Betz fails to explain satisfactorily why Paul has used this particular 'non-Jewish' phraseology to refer to the threat posed by Jewish Christian agitators. Nonetheless, his comments may point us in the right direction.

Thomas Witulski has recently gone much further down this path. He notes that the absence of any *explicit* reference to the sabbath, the most important day of all for Jews, rules out a reference to Jewish observances

[91] See G. N. Stanton, 'Galatians', in J. Barton and J. Muddiman, eds., *The Oxford Bible Commentary* (Oxford: Oxford University Press, 2001), pp. 1152–65.
[92] Betz, *Galatians* (above, n. 73), pp. 217–18.

here. Equally problematic for the consensus reading is the reference to 'years', for Jewish celebration of 'special years' was unknown in diaspora Judaism.[93] Witulski then presents a wealth of evidence to underpin his claim that the Galatian Christians were facing local pressures to participate in the imperial cult.[94]

In principle, it is highly likely that Galatian Christians did face strong social pressures, even though these may be more difficult to uncover from Paul's letter than the theological issues at stake between Paul and the agitators. Stephen Mitchell concludes his discussion of the imperial cult in Anatolia with these words:

> One cannot avoid the impression that the obstacle which stood in the way of the progress of Christianity, and the force which would have drawn new adherents back to conformity with the prevailing paganism, was the public worship of the emperors . . . It was not a change of heart that might win a Christian convert back to paganism, but the overwhelming pressure to conform imposed by the institutions of his city and the activities of his neighbours.[95]

Witulski notes that several celebrations of 'special days' were associated with Augustus. 'Months' may refer to the introduction of the new pattern of months referred to in the Calendar inscription, with its strong encouragement to begin the new year on the birthday of Augustus on 23 September. Careful observance of 'seasons' is taken to refer to festive celebrations in the context of the imperial cult, some of which extended over several days. 'Years' may reflect Augustus' reference in the *Res Gestae* to the decision of the Roman senate that every fifth year 'vows should be undertaken for my [i.e. Augustus'] health by the consuls and the priests. In fulfilment of these vows games have frequently been celebrated.' In this paragraph Augustus then notes that all citizens are included in these acts of devotion: 'individually and on behalf of their towns they offer . . . prayers at all the shrines for my health'.[96] I have summarized only part of the considerable evidence Witulski has amassed in building a cumulative case.

If this line of interpretation is followed, there is an obvious problem. How are social pressures to conform to the imperial cult linked to the particular concerns of the agitators in the Galatian churches over circumcision and observance of the law? Witulski's own solution smacks of desperation. He claims that two letters Paul wrote to the Galatians have been combined to form what became the canonical Galatians. The two letters originally had very different settings: in the earlier letter Paul attacks the agitators,

---

[93] Witulski, *Die Adressaten des Galaterbriefes*, pp. 155–6.   [94] Ibid., pp. 158–68.
[95] Mitchell, *Anatolia*, Vol. II, p. 10.   [96] Brunt and Moore, *Res Gestae Divi Augusti*, ch. 9, p. 23.

in the other (at least partly now in Gal. 4.8-20) he encourages resistance to pressures to observe the imperial cult. The first letter was written *before* the arrival of the imperial cult in Pisidian Antioch, the latter shortly after its arrival about AD 50. However, this dating (and the whole theory) is undermined by the more recent evidence sketched above, which indicates that the imperial cult arrived well before AD 50. And Gal. 4.8-20 is not the only part of Galatians which may have been heard against the background of the imperial cult.

(3) If Gal. 4.8-10 reflects the enormous social pressures to observe the imperial cult, then in 6.12-13, the opening verses of the carefully composed finale to the letter, we may perhaps be given a more specific explanation of the social pressures at work in the Galatian churches. Bruce Winter has recently proposed a solution that merits careful consideration. He notes that, immediately after Paul personally begins to pen the postscript to the Galatians, in his own hand, the apostle sums up his key concern in quasi-legal terminology in 6.12-13:

As many as wish to secure 'good' status by means of flesh, i.e. circumcision, [these people] compel you to be circumcised only in order that they may not be persecuted for the cross of Christ. 13. For those who themselves are circumcised do not keep the law, but only wish you to be circumcised in order that they may have confidence by means of your flesh, i.e. your circumcision.

Winter claims that avoidance of the imperial cult is connected to the central issue in Galatians. Gentile Christians were being encouraged by Jewish Christian agitators to 'look Jewish', i.e. to undergo circumcision and to keep the law as the means of circumventing their obligation to the imperial cult. 'Jewish Christians formulated this response to an extremely difficult civic obligation, for their own self-preservation and that of the Christian community was seen to be at stake.' The agitators believed that 'undergoing circumcision and keeping the law was one way of convincing the authorities that Christianity was part of a *religio licita*, for in Galatia these were cultural hallmarks of the one group that was recognized as being exempted from worship of the emperors.'[97]

This is certainly a provocative fresh reading of Galatians, which should not be dismissed without further ado. Winter correctly understands that the term *religio licita* is no more than a convenient way of referring to the

---

[97] B. W. Winter, 'The Imperial Cult and Early Christians in Roman Galatia (Acts XIII 13-50 and Galatians VI 11-18', in T. Drew-Bear, M. Tashalan, and C. M. Thomas, eds., *Actes du Ier Congrès International sur Antioche de Pisidie* (Université Lumière-Lyon 2 and Diffusion de Boccard, 2002), pp. 67–75.

special status Jews enjoyed: at this time there was no formal charter which underpinned that status. Even though we do not have specific evidence from the middle of the first century of the status of Jews in Roman eyes in the colony at Antioch,[98] it is highly likely that the Galatian Christians were being encouraged to accept circumcision in order to take advantage of the respect Jews enjoyed in society at large. John Barclay notes that 'by becoming proselytes the Galatians could hope to identify themselves with the local synagogues and thus hold at least a more understandable and recognizable place in society'.[99]

However, it is difficult to take a further step and suppose that the pressures on the Jewish Christian agitators were quite specific and involved the imperial cult. The final clause in Gal. 6.12 is one of the most difficult in Galatians: Paul claims that the agitators are trying to compel circumcision 'only that they may not be persecuted for the cross of Christ' (μόνον ἵνα τῷ σταυρῷ τοῦ Χριστοῦ μὴ διώκωνται). The agitators are wanting to avoid 'persecution' by compelling Gentiles to be circumcised. That much is clear. But who was responsible for the threat of persecution? Paul does not identify the alleged persecutors: he shelters them behind his use of the passive verb.

Some have suggested that too much weight should not be attached to this clause. Perhaps it is a 'throw-away' line, penned by Paul himself in a state of fury. Perhaps we can envisage strong arm-twisting from some quarter or other, but persecution? On the other hand, at 6.12 Paul uses the same verb (διώκω) as at Gal. 1.13, where he refers to his own 'pre-conversion' persecution of the church. So it is natural to suppose literal persecution. Plenty of candidates are on offer. The 'false brothers' of Gal. 2. 4-6, or 'hardline' Jews, whether local or new arrivals in Antioch, are often thought to have been the culprits.

Winter's theory offers a very different scenario. The Jewish Christian agitators were under severe pressure to participate in the imperial cult and thus prove that they merited the respect and toleration accorded to members of the Jewish community. Hence they urged Gentile converts in Antioch to 'look Jewish' and thus enjoy that same standing in society. In support of his theory Winter refers to Acts 13.50 and 14.12. 'The leading men of

---

[98] See especially J. M. G. Barclay's judicious appraisal of the limited evidence for the social status of Jews in the province of Asia, *Jews in the Mediterranean Diaspora* (Edinburgh: T & T Clark, 1996), pp. 259–81. He notes (p. 279) that it is frustrating that evidence for the social setting of Asian Jews in the first century is so paltry. He does not discuss Galatia. See also Paul Trebilco, *Jewish Communities in Asia Minor* (Cambridge: Cambridge University Press, 1991), pp. 167–85.

[99] J. M. G. Barclay, *Obeying the Truth: A Study of Paul's Ethics in Galatians* (Edinburgh: T & T Clark, 1988), p. 60.

the city' were involved in the ejection of Paul and Barnabas from Antioch. Antagonism towards the new movement is likely to have continued. Hence, on his return visit to Antioch, Paul warns the Christians there that they must expect to face continuing troubles. There is no reason to dismiss this evidence for Gentile opposition to Christians in Antioch out of hand, but there are no hints in Acts 13.50 and 14.12 that 'the leading men of the city' were enforcing observance of the imperial cult on Christians.

Winter acknowledges that we do not have evidence from the period that explains how Gentile Christians might have claimed exemption from participation in the imperial cult. This is a weak link in his argument, but not quite an Achilles' heel. Our knowledge of the imperial cult in Antioch in the middle of the first century has increased enormously in recent decades, but it is still limited. It is to be hoped that much-needed further archaeological work will enhance that knowledge. So it would be prudent to accept that at present we do not have evidence which would either confirm or undermine the envisaged scenario.[100]

(4) There is one further passage to be considered. Luke includes a lengthy account of Paul's preaching in the synagogue in Pisidian Antioch in Acts 13.14-41, one of the great set-piece speeches in the first half of Acts. Although it is extremely difficult to disentangle Luke's own colouring and shaping from any sources he may have used in the speeches in Acts, one should take seriously the fact that Luke sets this speech in Pisidian Antioch. For Luke regularly takes pains to shape the speeches in Acts to fit the local context. The preceding speech made by Peter to the Roman centurion Cornelius in Caesarea is a good example (Acts 10.34-43), as is Paul's Areopagus speech (Acts 17.22-31). So, even if we are sceptical about the extent to which Luke has used sources in the speech in Acts 13.14-41, some of its themes may have been intended to fit the context envisaged, as is clearly the case in the speech set in Lystra (Acts 14.15-17).

If we bear in mind that in Pisidian Antioch the synagogue would have stood in the shadow of the huge imperial temple, then there may be a ready explanation for two surprises Luke springs in this speech. The first Christological note sounded is that God has brought to Israel a Saviour, Jesus, as he promised (13.23); 'to us, this message of salvation has been sent' (13.26; see also 13.47). 'Saviour' (σωτήρ) is found in only one other passage in Acts (5.31) and is rare in the NT. 'Salvation' (σωτηρία) is used sparingly by Luke (only here and at Acts 4.12; 7.25; 16.17; 27.34).

[100] My comments on Gal. 6.12 have benefited from discussion with my colleague Dr James Carleton Paget, but he is not responsible for their formulation.

Is it a coincidence that 'saviour' and 'salvation' were prominent in the terminology of the imperial cult, that the imperial cult was prominent in Antioch, and that both terms were included in Luke's account of Paul's speech in this city?[101] As we noted above, according to Philo, the accession of the Emperor Gaius was announced as good news, for he had at first been regarded as a 'saviour and benefactor'. Σωτήρ is particularly common in inscriptions referring to the Emperor Claudius.[102] So the listeners to the speech in Luke's day may well have been reminded that Jesus, not the emperor or any other person or god, was Saviour, God's provision of salvation. However, it is unlikely that this theme goes back to Paul himself, for, with the exception of Phil. 3.20, in the undisputed Pauline letters σωτήρ is not used at all. The only possible link between the speech and Galatians is at Acts 13.38-9, which might be taken as a partial paraphrase of Gal. 2.16.

A Son of God Christology is also found only once in Acts up to this point (at 9.20), and is not repeated.[103] At the climax of the speech Luke's Paul proclaims the good news (εὐαγγελιζόμεθα, 13.32) that Jesus is the Son of God. God has fulfilled his promises: Jesus is the one of whom it is written in Psalm 2, 'You are my Son; today I have begotten you', the fulfilment of Psalm 2.7 and II Sam. 7.12 (13.23, 32-3). As we have seen, both 'son of god' and 'announcement of good news' are often associated with the imperial cult. So once again the readers of Acts are being reminded that Jesus, not the emperor, is to be acclaimed as Son of God. If we take seriously the setting of the speech in Acts 13.14-41 in Pisidian Antioch, we are forced to consider a reading which has been largely overlooked.

In the preceding paragraphs of this section I have suggested that Paul's initial proclamation of the Gospel, as well as his letter to the Galatian churches, would have been heard in the Roman colonies of Pisidian Antioch, Iconium, and Lystra against the backdrop of the all-pervasive imperial cult. This claim is strengthened by the use of the 'gospel' word group in both settings, but it is not dependent on this verbal link. For the whole ideology of Providence's provision of the emperor as the supreme benefactor, son of god and saviour was in 'rivalry' with Paul's claim concerning God's provision in grace / benefaction of Jesus Christ as God's Son.

[101] For details, see Peter Oakes, *Philippians: From People to Letter* (Cambridge: Cambridge University Press, 2001), pp. 138–47. See also W. Foerster, art. σωτήρ, *TDNT* VII, pp. 1010–12.
[102] See Oakes, *Philippians*, p. 140 for details.
[103] The confessional response of the Ethiopian eunuch, 'I believe that Jesus Christ is the Son of God' (Acts 8.37), is clearly a later addition to the text.

2.7 'GOSPEL' IN THESSALONICA AND PHILIPPI

There is even stronger evidence for this contention from some of Paul's other letters.[104] I shall limit myself to two examples, one from the beginning and one from the close of Paul's letter-writing ministry: the Thessalonian correspondence, and Philippians. Thessalonica was strongly Romanized, and Philippi was a Roman colony.

J. R. Harrison has recently argued that 'a pivotal claim of early first century propaganda – that providence would never provide a better Saviour than Augustus – increasingly faced challenge at Thessaloniki and elsewhere'.[105] The accusation that Paul and Silas acted 'against the decrees of Caesar, saying there is another king Jesus' (Acts 17.7) is the obvious starting point. Harrison lists no fewer than six words from the Thessalonian correspondence which are common to the imperial and early Christian eschatology: εἰρήνη ('peace': I Thess. 1.1; 5.3, 23); ἐπιφάνεια ('appearance': 2 Thess. 2.8); ἐλπίς ('hope': I Thess. 1.3; 2.19; 4.13; 5.8; 2 Thess. 2.16); εὐαγγέλιον ('good news': I Thess. 1.5; 2.2, 4, 8, 9; 3.2; II Thess. 1.8; 2.14); σωτηρία ('salvation': I Thess. 5.8, 9; II Thess. 2.13); χάρα ('joy': I Thess. 1.6; 2.19, 20; 3.9). He claims that Paul countered and subverted the aggressive influence of the eschatology of the imperial gospel by proclaiming the eschatological hope of the risen and reigning heavenly Lord.[106] In my judgement, his revival of the theory that at I Thess. 5.3 Paul prophesies the destruction of the proponents of the imperial *pax et securitas* is particularly strong. Equally plausible is the claim that the phrases 'the hope of salvation' and 'salvation through our Lord Jesus Christ' in I Thess. 5.8-9 would have evoked imperial associations.

Given that in the Thessalonian letters the most frequently used of the six words listed in the preceding paragraph is εὐαγγέλιον, it is surprising that Harrison does not discuss this term. For our current preoccupation with the gospel word group, two points are especially important. First, in I Thessalonians, probably Paul's earliest letter, Paul uses 'the word' (ὁ λόγος) and 'the gospel' (τὸ εὐαγγέλιον) almost synonymously (I Thess. 1.6, 8 and 2.13; see also II Thess 3.1). In the opening thanksgiving in I Thessalonians, the Spirit is associated closely with the reception both of 'the gospel' and of 'the word' (1.5-6); the terms could easily be interchanged in these verses.

---

[104] See R. A. Horsley, *Paul and Politics: Ekklesia, Imperium, Interpretation* (Harrisburg, Pa.: Trinity Press International, 2000). For Romans see N. T. Wright, 'A Fresh perspective on Paul?', *BJRL* 83 (2001) 21–39. For the imperial cult in Corinth see J. K. Chow, *Patronage and Power: A Study of Social Networks in Corinth* (Sheffield: JSOT Press, 1992).

[105] J. R. Harrison, 'Paul and the Imperial Gospel at Thessaloniki', *JSNT* 25 (2002) 71–96.

[106] Ibid., p. 92.

Both are 'shorthand' phrases whose content could be readily filled out by the Thessalonian Christians. In some cases Paul himself expands both terms slightly by adding 'of God' or 'of Christ' to 'the gospel' (I Thess. 2.2, 8, 9; 3.2) and 'of the Lord' or 'of God' to 'the word' (I Thess 1.8; 2.13; II Thess 3.1). I shall comment further on the 'shorthand' character of both terms in section 2.8.

In I Thessalonians, the apostle takes considerable pains to emphasize that the Gospel or the word is *God's* – it is from God, and it is about what God has done (2.2, 8, 9, 13). The Gospel and the word make their appeal not by means of fancy rhetoric, but on the basis of God's power or Spirit (1.5). The Gospel is *God's* glad tiding about Christ (3.2). The repeated emphasis in this letter on the Gospel as *God's* good news is striking. Why does Paul need to do this when he assumes that the Thessalonians will be able to unpack his shorthand? Surely there is at least an implicit subversion of the imperial gospel of Providence's provision of the emperor for salvation, for 'peace and security'. This is how Paul's words would have been heard in Thessalonica, whether or not that was part of Paul's intention.

And so briefly to Paul's letter to Christians in the Roman colony, Philippi. Phil. 3.20 has often been read against the background of the imperial cult: 'our citizenship is in heaven, and it is from there that we are expecting a *Saviour* (σωτήρ), the Lord Jesus Christ'. The so-called Christ hymn in Phil. 2.6-11, with its climax in the confession that Jesus Christ is κύριος, has been read similarly, but less often. Peter Oakes has recently built on earlier readings along these lines by showing that some of the key words and phrases in these passages (especially σωτήρ and κύριος) were prominent in the imperial cult. His cumulative case for reading the whole of Phil. 2.6-11 as an extended comparison between Christ and the emperor is provocative and may not win the day. Nonetheless, in the light of what has been said above, surely his main point is plausible: this is how many of the Philippians would have *heard* this passage.[107]

Peter Oakes provides plenty of literary, inscriptional, and numismatic evidence to back up his case, but hardly any of it is *local* to Philippi. Perhaps this is why he accepts that this cult is unlikely to have been the most pressing of the issues faced by the Philippians.[108] In effect, Oakes is offering a timely warning against the dangers of 'mirror-reading', i.e. of assuming too readily that every phrase in Paul's letters was either crafted by the apostle or heard by the Philippians in the light of the imperial cult.

In spite of this caveat, there is a striking feature of this letter, not mentioned by Peter Oakes, which may be related indirectly to the imperial cult.

[107] Oakes, *Philippians*, pp. 147–74. [108] Ibid., p. 137.

The phrase 'the gospel' is more prominent in this letter than in any other early Christian writing. In the opening chapter Paul uses the phrase τὸ εὐαγγέλιον six times, five of which are in absolute construction (Phil. 1.5, 7, 12, 16, 27), i.e. without any explanatory phrase. Phil. 1.27 is the exception that proves the rule, for here we find 'the gospel of Christ'. In three further passages in this letter the phrase is used absolutely (Phil. 2.22; 4.3, 15). The verb is not used at all. Once again 'the word' (ὁ λόγος) is used in the absolute, and synonymously with 'the gospel' (Phil. 1.14).[109]

Paul does mention that 'the gospel' has become known throughout the whole Praetorian Guard (Phil. 1.13). Members of the imperial guard would certainly have known the rival 'gospels' concerning Providence's provision of emperors. And so too, we may surmise, Christians in the Roman colony at Philippi.

Paul's repeated use of 'the gospel' and his use of 'the word' (Phil 1.14) as shorthand terms is striking. The Philippian Christians are able fill out their content on the basis of Paul's initial proclamation in their city and his continuing concern for them. Indeed, unlike Galatians, from this letter alone it is difficult to set out the *content* of 'the gospel'. What we have in Philippians, as in Paul's other letters, is use of a cluster of shorthand terms well known to the recipients – terms which are filled with distinctively Christian content and which are used in ways which are out of kilter with wider use in non-Christian first-century settings. I shall take this point further in the next section of this chapter.

2.8 'GOSPEL' AS PART OF AN EARLY CHRISTIAN SOCIOLECT

In an important article on the rhetorical functions of 'the gospel' in the Corinthian correspondence, Margaret Mitchell has built on Wayne Meeks's earlier observation that Paul's letters are packed with 'extremely compact formulas'. She notes that the phrase τὸ εὐαγγέλιον serves as a 'superabbreviation' of the whole narrative sequence of events which describe God's salvific acts on behalf of humankind. The phrase functions as a title which both characterizes the full contents of 'the gospel' and interprets its meaning for the hearer.[110]

---

[109] There is strong manuscript support for 'the word of God' (τὸν λόγον τοῦ θεοῦ); indeed, this reading was adopted in NA 26. F and G read τὸν λόγον κυρίου. NA 27 follows the lead of 𝔓46 and omits τοῦ θεοῦ. This is not always a wise move, given that 𝔓46, our earliest MS of Paul's letters, is riddled with minor slips. In this case, however, the shorter reading is preferable; later scribes failed to appreciate Paul's shorthand use of 'the word'.

[110] M. M. Mitchell, 'Rhetorical Shorthand in Pauline Argumentation: The Functions of "the Gospel" in the Corinthian Correspondence', in L. A. Jervis and P. Richardson, eds., *Gospel in Paul*, FS

This is a helpful observation. I have already borrowed Margaret Mitchell's phrase, 'Paul's shorthand'. I fully endorse her main conclusion. 'Paul's punctuated abbreviations unite his readers with himself and one another in a common bond of shared language and assumptions, a task central to the formation of ecclesial self-identity and social cohesion, and at the same time allow for elegant economy of expression in the new literary creations, the letters.'[111] However, I am not yet persuaded that we need to follow Margaret Mitchell's path in order to reach that conclusion. She claims that Paul is using effectively three forms of ancient rhetorical shorthand, described in rhetorical theory as 'brevity', 'synecdoche', and 'metaphor'. However, the extent to which Paul draws on ancient rhetorical theory is much disputed.[112] I am much more inclined to view Paul's use of shorthand as a classic example of the use of language patterns as identity markers, and here we can turn to sociolinguists for assistance.

The discipline of sociolinguistics is barely four decades old. Whereas Durkheim and Weber, the fathers of sociology, paid little attention to language, sociolinguists are now busy making up for lost time. A major theme in their research is the function of language as a means of group formation. In 1966 William Labov, one of the pioneers, observed the linguistic acts of identity made by those who wished to be recognized as natives of the summer resort Martha's Vineyard.[113] Lesley Milroy has made similar observations about language used on the streets of Belfast.[114] J. K. Chambers, one of the leaders in the field, emphasizes that 'the underlying cause of sociological differences . . . is the human instinct to establish and maintain social identity'. People have a profound need to show that they belong somewhere, and to define themselves by the use of language. 'We must also mark ourselves as belonging to the territory, and one of the most convincing markers is speaking like the people who live there.'[115]

Religious, political, ethnic, and other social groups (even teenagers) do develop their own 'insider' terminology, often by adapting the vocabulary

R. N. Longenecker (Sheffield: JSOT Press, 1994), pp. 63–88; here 63–4; W. Meeks, *The First Urban Christians: The Social World of the Apostle Paul* (New Haven: Yale, 1983), p. 93. See also Betz, *Galatians*, pp. 27–8, who lists a number of Pauline 'theological abbreviations', but not (surprisingly) τὸ εὐαγγέλιον.

[111] Mitchell, 'Rhetorical Shorthand', p. 88.
[112] See especially P. H. Kern, *Rhetoric and Galatians* (Cambridge: Cambridge University Press, 1998).
[113] For a helpful survey of the development of the discipline, see R. B. Le Page, 'The Evolution of a Sociolinguistic Theory of Language', in Florian Coulmas, ed., *The Handbook of Sociolinguistics* (Oxford: Blackwell, 1997), pp. 15–32.
[114] Lesley Milroy, *Language and Social Networks*, 2nd edn (Oxford: Blackwell, 1987).
[115] J. K. Chambers, *Sociolinguistic Theory* (Oxford: Blackwell, 1995), p. 250.

used by 'outsiders' so radically that the language of the 'in-group' is virtually incomprehensible beyond its own boundaries.

Biblical scholars should not be surprised to learn that there is a strong link between language and identity, and that even a single feature of language suffices to identify someone's membership of a given group. In Judg. 12.5-6 we read that, when any escaping Ephraimite wished to cross the Jordan, the men of Gilead would ask, 'Are you an Ephraimite?', and if he said, 'No', they would retort, 'Say "Shibboleth".' He would say 'Sibboleth', thus disclosing his identity and sealing his fate.[116]

I have argued above that in the middle of the first century the difference between 'gospel' in the singular and 'gospels' in the plural was just as significant. 'Gospel' in the singular was developed and used in the very earliest post-Easter communities to summarize the good news of God's once for all provision of Jesus Christ. This linguistic pattern was honed in the teeth of the rival 'gospels' of imperial propaganda. It quickly became part of the shared assumptions of Paul, his co-workers, and the communities he established. In Paul's early letters, the Thessalonian correspondence and Galatians, an explanatory phrase is often tacked on to 'the gospel'; absolute use of the phrase is uncommon. In what is probably Paul's final letter, Philippians, 'the gospel' is nearly always used absolutely. By then there was no need to add explanatory phrases, for 'the gospel' was set in stone as a key building block in a distinctively Christian language pattern.

Early Christian use of the gospel word group, and especially the noun, is one of the most prominent tips of a large iceberg. Here we have a term which had very different associations for insiders and outsiders. There were others. I have mentioned more than once that 'the word' was used by Paul as a synonym for 'the gospel', and that it was used similarly as shorthand, often in the absolute. In fact, it is arguable that 'the word' as a compact summary of the Christian message was used even more widely in the first century than 'the gospel'. It was used, for example, by the author of Hebrews and by Luke, both of whom shunned the phrase 'the gospel'.

Other early Christian near-synonyms for 'the gospel', such as 'the faith' (ἡ πίστις, Gal. 1.23), 'proclamation' (τὸ κήρυγμα), 'the message' (ἡ ἀκοή, e.g. Gal. 3.5), and also ἡ ἀγγελία (I John 1.5), and 'witness' (τὸ μαρτύριον) functioned similarly. They were not unknown to 'outsiders', but to 'insiders' they had a distinctive nuance.

The term χάρις ('grace'/'benefaction') is a first cousin of τὸ εὐαγγέλιον. J. R. Harrison's fine study of χάρις complements some of the key points

---

[116] See further, A. Tabouret-Keller, 'Language and Identity', in Coulmas, *Sociolinguistics*, pp. 315–26.

made in this chapter.[117] He notes that, in sharp contrast to the LXX, Paul chose χάρις over against ἔλεος. In Paul's day χάρις was normally used in the plural, and often to denote the beneficent dispensations of the Roman emperor. Paul always uses the term in the singular, and fills it with Biblical and distinctively Christian content. 'The χάριτες of Augustus had acquired soteriological, eschatological, and cosmological status within his own lifetime throughout the Graeco-Roman world. The grace of the Caesars would remain a continuing refrain. It was precisely in this context that Paul announced God's reign of grace through Christ . . . The paradox is that God accords the status of righteousness to believers through a dishonoured Benefactor.'[118]

I hope that I have said enough to make out my case. The very earliest Christians developed their own 'in-house' language patterns, partly on the basis of Scripture, especially the Septuagint, partly in the light of their distinctive Christian convictions, but partly by way of modifying contemporary 'street' language. In this way they developed their own 'social dialect', and in turn this was very influential on their self-understanding, and their worldview.

They did not, however, develop a wholly new language. If they had done so, obviously evangelism would have been impossible. Here we have a continuing dilemma for Christian theology, one which is underlined by the fact that today there is an increasingly wide gap between the ways insiders and outsiders understand the term 'gospel'. How are Christians to develop language which expresses Christian convictions and yet is intelligible to all and sundry? This is part of an even grander theme, the relationship of the Christian Gospel to culture.

2.9   FROM ORAL PROCLAMATION TO WRITTEN NARRATIVE

Sociolinguists would surely be fascinated by one of the most startling developments in the linguistic usage of the first Christians. In the earliest post-Easter decades τὸ εὐαγγέλιον refers to oral proclamation of the significance of the death and resurrection of Jesus, not to a written account of the story of Jesus. There is general agreement that by no later than the second half of the second century τὸ εὐαγγέλιον was used to refer to a 'gospel-book'.

---

[117] J. R. Harrison, 'Paul's Language of Grace (Χάρις) in its Graeco-Roman Context', Ph.D. thesis, Macquarie University, 1996, to be published in the WUNT series by J. C. B. Mohr, Tübingen. See also his 'Paul, Eschatology and the Augustan Age of Grace', *TB* 50 (1999) 79–91.

[118] Harrison, 'Paul's Language of Grace', p. 201 and p. 210.

There were two phases to this very considerable linguistic development, the first less radical than the second. The evangelist Mark envisages that 'the gospel' includes an account of the teaching of Jesus and narratives of his actions. Mark is expanding the semantic field associated with earlier Christian usage of the noun, especially in Pauline circles. The actions and words of Jesus are now integrated fully into Christian proclamation of God's glad tiding concerning the death and resurrection of Jesus Christ. Although this is often singled out as Mark's most important theological achievement, I do not think that Mark was as innovative as most suppose. For I have long been persuaded that oral proclamation of 'Christ crucified and raised' by Paul and his co-workers would hardly have made sense without at least a sketch of the story of Jesus.[119] Pauline specialists are now more willing to acknowledge that there is a narrative sub-structure to Paul's theology.[120] Nonetheless, the term 'gospel' has undergone considerable development between Paul and Mark.

An even more considerable development in early Christian usage of 'gospel' came with the use of this term to refer to a *written* account of the teaching and actions of Jesus. Who was responsible for this extension of the linguistic usage of the very first Christians? Opinions differ markedly. Was it Mark, or Marcion, or should we look elsewhere?

Luke and John rule themselves out of contention immediately. Luke does not use the noun at all in his account of the life of Jesus. No one has ever explained satisfactorily why he did not do so. The Fourth evangelist uses neither the noun nor the verb. This is no surprise, for he transposes a great deal of earlier Christian vocabulary into a different key.

So who first used 'gospel' to refer to a writing?[121] In tackling questions of this kind it is often helpful to work backwards from the point at which a new development is well attested. From the end of the second century and the first half of the third century there is clear evidence from papyri, the Old Latin and the Coptic versions, and from Irenaeus, Clement of Alexandria, and Tertullian, that the titles 'the Gospel according to Matthew, Mark etc.' (εὐαγγέλιον κατὰ Μαθθαῖον, Μάρκον κτλ.) were widely used.[122] In the middle of the second century Justin, *I Apol.* 66.3, provides the first example

---

[119] See G. N. Stanton, *Jesus of Nazareth in New Testament Preaching* (Cambridge: Cambridge University Press, 1974), pp. 86–116.

[120] See Longenecker, *Narrative Dynamics in Paul.*

[121] The remaining paragraphs in section 2.9 are an abbreviated version of part of my contribution to the *Festschrift* in honour of Franz Neirynck: 'Matthew: βίβλος, εὐαγγέλιον, or βίος?', F. Van Segbroeck et al., eds., *The Four Gospels 1992*, Vol. II (Leuven: Leuven University Press, 1992), pp. 1190–5.

[122] See M. Hengel, 'The Titles of the Gospels and the Gospel of Mark', in his *Studies in the Gospel of Mark* (London: SCM, 1985), p. 66f. Hengel argues convincingly against the widely held view

of the plural εὐαγγέλια to refer to 'gospel books'. Justin states explicitly
that the ἀπομνημονεύματα τῶν ἀποστόλων (a phrase he uses thirteen
times in *Dialogue* 100-7 and once more in *I Apol.* 67.3-4) are εὐαγγέλια.[123]

About a decade earlier Marcion almost certainly referred to his version
of Luke as 'the gospel'.[124] H. Koester has claimed that Marcion's concept
of a written gospel was a 'revolutionary innovation' which Justin took
over.[125] However, Koester partly undermines his own case by making two
concessions. (1) Even before Marcion's day, liturgical readings from the
written gospels may well have been introduced as 'the gospel'.[126] (2) Koester
accepts Hengel's claim that the canonical gospels must have circulated under
the name of a specific author from the very beginning, but he denies that
the original titles were identical with the later 'Gospel according to . . .'.[127]
It is almost inconceivable that the name of the author would have been
attached to copies of the gospels without a title of some kind.[128] But what
title would have been used, if not τὸ εὐαγγέλιον?[129]

There is in fact evidence that εὐαγγέλιον was beginning to be used
to refer to a writing in the decades before Marcion. (a) II Clement 8.5
introduces one of his quotations of words of Jesus with 'the Lord says in the
Gospel' (λέγει γὰρ ὁ κύριος ἐν τῷ εὐαγγελίῳ). The writing concerned is
probably Luke's Gospel, 16.10a and 11.

(b) In two of his letters, Ignatius (c. AD 110) uses 'the Gospel' (τὸ
εὐαγγέλιον) to refer to proclamation of the cross and resurrection of
Jesus. At *Philad.* 9.2, τὸ εὐαγγέλιον includes the coming (παρουσία here

---

    (which is reflected in the titles of the four gospels in the 26th (and also the 27th) edition of the
    Nestle–Aland text) that a shorter form (κατὰ Μαθθαῖον etc.) of the later titles was original.

[123] See Chapter 4.

[124] See A. von Harnack, *Marcion: Das Evangelium vom fremden Gott* (Leipzig: J. C. Hinrichs, 1921),
    pp. 165–6*.

[125] H. Koester, 'From the Kerygma-Gospel to Written Gospels', *NTS* 35 (1989) 361–81, esp. 377–81; the
    phrase quoted is used on p. 381. While at first sight it does seem unlikely that Justin would adopt
    a usage introduced for the first time by his arch-rival Marcion, this is not impossible. Rivals often
    influence one another to a much greater extent than they are aware.

[126] Ibid., p. 381 n. 1. M. Hengel had made the same point in some detail earlier. See his 'Titles',
    pp. 74–81.

[127] 'Kerygma-Gospel', p. 373 n. 2.

[128] See M. Hengel, 'Titles', p. 65. At a very early point Papias refers to the names of the writers of
    the gospels without using εὐαγγέλιον, but he is commenting on the origin of the writings – not
    referring to the title of a manuscript.

[129] Koester, 'Kerygma-Gospel', p. 374 suggests that what Papias says about both Matthew and Mark
    reveals that these 'gospels' had incipits which were similar to those still preserved in the gospels
    from the Nag Hammadi Library. But this does not take us further forward. According to Koester's
    own survey in his *Ancient Christian Gospels: Their History and Development* (London: SCM and
    Philadelphia: Trinity, 1990), pp. 20–3, most of the incipits and colophons of the Nag Hammadi
    'gospels' are either missing or clearly later additions to the manuscripts. Matthew and Mark are
    most unlikely ever to have been referred to as 'Secret Sayings', or 'Secret Book'!

undoubtedly refers to the life) of Jesus Christ, as well as his suffering and resurrection. This suggests that a writing rather than oral proclamation is being referred to, but the latter interpretation is possible.[130]

In the letter to the Smyrnaeans, however, there is less room for doubt. The letter opens with a credal summary of Christological convictions which refers to the baptism of Jesus by John, 'so that all righteousness might be fulfilled by him' (ἵνα πληρωθῇ πᾶσα δικαιοσύνη ὑπ' αὐτοῦ). The verbal agreement with Matt. 3.15, a verse which bears the stamp of Matthew's redactional hand, is sufficiently close to persuade most scholars that Ignatius is here quoting Matthew's Gospel.[131]

In the same letter (5.1) Ignatius notes that neither the prophecies, nor the law of Moses, nor τὸ εὐαγγέλιον has persuaded his opponents. The juxtaposition of τὸ εὐαγγέλιον with Scriptural writings strongly suggests that, in this letter at least, Ignatius is referring to a writing – most probably Matthew's Gospel, which he has quoted just a few paragraphs earlier. A similar juxtaposition of τὸ εὐαγγέλιον with Scriptural writings is found two paragraphs later at 7.2. Here Ignatius urges his readers to 'pay attention to the prophets and especially to the gospel (τῷ εὐαγγελίῳ) in which the Passion has been made clear to us and the resurrection has been accomplished'.[132]

(c) In Didache 8.2; 11.3; 15.3-4f. there are four references to τὸ εὐαγγέλιον. The first passage introduces a quotation of the Lord's prayer with wording which is close to Matt. 6.9-13. The other two passages allude to Matthew's versions of sayings of Jesus. Since few scholars doubt that the Didache is dependent on Matthew, these references confirm that τὸ εὐαγγέλιον was used to refer to a gospel writing, almost certainly Matthew, some decades before Marcion.[133]

If Marcion was not the first to use the term εὐαγγέλιον to refer to a written account of the story of Jesus, was Mark the innovator, some

---

[130] W. R. Schoedel insists (but in my view without compelling arguments) that Ignatius always uses τὸ εὐαγγέλιον to refer to oral proclamation, not to a writing. See his *Ignatius of Antioch*, Hermeneia (Philadelphia: Fortress, 1985), p. 208 n. 6; p. 234.

[131] See W. Köhler, *Die Rezeption des Matthäusevangeliums in der Zeit vor Irenäus*, WUNT 24 (Tübingen: Mohr, 1987); O. Knoch, 'Kenntnis und Verwendung des Matthäus-Evangeliums bei den Apostolischen Vätern', in L. Schenke, ed., *Studien zum Matthäusevangeliums*, FS W. Pesch (Stuttgart: Katholisches Bibelwerk, 1988), pp. 167–8.

[132] I have quoted M. W. Holmes's light revision of J. B. Lightfoot's *The Apostolic Fathers*: M. W. Holmes, ed., *The Apostolic Fathers: Greek Texts and English Translations*, 2nd edn (Grand Rapids: Baker, 1992).

[133] Koester, 'Kerygma-Gospel', pp. 371f., assigns these passages rather arbitrarily to the final redaction of the Didache, which he dates to the end of the second century. This late dating and his denial of the dependence of the Didache on Matthew are accepted by few other scholars.

seventy years earlier? For Mark, τὸ εὐαγγέλιον is the proclaimed message
about Jesus Christ. His usage is close to Paul's, even though Mark, unlike
Paul, sets out a narrative of the teaching and actions of Jesus as a 'sermon'
on, or expression of, the Gospel.[134] This is how Mark's opening line, 'the
beginning of the gospel of Jesus Christ' (ἀρχὴ τοῦ εὐαγγελίου Ἰησοῦ
Χριστοῦ), should be interpreted. Whether τοῦ εὐαγγελίου is taken as a
subjective or as an objective genitive, Mark 1.1 refers to 'proclamation', not
a 'written report'.[135] While it is true that Mark's development of Paul's use
of τὸ εὐαγγέλιον paves the way for later reference to the written story of
the life of Jesus as τὸ εὐαγγέλιον, Mark did not take that step himself.

Matthew, however, did so. In order to show this, we must examine
closely the differences between the use of 'gospel' in Matthew and in
Mark. Matthew omits five of Mark's uses of εὐαγγέλιον (Mark 1.1; 1.14
and 15; 8.35; 10.29) and expands the other two (Mark 13.10 and 14.9). With
the exception of Mark 1.1, in all these passages Matthew is following Mark
closely, so the omissions are striking. They have led M. Hengel to conclude
that Matthew uses τὸ εὐαγγέλιον 'only in a markedly reduced sense'.[136]
Since in his very much longer gospel Matthew retains only two of Mark's
seven uses of the noun and adds it to only two other passages, this seems to
be a reasonable conclusion. On closer inspection, however, it is clear that
Matthew's use of this key word is an important new development.

First of all we must account for Matthew's omission of five of Mark's
uses of εὐαγγέλιον. Mark 1.1 is omitted as it would have been an inap-
propriate introduction to the genealogy Matthew included. Mark 1.14 and
15 are omitted as part of Matthew's concern to bring out clearly the close
correspondence between the proclamation of John the Baptist (Matt. 3.2),
Jesus (4.17), and the disciples (and followers of Jesus in his own day) (10.7):
they all proclaim the coming of the kingdom of heaven.

Mark 8.35; 10.29 are omitted because the phrases 'for the sake of the
gospel' and 'for the sake of Jesus himself' are almost synonymous, and
point to a post-Easter setting. Matthew, however, saw the earthly Jesus, his
teaching and actions, as 'gospel', and so omitted the Marcan passages.

---

[134] W. Marxsen's discussion of Mark's use of τὸ εὐαγγέλιον has been influential. See his *Mark the
Evangelist*, especially pp. 126–38.
[135] W. Marxsen suggests that it is almost accidental that something in the way of report also appears,
Mark the Evangelist, p. 131. R. Guelich argues strongly that 1.1 is not a title for the whole work
since syntactically it must be linked with the sentence which follows. See his *Mark*, Word Biblical
Commentary (Dallas: Word, 1989), p. 9, and, more fully, 'The Gospel Genre', in P. Stuhlmacher,
ed., *Das Evangelium und die Evangelien* (Tübingen: Mohr, 1983), pp. 183–219, esp. pp. 204–8.
[136] Hengel, 'Titles', p. 83.

Unlike Luke, Matthew is not averse to the noun. He uses it in two key passages, 4.23 and 9.35, to summarize the proclamation of Jesus as 'the gospel of the kingdom' (τὸ εὐαγγέλιον τῆς βασιλείας). From the context it is clear that in both passages he has the teaching of Jesus in mind. These passages are central pillars in Matthew's construction of the first half of his gospel: between these pillars he places the Sermon on the Mount in chapters 5–7 and his cycle of miracle traditions in chapters 8–9.

The two passages in which Matthew retains Mark's use of εὐαγγέλιον are equally revealing. In 24.14 Matthew expands Mark's absolute use of the noun at 13.10 to 'this gospel of the kingdom' (τοῦτο τὸ εὐαγγέλιον τῆς βασιλείας). In 26.13 Matthew has 'this gospel' (τὸ εὐαγγέλιον τοῦτο); once again Mark's absolute use of the noun at 14.9 is modified. In both passages the addition of τοῦτο is very striking. The redactional phrase 'the word of the kingdom' (ὁ λόγος τῆς βασιλείας) at Matt. 13.19 is clearly closely related to 24.14 and 26.13.

What is 'this gospel of the kingdom' (or 'word of the kingdom', 13.19) with which the readers of Matthew are to confront the whole world? No definition or explanation is given in any of these three passages, but Matt. 26.13 provides an important clue. This verse, which refers to the woman's act of anointing the head of Jesus with costly oil, shows that for Matthew 'this gospel of the kingdom' includes not only the teaching of Jesus, but also accounts of his actions.[137]

As J. D. Kingsbury notes, the evangelist simply assumes that his readers will know what 'this gospel' is on the basis of their acquaintance with his written document.[138] We may conclude with Kingsbury that the phrase 'this gospel of the kingdom' is Matthew's own capsule-summary of his work.[139]

Matthew probably did not provide a title for his writing, but he intended his full account of the teaching and actions of Jesus to set out for his readers

---

[137] Marxsen, *Mark the Evangelist*, p. 124, claims that for Matthew the 'gospel is of a piece with his speech complexes', but 26.13 surely rules that out. On p. 141 he concedes that there is 'a kernel of truth' in the hypothesis that Matthew's addition of τοῦτο is intended to set up a connection between the Gospel as such and the book of Matthew.

[138] J. D. Kingsbury, *Matthew: Structure, Christology, Kingdom* (London: SPCK, 1975), p. 130, and also p. 163.

[139] Ibid., 131. Kingsbury refers to several earlier writers who have supported the same conclusion. See now also W. Schenk, *Die Sprache des Matthäus* (Göttingen, Vandenhoeck & Ruprecht, 1987), p. 265. U. Luz, *Matthäus*, p. 249 is sympathetic to this view, but suggests that a direct link is not yet drawn. In *Ancient Gospels*, p. 11, n. 4, H. Koester rather rashly claims that all modern commentaries agree that 'this gospel' at Matt. 26.13 cannot refer to Matthew's Gospel, thus overlooking the commentaries of J. Schniewind (on Matt. 24.14) and W. Grundmann. For a different view, see R. H. Gundry, ΕΥΑΓΓΕΛΙΟΝ: How Soon a Book?', *JBL* 115 (1996) 321–5.

the content of 'this gospel of the kingdom'. As soon as an individual or a community had access to more than one narrative account of the life of Jesus, it would have been necessary to distinguish between them by means of a title, especially in the context of readings at worship.[140] That first happened as soon as Matthew had completed his writing, for the evangelist (and perhaps some of the communities to which he wrote) then had two accounts of the story of Jesus: his own, and Mark's.

We may conclude, then, that long before Marcion's day 'gospel' was used for a written account of the story of Jesus. But, since Mark's usage is closer to Paul's and is very different from Matthew's, Mark is not the 'radical innovator'.[141] Need we look any further than the evangelist Matthew? By his insistence that the teaching and actions of Jesus are 'gospel' (4.23 and 9.35) and by his addition of 'this' to Mark's 'the gospel' in 24. 14 and 26.13 (τοῦτο τὸ εὐαγγέλιον), he indicates clearly to his readers that there is a close correspondence between the 'gospel of Jesus' and 'the gospel' which is to be proclaimed in his own day. He also emphasizes that his own writing is 'a gospel'.[142]

We should not suppose that, once τὸ εὐαγγέλιον began to be used for a written account of the life and teaching of Jesus, it ceased to be used to refer to Christian oral proclamation. That double usage continues to this day.

The preceding paragraphs confirm that in early Christian writings it is often difficult to determine whether τὸ εὐαγγέλιον refers to oral proclamation or to a writing. Oral traditions did not disappear the moment Mark wrote. As we shall see in Chapters 3 and 4, oral traditions and written gospels continued to exist side by side until at least the end of the second century.

Language is rarely static. The term τὸ εὐαγγέλιον is a prime example. In Paul's day it referred to the *one* oral Gospel of God's provision of Jesus Christ, in contrast to Providence's repeatable 'gospels' of the provision of Roman emperors. By the end of the second century Irenaeus drops his

---

[140] This point is made most impressively by M. Hengel in 'Titles'; see his section entitled 'The Practical Necessity of the Titles', pp. 74–81.

[141] M. Hengel, who sees Mark as the innovator, does not discuss the differences between Matthew and Mark in 'Titles'. I accept Hengel's point that Mark may have been referred to as 'the gospel' as soon as it began to be used in readings in worship. If so, then this usage would have influenced Matthew. However, the first *explicit* evidence for the use of τὸ εὐαγγέλιον for a writing is found in Matthew's Gospel, not Mark's.

[142] For a very different view, see H. Frankemölle, *Jahwebund und Kirche Christi* (Münster: Aschendorff, 1974), who claims that Matthew is a literary work, a *Buch der Geschichte* modelled on Jewish history writing such as Deuteronomy and Chronicles. This claim does not do justice to the importance for Matthew of the OT prophetic writings and of Mark's Gospel.

guard and refers to four *written* gospels, even though he emphasizes that there is *one Gospel* according to four individual evangelists.

2.10 CONCLUSIONS

This discussion of the origin and use of τὸ εὐαγγέλιον in earliest Christianity has necessarily ranged far and wide. I do not intend to weary readers with summaries of my main conclusions. They can be found at the end of most of the individual sections of this chapter. Nonetheless, several points cry out for brief further comment.

I have suggested that, very soon after Easter, Greek-speaking Jewish followers of Jesus began to use the 'gospel' word group to refer to proclamation of God's one glad tiding concerning Jesus Christ. The content of that proclamation would have been *heard* by many with the language of the imperial cult ringing in their ears, whether or not that was intended by Christian missionaries and teachers who used this terminology. Of course, the imperial cult did not provide the first Christians with their central theological themes. Those themes were shaped by Scripture and by convictions concerning the life, death, and resurrection of Christ. Although there were some superficial similarities between the two forms of 'good news', early Christian proclamation of the Gospel was distinctive, and ultimately subversive of its rival. The key question was: whose good news? Providence's provision of Caesars and their benefactions, or God's once for all provision of grace through 'a dishonoured Benefactor, Jesus Christ?'[143]

As we shall see in Chapter 6, long before the downfall of Jesus, his own proclamation of God's glad tiding was deemed by some to be subversive. The key question was: was Jesus a demon-possessed magician and a false prophet? Or was Jesus proclaiming in word and action God's good news to the poor as a messianic prophet?

Contemporary Christian theological statements regularly assume that a straight line of continuity concerning 'gospel' can be traced from Jesus to the post-Easter church. This has long been the traditional view. It was defended in 1908 by James Denney in an influential book whose title aptly sums up his argument: *Jesus and the Gospel: Christianity Justified in the Mind of Christ.*[144] It is expressed very forcefully in the Second Vatican Council's *Constitution on Divine Revelation 'Dei Verbum'*, chapter 2 §7 (1965). After

---

[143] I owe the striking phrase 'dishonoured benefactor' to Harrison, 'Paul's Language of Grace', p. 210.
[144] (London: Hodder & Stoughton, 1908). In spite of his title, James Denney includes only one paragraph on the term 'gospel'. Somewhat surprisingly, he does not hesitate to accept that Mark uses the term 'gospel' in the sense of the apostolic church (p. 57).

noting that Christ had 'commissioned the Apostles to preach to all men that Gospel which is the source of all saving truth and moral teaching, and to impart to them heavenly gifts', the statement continues: 'This Gospel had been promised in former times through the prophets, and Christ Himself had fulfilled it and promulgated it with His lips.'

My own line of continuity between Jesus' own proclamation and post-Easter proclamation of him is less neat and tidy. It is curved in places, and dotted in others. Nonetheless, there is continuity at some points. Jesus of Nazareth was more than a proclaimer of good news. Key phrases in 4Q521 strongly suggest that in his use of Isaiah 61 Jesus was making an indirect messianic claim: he was himself part of God's good news.

It is often overlooked that the evangelists have less hesitation than modern scholars in drawing that line of continuity. As we have seen, Mark does this through his use of τὸ εὐαγγέλιον. This is confirmed by the interpretation of the parable of the sower (4.13-20). Here we are told that the seed sown by the sower is 'the word', and from the context this can only be a reference to the Gospel; it is clearly implied that the sower of the word or the Gospel is Jesus himself. In fact 'the word' and 'the gospel' are synonymous here, as in several passages in Paul's letters, and also in Matthew, as Matt. 13.19 confirms.

Matthew's line of continuity is even thicker. In his first two uses of τὸ εὐαγγέλιον he has in mind the teaching of Jesus (Matt. 4.23 and 9.35). In his only two other uses of the phrase (Matt. 24.14 and 26.13), he envisages that his own writing will serve as 'gospel' proclaimed 'throughout the world'.

Luke does not use the phrase τὸ εὐαγγέλιον. Nonetheless, he also stresses that the proclamation of Jesus and post-Easter proclamation are identical. He does this by means of the verb 'to proclaim good news' (εὐαγγελίζεσθαι) and the phrases 'the word' and 'the word of God'. Just as Jesus proclaims God's good news (Luke 4.18, 43; 7.22; 8.1; 9.6; 16.16; 20.1), numerous passages in Acts report that the apostles did likewise. At Luke 5.1 we read that the crowd pressed in on Jesus 'to hear the word of God'. The phrase echoes the words of Jesus two verses earlier (4.43): 'I must proclaim the good news of the kingdom of God' (εὐαγγελίσασθαί με δεῖ τὴν βασιλείαν τοῦ θεοῦ). In Luke 5.1 and in three other verses in his gospel (8.11, 21; 11.28) Luke reshapes his sources in order to emphasize that Jesus proclaimed 'the word of God'. In Acts this phrase frequently refers to post-Easter proclamation and once (10.36) to Jesus' own pre-Easter proclamation.

The lines of continuity between pre- and post-Easter proclamation drawn by all three synoptic evangelists are clear.[145] Equally significant is the fact that in differing ways the evangelists indicate that the gospel word group is synonymous with 'the word' or 'the word of God'. In section 2.7 I noted that in several passages in Paul's earliest letter 'the word' (I Thess. 1.6, 8 and 2.13; cf. II Thess. 3.1) and 'the gospel' (I Thess. 1.5; 2.2, 4, 8, 9; 3.2; II Thess. 1.8 and 2.14) are almost synonymous terms. At Gal. 1.23 Paul uses 'the faith' to refer to Christian proclamation (probably for the only time), where 'the gospel' might well have been used. Similarly with Paul's four uses of τὸ κήρυγμα ('proclamation') (I Cor. 1.21; 2.4; 15.14; Rom. 16.25).

In short, as I emphasized at the outset, a basket of near-synonymous words and phrases is used in early Christian writings to refer to God's good news or word concerning Jesus Christ. *Only the gospel word group has verbal links with the language of the imperial cult.* Hence we must be wary of assuming that with every early Christian use of this word group the imperial cult is lurking in the background. The content of Christian proclamation, however, was sufficiently close to the central themes of imperial propaganda for it to be understood by many as a rival, and in due course as a threat.

In section 2.8 attention was drawn to the ways in which 'the gospel' was used in earliest Christianity (and especially by Paul) as a shorthand term and identity marker. The phrase was part of the social dialect of several strands of early Christianity. Although Christian usage was quite distinctive, it was not incomprehensible to 'outsiders'. For it was of the very essence of the whole semantic field associated with this noun that τὸ εὐαγγέλιον was open proclamation, open heralding, to Jew and Gentile alike, of God's evangel or Gospel concerning Jesus Christ.

The pattern of usage I have sketched was replicated in a number of other cases. Key early Christian words such as ἐκκλησία, χάρις, ἀγάπη, and καταλλάσσω were not unknown outside the walls of the earliest house church communities, but they were developed considerably and linked with other words and phrases in order to express the newness of the content of the Gospel.

[145] It is usually assumed that the Fourth Evangelist has merged without remainder proclamation of Jesus and post-Easter proclamation, so that there is complete continuity between the two. This isn't quite the whole story, for the evangelist does distinguish between pre- and post-Easter by means of his 'memory' motif. When Jesus says, 'Destroy this temple, and in three days I will raise it up' (2.19), neither the Jewish leaders nor the disciples understand what he means. However, the evangelist explains that in the light of resurrection faith the disciples remembered this saying and understood its significance (2.22). So too with the entry into Jerusalem (12.16; see also 14.26 and 20.9).

I have suggested that early Christian use of the noun 'gospel' was developed in a quite precise social setting. The relationship between the Christian Gospel and culture must always be two-sided. Language has to be found which rings bells in any given cultural setting, but always with the recognition that Christian proclamation may be subversive, as it undoubtedly was in the first century.

In my Inaugural Lecture in the University of London in 1978 I quoted with approval Gerhard Ebeling's hermeneutical dictum: 'the same *word* can be said to another time only by being said differently'. I want to repeat that dictum today: the same *Gospel* can be said to another time only by being said differently.[146] So I do not want to suggest that Christians should necessarily sprinkle the noun 'gospel' like confetti over all their mission statements, for, in some strands of early Christianity, the noun is conspicuous by its absence. My hope is that Christians will find new ways to express *the concept* meaningfully. In taking up that challenge, we shall be helped by a keener appreciation of the rich and diverse ways the noun 'gospel' is used in the New Testament writings, and in particular by Paul.

---

[146] G. Ebeling, 'Time and Word', in J. M. Robinson, ed., *The Future of our Religious Past: Essays in Honour of Rudolf Bultmann* (E. tr. London: SCM, 1971), p. 265.

CHAPTER 3

The fourfold Gospel

The origins and the theological significance of the fourfold Gospel raise a set of teasing questions.[1] Why did the early church eventually accept four partly parallel foundation documents, no more, no less? There is no precedent for this either in the OT Scriptures or elsewhere in earliest Christianity. Did retention of four gospels assist or hinder the early church in the presentation of its claims concerning Jesus? No doubt, to some, insistence that there were four gospels implied that there were basic flaws in the single gospels. Was the second-century church's decision to bring together four separate gospels wise? What were, and what are, the theological implications of the fourfold Gospel? A critical theology cannot avoid asking these questions.

In the early decades of the twentieth century, the views of the great giants, Theodore Zahn and Adolf von Harnack, were influential: many scholars accepted their view that the fourfold Gospel emerged *very early* in the second century, well before Marcion.[2] More recently, particularly under the influence of Hans von Campenhausen, most scholars have accepted that the fourfold Gospel emerged in the *second half* of the second century and that the Muratorian Fragment and Irenaeus are our primary witnesses.[3]

However, the current consensus on the emergence of the fourfold Gospel is now being challenged from two entirely different starting points. The

---

[1] This chapter was my Presidential Address delivered on 7 August 1996 at the 51st General Meeting of Studiorum Novi Testamenti Societas in Strasbourg, France. It was published in *NTS* 43 (1997) 317–46, and has been lightly revised for this book.

[2] A. von Harnack, *The Origin of the New Testament and the Most Important Consequences of the New Creation* (London and New York, 1925), pp. 69–72; Th. Zahn, *Grundriss der Geschichte des Neutestamentlichen Kanons*, 2nd edn (Leipzig: Deichert, 1904), pp. 35–41. E. J. Goodspeed dated the origin of the fourfold Gospel to c. 125: see his *The Formation of the New Testament* (Chicago: University of Chicago Press, 1937), pp. 33–41. Five years later John Knox rejected Goodspeed's arguments and opted for the West between 150 and 175 as the time when 'we get our first glimpse of the existence of the fourfold Gospel', *Marcion and the New Testament* (Chicago: University of Chicago Press, 1942), pp. 140–67. K. L. Carroll, 'The Creation of the Fourfold Gospel', *BJRL* 37 (1954–5) 68–77 echoed Knox's claim that the fourfold Gospel was an answer to Marcion.

[3] Hans von Campenhausen, *Die Entstehung der christlichen Bibel* (Tübingen: Mohr, 1968); E. tr. *The Formation of the Christian Bible* (Philadelphia: Fortress; London: Black, 1972), chapter 5.

Muratorian Fragment is being assigned by some to the fourth century, and, as a corollary, Irenaeus' devotion to the fourfold Gospel is seen as 'something of an innovation' in a time of fluidity of gospel traditions and a proliferation of gospels.[4] The other challenge to the consensus approaches the question from a very different angle. Whereas the traditional way of discussing this question focusses on the use early Christian writers made of the four gospels, attention is now being given to the evidence of the earliest copies of the gospels themselves – especially to the predilection of Christian scribes for the codex and for *nomina sacra*.[5]

Theological reflection on the significance of Christianity's commitment to four gospels has been sparse in recent years. Very little has been written since Oscar Cullmann's important article first published in 1945.[6] However, in some circles a strong challenge has been mounted to the pre-eminence of the canonical four in historical reconstructions of the origin and development of early Christianity. Now and again this challenge is accompanied by hints of a theological agenda: we are told that by giving increased attention to non-canonical gospels it may be possible to construct a Jesus who will be more congenial in a post-modernist era.

I shall attempt to take account *both* of the ways second-century writers used, and referred to, the gospels *and* also of the evidence of the earliest manuscripts. I shall work backwards from Irenaeus, for I find that it is often helpful to work back from the full flowering of a concept or a development to its earlier roots. I shall insist that the decision to accept four gospels, along with the earlier acceptance of a plurality of gospels, was one of the most momentous ones taken within early Christianity, a decision which cries out for continuing theological reflection.

3.1 IRENAEUS

Book III of Irenaeus' *Adversus Haereses* was written about AD 180. Irenaeus comments on the origin of the four individual gospels, which he clearly

---

[4] See especially G. M. Hahneman, *The Muratorian Fragment and the Development of the Canon* (Oxford: Clarendon, 1992), p. 101. Note also, 'It is difficult therefore to acknowledge that the fourfold Gospel was "firmly established" in the last quarter of the second century' (p. 100; and cf. p. 108). Hahneman develops considerably the arguments for a fourth-century date first advanced by A. C. Sundberg in two articles: 'Towards a Revised History of the New Testament Canon', *Studia Evangelica* 4/1 (1968) 452–61; 'Canon Muratori: A Fourth Century List', *HTR* 66 (1973) 1–41.

[5] See below, pp. 71–5.

[6] O. Cullmann, 'Die Pluralität der Evangelien als theologisches Problem im Altertum', *Theologische Zeitschrift* 1 (1945) 23–42; E. tr. in Cullmann's *The Early Church*, ed. A. J. B. Higgins (London: SCM, 1956), pp. 37–54. See also R. C. Morgan, 'The Hermeneutical Significance of Four Gospels', *Interpretation* 33 (1979) 376–88; R. A. Burridge, *Four Gospels, One Jesus?* (London: SPCK, 1994), pp. 163–79.

accepts as 'Scripture', and sets out the earliest defence of the church's four-fold Gospel. His main point is clear: there is one Gospel in fourfold form, held together by one Spirit (*Adv. Haer.* iii.11.8).

Irenaeus frequently refers to 'the Gospel', 'the Gospel according to . . .' and only very rarely to 'four gospels'.[7] The Gospel is primarily the faith proclaimed and transmitted by the apostles, and only secondarily the written record 'reported' by such and such an evangelist.[8] If there is one Gospel, why are there four written accounts of it? Why four, no more, no less?

Irenaeus' attempt in iii.11.8 to defend the number 'four' with analogies from both the natural and the spiritual worlds is well known. His fourfold appeal to the four points of the compass and the four winds, the four-faced cherubim of Ezekiel 1 and the four living creatures of Rev. 4.7, the fourfold activity of the word of God, and God's four covenants with mankind has been derided as a 'fundamental error'[9] and seen as a quite desperate attempt to defend a recent innovation.[10]

I do not think that this reading of Irenaeus is accurate: his discussion of the fourfold Gospel is much more sophisticated than many writers have supposed. All too often Irenaeus' comments on the number four are wrenched out of context; they are in fact a digression in a lengthy and often perceptive discussion of the authority and reliability of the witness of the Scriptures to one God, the Creator of all.

Irenaeus' views on the four gospels are established long before he offers reasons why there are four gospels, no more, no less, in chapter 11 of Book iii. In the Preface to Book iii Irenaeus states clearly that the Gospel preached by the apostles has been 'handed on to us in the Scriptures, so that the Gospel may be the foundation and pillar of our faith'. This image of the Gospel as the 'foundation and pillar' of the church, an allusion to I Tim. 3.15, is repeated in chapter 11 and extended to the four gospels as the four pillars of the church.

---

[7] See A. Benoit, *Saint Irénée. Introduction à l'étude de sa théologie* (Paris: Presses Universitaires de France, 1960). Benoit notes that, in Book iii, 'gospel' is used in the singular forty-one times; twelve times for a particular gospel; only six times in the plural. See also Yves-Marie Blanchard, *Aux sources du canon, le témoinage d'Irénée, Cogitatio Fidei 174* (Paris: Cerf, 1993), p. 157, who counts seventy-five occurrences of 'gospel' in Book iii, only five of which are in the plural.

[8] See especially the Preface to Book iii, and iii.1.1. For a helpful discussion of the verbs used to refer to the 'reporting' or 'recording' activity of the evangelists, see Blanchard, *Aux sources du canon*, p. 161.

[9] Cullmann, *The Early Church*, pp. 50–2 claims that Irenaeus' justification of the fourfold Gospel 'is based on the same fundamental error as the Gnostics' "docetic" arguments against it': his appeal to four as a 'divinely ordained number' left out of account the purely human circumstances of the formation of the fourfold Gospel.

[10] Theodor Zahn, *Geschichte des neutestamentlichen Kanons* (2 vols., Erlangen: Deichert, 1888), Vol. i, p. 153, scornfully rejects attempts to write off Irenaeus' arguments as 'dogmatic assertions and theosophical trifles'.

In the important opening paragraphs of Book III Irenaeus comments further on the origins of the four gospels. After Pentecost the apostles proclaimed the Gospel orally; two of the apostles and two of their followers wrote gospels. Discussion of the human origins of the four written gospels is followed by emphasis on their theological unity: 'They have all declared to us that there is one God, Creator of heaven and earth, announced by the law and the prophets; and one Christ, the Son of God' (III.1.1-2).

So right from the outset of Book III the reader knows that the church has the one God-given Gospel as recorded by two apostles and two of their immediate associates. In other words, the Gospel has been given to the church in fourfold form, and chapter 11 with its set of four arguments, within each of which the number four plays a central role, is hardly necessary. We may even feel that the extended defence of the number four in 11.8 weakens rather than strengthens Irenaeus' case, but his first readers probably thought otherwise, for they were accustomed to seeing hidden meaning in numbers. At the outset of the *Adversus Haereses* Irenaeus summarizes the Valentinians' views and shows that the number four played an important role in their speculations.

For Irenaeus' readers, the number four would certainly have evoked solidity and harmonious proportion, precisely his intention. As an example of the evocative nature of the number four in Irenaeus' day, let me mention the Tetrapylon at Aphrodisias, completed just a few years before Irenaeus wrote. This superb gateway to Aphrodisias, one of the finest and most influential cities of the ancient world in the second century, has four recently re-erected columns, each one of which has four richly decorated faces. So Irenaeus' first readers may well have been impressed by his claims that the outward form of the Gospel should be harmoniously composed and well proportioned, just like God's creation (III.11.9).

Now to a rather different point. Irenaeus is fascinated by the beginnings of the four gospels. He refers to them three times in Book III, beginning at 11.9. Why does he cite and comment on the *openings* of the four gospels so fully? He could have made his general point concerning one God the Creator from many other passages from the gospels. The considerable variations in the openings of the four gospels must have baffled both Christian and non-Christian alike. Irenaeus does state that the Valentinians seized on the errors and contradictions of the gospels (III.2.1).[11] So, probably with an

---

[11] '. . . in accusationem convertuntur ipsarum Scripturarum, quasi non recte habeant, neque sint ex auctoritate et quia varie sint dictae . . .'. I have used the edition of the Latin text in *Irénée de Lyon. Contre les hérésies*, III, ed. A. Rousseau and L. Doutreleau, Sources Chrétiennes 211 (Paris: Cerf, 1974), which includes the Greek fragments and a retroversion of the Latin into Greek.

eye on his opponents, Irenaeus stresses that, in spite of their very different starting points, the four gospels do have a theological unity.[12] The Muratorian Fragment, to which we shall come in a moment, makes a similar point.

Although Irenaeus often cites passages from the four gospels accurately, he also regularly introduces sayings of Jesus with 'the Lord said', 'the Lord said in the Gospel', 'the Lord declared', without indicating from which particular gospel the sayings are taken. At the end of the Preface to Book III, for example, a version of Luke 10.18 is introduced with the words 'the Lord declared'. In this case, the text is cited in abbreviated form: it is difficult to decide whether the variation occurs as the result of faulty memory, Irenaeus' knowledge of an otherwise unattested textual tradition, or his use of oral tradition. In the middle of his extended discussion of the opening chapters of Luke's Gospel, Irenaeus refers to four verses from John 1, but without indicating that he has switched from Luke to John (III.10.3). Matt. 12.18-21 is quoted as part of the discussion of the opening chapters of John's Gospel, but, once again, the reader is not told about the change of gospels. Similar phenomena occur elsewhere. This is not surprising once we recognize that, for Irenaeus, 'the Gospel' and in particular the words of Jesus have a higher authority than the individual writings of the evangelists, even though the gospels are referred to occasionally as 'Scriptures'.

Irenaeus is able to cite the written gospels both carefully and carelessly,[13] to weave together loosely passages from two or more gospels, and to introduce sayings with 'the Lord said', some of which seem to be taken from the written gospels, some from oral tradition. The fact that these various phenomena are found in a writer for whom the fourfold Gospel is fundamental stands as a warning sign for all students of gospel traditions in the second century. Earlier Christian writers may also value the written gospels highly even though they appeal directly either to the words of Jesus or to oral tradition, or even though they link topically sayings of Jesus taken from two or more gospels. Irenaeus was not the only writer who cites 'words of the Lord', and does not tell us whether he is quoting from written gospels or from oral tradition.

By the time Irenaeus wrote in about AD 180, the fourfold Gospel was very well established. Irenaeus is not defending an innovation, but explaining why, unlike the heretics, the church has four gospels, no more, no less: she

---

[12] See Zahn, *Geschichte*, Vol. II, p. 43 and H. Merkel, *Die Widersprüche zwischen den Evangelien. Ihre polemische und apologetische Behandlung in der alten Kirche bis zu Augustin* (Tübingen: Mohr, 1971), pp. 42–3.

[13] Matt. 11.27 is cited in three different ways at IV.6.1, 3, 7.

has received four written accounts of the one Gospel from the apostles and their immediate followers.[14]

3.2   THE MURATORIAN FRAGMENT

The second pillar in most discussions of the origin of the fourfold Gospel has been the Muratorian Fragment, generally dated to just before, or just after, Irenaeus' *Adversus Haereses*. Is this view still tenable, in spite of attempts to date the Fragment to the fourth century? Or is this pillar beginning to crumble?

In 1992 Geoffrey Hahneman picked up and developed a case for a fourth-century date, first defended by A. Sundberg in 1968.[15] Even though they have now won a handful of converts, especially in the USA,[16] I do not think that the case for a fourth-century date has been made out.[17] I shall do no more than refer briefly to their three main points.

First, the cornerstone of the traditional dating has always been the Fragment's reference to Hermas' composition of the Shepherd 'nuperrime', very recently, in our times, in the city of Rome, while bishop Pius, his brother, was occupying the episcopal chair of the church of the city of Rome (lines 73–6) – i.e. not all that long after AD 140.[18] Hahneman, however, claims that all the Fragment's information about the Shepherd is 'erroneous or misleading'. He redates the Shepherd to c. AD 100 and then argues that the Fragment's attribution of the Shepherd to Hermas is fourth-century pseudonymity designed to discredit the Shepherd. But, since the Shepherd

---

[14] Cf. Benoit, *Saint Irénée*, p. 117: 'La justification irénéenne ne veut pas être une démonstration, elle ne fait qu'augmenter la crédibilité du fait accepté par ailleurs.' T. C. Skeat, 'Irenaeus and the Four-Gospel Canon', *NovT* 34 (1992) 193–9, claims that, in his celebrated identification of the four evangelists with the four living creatures of the Apocalypse, Irenaeus has used an earlier source. His case is strong but not conclusive, so I have not drawn on it in this chapter.

[15] See n. 4 above.

[16] In his article 'Muratorian Fragment' in *The Anchor Bible Dictionary*, ed. D. N. Freedman (New York: Doubleday 1992), Vol. IV, p. 929, G. A. Robbins claims that Sundberg's thesis 'has won considerable acceptance and further confirmation'. In his article 'Canon, New Testament' in the same dictionary, H. Y. Gamble accepts Sundberg's thesis cautiously (Vol. I, p. 856), as does H. Koester, *Ancient Christian Gospels: Their History and Development* (London: SCM; Philadelphia: Trinity, 1990), p. 243.

[17] See now J. Verheyden's detailed study, 'The Canon Muratori: A Matter of Dispute', in J.-M. Auwers and H. J. de Jonge, eds., *The Biblical Canons* (Leuven: Peeters, 2003), pp. 487–586. Verheyden concludes (p. 556) that 'the suggestion of a fourth century eastern origin for the Fragment should be put to rest not for a thousand years, but for eternity'.

[18] I have used the critical edition edited (with a facsimile reproduction) by S. P. Tregelles, *Canon Muratorianus* (Oxford: Clarendon, 1867). Tregelles's learned notes are still worth consulting. See also H. Lietzmann's edition, *Das Muratorische Fragment und die monarchianischen Prologe zu den Evangelien*, Kleine Texte, i (Bonn, 1902).

is still listed in the Fragment as 'recommended reading', this seems implausible.[19]

Secondly, the Fragment is said to fit naturally into fourth-century catalogues of canonical writings; it is an anomaly in the second century. This line of argument is well off the mark, for the Fragment is not a canonical list or catalogue at all. Its genre is that of 'Einleitung' comments about the origin and authority of early Christian writings; the only two later uses of the Fragment are in prologues, not lists.[20]

Thirdly, the Fragment is allegedly out of line with other evidence for the development of the canon. In my judgement none of the Fragment's comments is anomalous in a second-century setting; many fit much more readily into that setting than into a fourth-century context.[21] I shall now explore this point with reference to the Fragment's comments on the gospels.

There is general agreement that the Fragment's comments on Luke were preceded by comments on Matthew and Mark. The second line could well be a title for Luke's Gospel: the third book of the Gospel according to Luke.[22] Just like Irenaeus, the Fragment uses both the formal phrase, 'Gospel according to Luke', 'evangelium secundum Lucam', a direct translation of εὐαγγέλιον κατὰ Λουκᾶν (a phrase to which I shall return later), and also uses the plural, 'fourth of the gospels' (line 9, and similarly in lines 17 and 20).

The Fragment comments more fully on the origin of 'the fourth of the gospels' than on any other writing.[23] The attempt to link the origin of this gospel to the whole apostolic circle smacks of apologetic: the Fourth Gospel, it is claimed, stems ultimately from revelation. This thoroughgoing defence of the Fourth Gospel would surely not have been needed in

[19] Similarly, E. Ferguson in his critical review of Hahneman's monograph in *JTS* 44 (1993) 691–7: 'The pseudonymity would seem to be of doubtful value in a polemic against the Shepherd in the fourth century.' See also E. Ferguson's discussion of Sundberg's theory in 'Canon Muratori: Date and Provenance', *Studia Patristica* 18 (1982) 677–83.

[20] Cf. J.-D. Kaestli: 'Par son contenu et par sa forme, le *CM* (Canon de Muratori) est plus proche du genre des "prologues" que de celui des "listes canoniques": 'La Place du *Fragment de Muratori* dans l'histoire du canon. A propos de la thèse de Sundberg et Hahneman', *Cristianesimo nella Storia* 15 (1994) 609–34, here 616. Similarly Ferguson, *JTS* 44 (1993) 696.

[21] For similar conclusions, see Ferguson, *JTS* 44 (1993) 691–7; Kaestli, 'La Place du *Fragment de Muratori*'; P. Henne, 'La Datation du *Canon de Muratori*', *RB* 100 (1993) 54–75; and W. Horbury, 'The Wisdom of Solomon in the Muratorian Fragment', *JTS* 45 (1994) 149–59.

[22] A. T. Ehrhardt suggests that the comment about Luke in lines 6–7, 'dominum tamen nec ipse vidit in carne', is sufficient evidence 'to assume that Papias was responsible for the fragmentary remark about St. Mark in the Muratorian Fragment': 'The Gospels in the Muratorian Fragment', in his *The Framework of the New Testament Stories* (Manchester: Manchester University Press, 1964), pp. 11–36, here p. 13; this chapter was first published in German in *Ostkirchen Studien* 2 (1953) 121–38.

[23] See especially Ehrhardt, *Framework*, pp. 18–25.

the fourth century, but we do know that in the latter part of the second century there were doubts in some circles about the Fourth Gospel, most notably among the Alogi and the followers of the anti-Montanist Gaius.

Andrew is the only apostle who is named at this point. This is not surprising, since in John 1.40 Andrew is identified by name as the first person to respond to John's witness to Jesus. In the Fourth Gospel Andrew is given a prominence which he does not have in the other three gospels. As we shall see shortly, Papias also singles out Andrew for special mention and in so doing reveals his knowledge of the Fourth Gospel.

The Fragment's lengthy defence of the Fourth Gospel includes in lines 16–26 an important reference to the fourfold Gospel. The Fragment concedes that different beginnings are taught in the various gospel books, yet insists that they are held together by one primary Spirit. This is surely a response to critics who have pounced on the different beginnings of the gospels.[24] As in other lines, we are close to Irenaeus, though there is no sign of verbal dependence. I have already drawn attention to the way Irenaeus comments at length on the beginnings of the gospels, probably partly in response to critics. Similarly in the Fragment.[25] In lines 7–8 the opening of Luke's story is referred to. In lines 16–26 a theological response is made to the criticism that the gospels have different beginnings: by the one primary Spirit, the central themes of the story of Christ are found in all four gospels. As with Irenaeus, the fourfold Gospel is not an innovation, but it does need to be defended against the jibes of critics who poke fun at the different openings of the gospels.

Who did this? As I noted above, Irenaeus refers to the Valentinians. I also suspect that Celsus or some other pagan critic may well be lurking behind Irenaeus' comments and lines 16–26 of the Fragment. Writing between 177 and 180, just a few years before Irenaeus wrote Book III of the *Adversus Haereses*, Celsus knew all four gospels and had a particular interest in their early chapters. According to Origen, Celsus' Jew claimed that some Christians, as if somewhat the worse from drink, 'alter the original text of the Gospel three or four or several times over, and they change its character to enable them to deny difficulties in the face of criticism'.[26] I take

---

[24] So also R. M. Grant, *The Earliest Lives of Jesus* (London: SPCK, 1961), p. 31.

[25] See also Zahn, *Geschichte* (above, n. 2), Vol. II, p. 43.

[26] *Contra Celsum* II.27, ed. and trans. H. Chadwick (Cambridge: Cambridge University Press, 1953), p. 90. See also v.56, where Origen responds to Celsus' jibes concerning the number of angels at the tomb of Jesus. For other evidence of the problems caused by differences in the gospels, see H. Merkel, *Die Widersprüche* (above, n. 12), and *Die Pluralität der Evangelien als theologisches und exegetisches Problem in der alten Kirche* (Bern: Peter Lang, 1978).

this to be a reference to differences between the 'three or four' canonical gospels.[27]

The Fragment refers to the two parousias of Christ and rather optimistically claims that this schema is found in all four gospels. 'Everything is declared in all the gospels . . . concerning his two comings, the first in humility when he was despised, which is past, the second, glorious in royal power, which is still in the future.' This schema is first developed fully by Justin Martyr, though I have argued that it is partly anticipated in Matthew's Gospel.[28] The two parousias schema is very prominent in Justin's writings; it is also found in his *Apology*, in Irenaeus, Tertullian, Hippolytus, Origen, and the *Anabathmoi Iakobou*, but not, as far as I can discover, in fourth-century writings.

The Fragment confirms that the fourfold Gospel was well established towards the end of the second century.[29] Quite independently, the Fragment and Irenaeus make similar points concerning the fourfold Gospel: in spite of what critics may say about the different beginnings of the gospels, there is one Gospel in fourfold form, held together by one Spirit.[30] Needless to say, the points I have emphasized are conspicuous by their absence in the recent attempts to locate the Fragment in the fourth century.

3.3 EARLY FOUR-GOSPEL CODICES

Could Irenaeus and the writer of the Muratorian Fragment have used codices containing all four gospels? In 1968 von Campenhausen denied vigorously that the references to the fourfold Gospel in Irenaeus and the Muratorian Fragment had anything to do with 'book production' or Christian use of a four-gospel codex.[31] In 1933, however, F. G. Kenyon had edited the recently discovered $\mathfrak{P}$45, the Chester Beatty codex of the four gospels and Acts, and had noted that this new evidence meant that it was

---

[27] So too Merkel, *Die Widersprüche*, p. 11. See also T. Baarda, 'ΔΙΑΦωΝΙΑ – ΣΥΜΦωΝΙΑ: Factors in the Harmonization of the Gospels, Especially in the Diatessaron of Tatian', in W. L. Petersen, ed., *Gospel Traditions in the Second Century* (Notre Dame and London: University of Notre Dame Press, 1989), pp. 133–5, reprinted in his *Essays on the Diatessaron* (Kampen: Kok Pharos, 1994), pp. 29–48; Grant, *Earliest Lives*, pp. 59–60.

[28] G. N. Stanton, 'The Two Parousias of Christ: Justin Martyr and Matthew', in M. C. de Boer, ed., *From Jesus to John, FS M. de Jonge* (Sheffield: JSOT Press, 1993), pp. 183–96.

[29] Ehrhardt, *Framework*, p. 11 suggests that the Fragment was produced at Rome, probably under Zephyrinus, AD 197–217.

[30] I am not convinced by A. Ehrhardt's claim (ibid., pp. 14–15) that the reference to John as 'ex discipulis' in line 16 betrays its origin in Irenaeus, who refers to John the evangelist as 'the disciple of the Lord', but never refers to him as the son of Zebedee; this similarity could have arisen from independent use of the same tradition.

[31] Von Campenhausen, *Formation* (above, n. 3), pp. 173–4.

possible to believe that Irenaeus may have been accustomed to the sight of codices which contained all four gospels.[32] Kenyon dated the codex to the first half of the third century and concluded that it was the earliest example of a codex containing all four gospels.

Kenyon's dating of 𝔓45 and his general observations on this codex have been widely accepted, though most scholars have overlooked his important comment on Irenaeus' probable knowledge of four-gospel codices. In recent years our knowedge of Biblical papyri and codices has increased very considerably: we now have fairly solid evidence for two further four-gospel codices which are even earlier than 𝔓45.

𝔓75, the Bodmer papyrus of Luke and John, has attracted plenty of attention from text critics. There is general agreement that it dates from early in the third century; the editors dated it to between AD 175 and 225. However, the possibility that its fragments of Luke and John formed the second of two single-quire codices sewn together does not seem to have been considered until 1994.[33] Why would Luke and John be bound together without Matthew and Mark? It is just possible to imagine a codex containing Matthew and John, the two gospels considered to have been written by apostles. But a codex containing only Luke and John is most unexpected. In fact we have no other example of a two-gospel codex.[34] T. C. Skeat has calculated that 𝔓75 contained seventy-two leaves, and noted that a codex of double this size would have been almost impossible to handle. So he concludes that 𝔓75 may have originally consisted of a single-quire codex containing Matthew and Mark, sewn together with another containing Luke and John, and then bound.[35]

A strong case has recently been made out by T. C. Skeat for an even earlier four-gospel codex.[36] 𝔓64, the fragments of Matthew held at Magdalen College, Oxford, was first edited by Colin Roberts in 1953 and dated to

---

[32] *The Chester Beatty Biblical Papyri*, Fasciculi I and II, *The Gospels and Acts*, General Introduction and Text (London: Emery Walker, 1933), here I, p. 13. 𝔓45 is made up of quires of two leaves – a single sheet of papyrus folded into two. The letters are small; the scribe was no calligrapher.

[33] T. C. Skeat, 'The Origin of the Christian Codex', *ZPE* 102 (1994) 263–8, here 264.

[34] 𝔓53, third century, with fragments of Matthew and Acts in the same hand, is an interesting possible partial exception, though the fragments may not be from the same codex. If they are, and if the codex included all four gospels, it would have run to a highly improbable 300–50 leaves. So a codex with one or two gospels, plus Acts, is possible. Cf. K. Aland, *Repertorium der griechischen christlichen Papyri*, Vol. 1 (Berlin and New York: De Gruyter, 1976), pp. 53 and 283. See also J. van Haelst, *Catalogue des papyrus littéraires juifs et chrétiens*, Papyrologie 1 (Paris: Publications de la Sorbonne, 1976), nos. 380, 381.

[35] Skeat, 'Origin', p. 264. In 'The Oldest Manuscript of the Four Gospels?' *NTS* 43 (1997) 31, Skeat mentions in passing the possibility that perhaps there were two volumes, i.e. two single-quire codices bound separately.

[36] Skeat, 'Oldest Manuscript', pp. 1–34.

the late second century on the grounds that its hand is a precursor of the style known as Biblical Uncial or Biblical Majuscule. These are the three fragments which have attracted so much attention in the media since a sensationalist article published in *The Times* of London on 24 December 1994 reported C. P. Thiede's claim that they date from the mid first century.[37]

There has never been any doubt that $\mathfrak{P}67$, with its further fragments of Matthew now in Barcelona, was from the same codex as $\mathfrak{P}64$. For some six months before the media became interested in $\mathfrak{P}64$, T. C. Skeat had been working intensively on $\mathfrak{P}64 + \mathfrak{P}67$, as well as $\mathfrak{P}4$, fragments of Luke in the Bibliothèque nationale in Paris. Skeat has now shown beyond reasonable doubt that $\mathfrak{P}64 + \mathfrak{P}67 + \mathfrak{P}4$ are from the same single-quire codex, probably our earliest four-gospel codex, which may date from the late second century.

In his *NTS* article Skeat does not comment on the significance of one of the codex's most striking features, its double columns.[38] The format of two columns to the page is rare in papyrus codices. This is the only example of a two-column Greek New Testament papyrus manuscript, though there are four examples in early fragments of OT papyri.[39] The narrow columns, with only about fifteen letters in each column, would have assisted reading aloud in the context of worship.[40] The columns have about the same number of letters as each of the three columns of Codex Vaticanus, and only about

---

[37] See G. N. Stanton, *Gospel Truth? New Light on Jesus and the Gospels* (London: HarperCollins, 1995), pp. 1–19. For Thiede's theory, see his 'Papyrus Magdalen Greek 17 (Gregory–Aland $\mathfrak{P}64$): A Reappraisal', *ZPE* 105 (1995) 13–20; reprinted in *TB* 46 (1995) 29–42. The theory has been rejected by numerous scholars, all of whom accept Roberts's original date for $\mathfrak{P}64$, the late second century. See especially J. Neville Birdsall, 'The Dating of the Magdalen Papyrus', *Church Times*, 6 January 1995; Klaus Wachtel, 'Π64/67: Fragmente des Matthäusevangeliums aus dem 1. Jahrhundert?', *ZPE* 107 (1995) 73–80; Peter M. Head, 'The Date of the Magdalen Papyrus of Matthew (*P. Magd. Gr.* 17 = P64): A Response to C. P. Thiede', *TB* 46 (1995) 251–85; D. C. Parker, 'Was Matthew Written before 50 CE? The Magdalen Papyrus of Matthew', *Expository Times* 107 (1995) 40–3; S. R. Pickering in *NT Textual Research Update* 2 (1994) 94–8 and 3 (1995) 22–5; P. Grelot, 'Remarques sur un manuscrit de l'Evangile de Matthieu', *RSR* 83 (1995) 403–5; J. K. Elliott in *NovT* 38 (1996) 393–9; H. Vocke, 'Papyrus Magdalen 17 – Weitere Argumente gegen die Frühdatierung des angeblichen Jesus-Papyrus', *ZPE* 113 (1996) 153–7.

[38] After I had completed the research summarized in this paragraph, T. C. Skeat wrote to me (10 July 1996) as follows: 'The two-column format became the standard form throughout the whole of the Middle Ages, and has survived almost down to the present day in printed bibles and prayer-books. Why? I have never seen this considered, but I suppose the answer must be that this is the easiest to read. Certainly reading the lessons from $\mathfrak{P}45$ with its very long lines and small script would have been quite difficult, and no doubt it wasn't intended for liturgical use.'

[39] See E. G. Turner's list of papyrus codices written in two columns, *The Typology of the Early Codex* (Philadelphia: University of Pennsylvania Press, 1977), p. 36.

[40] In 1970 the NEB was published with one single wide column on each page. In 1989 the REB reverted to the more traditional two-column format, partly in order to facilitate reading aloud in the context of worship.

three fewer than the four columns of Codex Sinaiticus. The two great fourth-century manuscripts were clearly intended for liturgical use. So the use of two columns in $\mathfrak{P}64 + \mathfrak{P}67 + \mathfrak{P}4$ is almost certainly an indication of a high-class codex, a splendid 'pulpit edition' intended for liturgical use.[41]

There are several other indications that this codex was an *édition de luxe*.[42] The codex was planned and executed meticulously: the skill of the scribe in constructing it is most impressive.[43] All these features indicate a most handsome edition of the four gospels, which would have been expensive to produce. This codex does not look at all like an experiment by a scribe working out ways to include four gospels in one codex: it certainly had predecessors much earlier in the second century.

The three early codices are not clones of one another, for they are all constructed and executed quite differently.[44] In all probability they had a number of predecessors. So well before the end of the second century there was a very well-established tradition of four-gospel codices. All three papyrus codices were found in Egypt; the evidence of Irenaeus and the Muratorian Fragment points towards the West. So the fourfold Gospel seems to have been well established in both East and West at the end of the second century, and probably very much earlier.

However, for two reasons some caution is necessary. First, it is just possible that one or more of these three codices was in fact written in the West. If that seems an unlikely scenario, we need to bear in mind that a fragment of Irenaeus, P. Oxy. 405 (from a roll) travelled from Lyons to Oxyrhynchus within twenty years of its production, 'not long after the ink was dry on the author's manuscript', to quote Roberts's memorable comment.[45]

Secondly, papyrologists are always, rightly, extremely cautious about dating handwriting styles and developments in the production of manuscripts. On the other hand, the recent media attention has ensured that the dating

---

[41] Cf. Turner, *Typology*, pp. 36–7. Van Haelst, *Catalogue*, no. 336, even says that this is the oldest example of a codex with two columns; presumably he means the oldest *Biblical* codex, though, in the light of Turner's list, this is a doubtful claim.

[42] This is T. C. Skeat's phrase, 'Oldest Manuscript', p. 26.

[43] C. H. Roberts noted that 'in its handsome script as well as in its organization . . . it is a thoroughgoing literary production'. *Manuscript, Society and Belief in Early Christian Egypt* (London: Oxford University Press for The British Academy, 1979), p. 23. Although Skeat, 'Oldest Manuscript', 2 and 7, has been unable to find any trace of two of the examples given by Roberts – three different positions for punctuation as well as omission and quotation signs – he concurs with Roberts's general conclusions.

[44] $\mathfrak{P}45$, the latest of the three, is the least impressive hand. Whereas $\mathfrak{P}45$ is made up of quires of two leaves – a single sheet of papyrus folded in two – $\mathfrak{P}75$ probably contained two single-quire codices bound together. $\mathfrak{P}64 + \mathfrak{P}67 + \mathfrak{P}4$ is a two-column, single-quire codex.

[45] Roberts, *Manuscript*, p. 53; Roberts notes some similarities with $\mathfrak{P}64 + \mathfrak{P}67 + \mathfrak{P}4$, p. 23.

of $\mathfrak{P}64 + \mathfrak{P}67 + \mathfrak{P}4$ has been considered carefully by several papyrologists. Working independently, they have all dated this codex to the end of the second century.[46]

3.4 EARLIER ROOTS

Irenaeus, the Muratorian Fragment, and the three earliest codices of the gospels all suggest that, by the latter decades of the second century and probably much earlier, the fourfold Gospel was well established and widely accepted. At what point, and under what circumstances, were four gospels brought together? Since this was a major development within early Christianity, our critical instincts encourage us to search for answers. Before we resume the search, however, it is important to recall that there are no explicit comments on the fourfold Gospel before Irenaeus, and to note that knowledge and use of a plurality of gospels is not necessarily to be equated with acceptance of the fourfold Gospel.

Is it possible to trace the *roots* of the development of the fourfold Gospel to the first half of the second century? In discussion of this question, three issues are particularly important.

(1) I turn first to Justin Martyr, whose knowledge and use of the gospels shortly after the middle of the century is still much disputed, in spite of intense research and debate. I am concerned with only one issue: did Justin anticipate the adoption of the fourfold Gospel, or did he anticipate his pupil Tatian's harmony?

In Justin's well-known account of eucharistic worship in *I Apol.* 67, he refers to the reading of 'the memoirs of the apostles or the writings of the prophets, as long as time allows'. Here apostolic writings are being accorded a similar authority to that of the writings of the prophets, which, as for Irenaeus, is a Christian short-hand way of referring to the OT Scriptures. But what are the 'memoirs of the apostles'? In the preceding chapter the reader is told explicitly that they are 'the gospels' (*I Apol.* 66), the first Christian occurrence of the plural. This is not a later gloss, for, as Luise Abramowski has shown, Justin does add similar explanatory phrases for his readers.[47]

In addition to these two references to 'the memoirs of the apostles' in the *Apology*, Justin uses the phrase thirteen times in one section of the

---

[46] See above, n. 37.
[47] L. Abramowski, 'Die "Erinnerungen der Apostel" bei Justin', in P. Stuhlmacher, ed., *Das Evangelium und die Evangelien* (Tübingen: Mohr, 1983), pp. 341–54, esp. p. 341.

Dialogue, chapters 98–107, in which he seems to have incorporated his own, earlier extended anti-gnostic exposition of Psalm 22, and in which he emphasizes the 'writtenness' of 'the memoirs of the apostles'. At one point in this exposition Justin refers to Peter's memoirs; from the context this is a reference to Mark's Gospel (*Dialogue* 106.3). So in both the *Apology* and the *Dialogue* the 'memoirs' are identified as written gospels.

How many gospels does Justin accept? In *Dialogue* 103.8 he refers to 'the memoirs composed by his apostles and those who followed them' (ἐν γὰρ τοῖς ἀπομνημονεύμασιν, ἅ φημι ὑπὸ τῶν ἀποστόλων αὐτοῦ καὶ τῶν ἐκείνοις παρακολουθησάντων συντετάχθαι . . .). Although Justin never refers to the number of the gospels he accepts, this passage implies that there were at least four. It is surprising how many recent writers have ignored this point.[48] There is general agreement that Justin used Matthew and Luke regularly, and that Mark's Gospel is referred to once (*Dialogue* 106.3). Justin's knowledge of the Fourth Gospel is much disputed, but I am convinced that *I Apology* 61.4 draws on John 3.3-5, and that *Dialogue* 88.7 shows knowledge of John 1.19-20. Justin's failure to refer to John's Gospel more frequently is puzzling, but it may be related to his strong interest in infancy narratives, and in ethical teaching and futurist eschatological sayings – all in somewhat short supply in this gospel. Since there is no clear evidence for Justin's knowledge of any gospels other than the canonical four, we can be all but certain that he had in mind Matthew, Mark, Luke, and John, no more, no less.

Justin uses the singular 'Gospel' in only two passages, but in both cases he is referring to written traditions. At *Dialogue* 10.2 Justin's opponent Trypho states that he has *read* with appreciation the commands of Jesus 'in the so-called Gospel'. At *Dialogue* 100.1 there is a similar usage: a citation of Matt. 11.27 is introduced with the words, 'in the Gospel it is written . . .' (ἐν τῷ εὐαγγελίῳ γέγραπται εἰπὼν . . .) These two references recall Irenaeus' much more frequent use of the phrase 'in the Gospel'. For Justin, as for Irenaeus, the sayings of Jesus are of special importance: they are recorded 'in the Gospel', 'in the memoirs of the apostles'.

Unlike Irenaeus, Justin is not interested in the authorship or distinctive features of the individual gospels. However, like Irenaeus, Justin knows at least four written 'memoirs' or gospels, which can be referred to collectively as 'the Gospel'. Of course, Justin does not have Irenaeus' clear conception of the fourfold Gospel, but the references in his extant writings to

[48] It was noted already by S. P. Tregelles in 1867 (*Canon Muratorianus* (above, n. 18), p. 71): 'no smaller number [than four] could be implied by the two groups'.

written gospels suggest that he may well have had a four-gospel codex in his catechetical school in Rome by about AD 150.[49]

At this point account must be taken of the ways Justin cites sayings of Jesus. The textual evidence is undeniably complex, and it is not easy to account for the variations in wording from Matthew and Luke.[50] In his important recent study W. L. Petersen has shown that some of Justin's harmonized traditions can be traced in his pupil Tatian's more thorough-going harmony.[51] Helmut Koester has gone further and suggested that 'Justin was composing the *one* inclusive new Gospel which would make its predecessors, Matthew and Luke (and possibly Mark), obsolete'.[52] If one focusses attention on the wording of the citations, Justin's use of, or even composition of, a harmony of sayings of Jesus is undeniable.

But how can such a conclusion be squared with Justin's references to written gospels? I think it is likely that for catechetical purposes (and possibly even to disarm critics)[53] Justin himself gathered together topically harmonized clusters of sayings of Jesus from written gospels, primarily Matthew and Luke.[54] In this respect he partially anticipates Tatian, but I do not believe that the corollary is an intention to do away with the 'memoirs of the apostles', i.e. the written gospels in which the Saviour's words were recorded (cf. *Dialogue* 8.2).

The opening programmatic exchange between Justin and Trypho in the *Dialogue* strongly suggests that Justin's references to the sayings of Jesus are based on written gospels. Justin recalls his own conversion experience and the passionate desire which possessed him for the prophets, and for those great men who are 'the friends of Christ', surely the apostles (8.2). Justin refers immediately to the 'dreadful majesty' of the Saviour's words and the importance of carrying them out: there is a clear implication that the words of Jesus have been written down by 'the friends of Christ'. Trypho responds with a taunt: Justin has been deceived, for he has been following

---

[49] E. J. Goodspeed (*Formation*, p. 38) is much less cautious: 'Justin became a Christian at Ephesus as early as 135 AD, and probably there became attached to the fourfold gospel.'

[50] See especially, A. J. Bellinzoni, *The Sayings of Jesus in the Writings of Justin Martyr* (Leiden: Brill, 1967) and Koester, *Ancient Christian Gospels*, pp. 360–402.

[51] See W. L. Petersen, 'Textual Evidence of Tatian's Dependence upon Justin's ΑΠΟΜΝΗ-ΜΟΝΕΥΜΑΤΑ', *NTS* 36 (1990) 512–34.

[52] H. Koester, 'The Text of the Synoptic Gospels in the Second Century', in W. L. Petersen, ed., *Gospel Traditions in the Second Century* (Notre Dame and London: University of Notre Dame Press, 1989), p. 30, and cf. p. 32.

[53] W. L. Petersen mentioned the latter possibility to me in a letter dated 1 September 1996.

[54] Similarly Bellinzoni, *Sayings of Jesus*; E. Osborn, *Justin Martyr* (Tübingen: Mohr, 1973), p. 132; and L. Abramowski, 'Die "Erinnerungen"', 352–3.

men (plural) of no account, once again, surely, a reference to the apostles who have recorded the words of the Saviour.

Like Irenaeus, Justin set great store by the words of Jesus. So for catechetical purposes he seems to have used written gospels to make his own harmonized collections of sayings of Jesus, linking them together topically. On the other hand, Justin's knowledge and use of four written gospels is clear. Although in some respects he anticipates Tatian, in the use of written gospels alongside harmonized sayings of Jesus his successor is Irenaeus. In the light of our earlier conclusions, Justin's reference to at least four written gospels in *Dialogue* 103.8 suggests that he may well have possessed a four-gospel codex in the library of his catechetical school.

(2) Martin Hengel has drawn attention to Zahn's and Harnack's views on the titles of the gospels.[55] In my judgement all three scholars have correctly insisted that from early in the second century there was a profound conviction that there was *one* Gospel 'according to' individual evangelists. The evidence is so strong and so widespread that here we are surely in touch with another of the roots of Irenaeus' conviction that there is one Gospel in fourfold form.

Hengel rightly attached weight to the evidence of the papyri. The opening and closing leaves of papyri codices are usually missing, so the clear inscriptio εὐαγγέλιον κατὰ Ἰωάννην ('the Gospel according to John') in 𝔓66 from about 200 is striking. It is in the same hand as the rest of the text, but it has been added to the opening page a little awkwardly; the subscriptio would have been identical. In 𝔓75, perhaps only a couple of decades later, we have two examples on the same page of εὐαγγέλιον κατά . . . , a subscriptio to Luke and an inscriptio to John.[56]

The evidence of 𝔓66 and 𝔓75 is consistent with the evidence of Irenaeus and the Muratorian Fragment: in the second half of the second century in many circles there was a strong conviction that there was *one* Gospel, according to a particular evangelist. But what about the first half of the second century? Helmut Koester rejects Martin Hengel's theory that from early in the second century the gospels must have had εὐαγγέλιον κατά . . . attached to them as titles by claiming that Hengel has anachronistically read

---

[55] M. Hengel, 'The Titles of the Gospels and the Gospel of Mark', in *Studies in the Gospel of Mark* (London: SCM, 1985), pp. 64–84.

[56] M . Hengel also notes that a page from 𝔓64 + 𝔓67 + 𝔓4, 'which belong together', has the inscriptio εὐαγγέλιον κατὰ Μαθθαῖον ('Titles', p. 66). However, this example should not be set alongside the evidence of 𝔓66 and 𝔓75, for the inscriptio (which is now located with the 𝔓4 fragments of Luke) is not in the same hand; it probably comes from a fly-leaf added to the codex at a later point.

back to the beginning of the century evidence of papyri from the end of the second century.[57]

However, Koester and Hengel agree on one crucial point: as soon as Christian communities regularly used more than one written account of the actions and teaching of Jesus, it would have been necessary to distinguish them by some form of title, especially in the context of readings at worship.[58] That first happened as soon as Matthew had completed his writing, for many Christians then had two accounts of the story of Jesus, Matthew's and Mark's.

There is plenty of evidence for use of a plurality of gospels in many circles in the first half of the second century. Papias, now dated to c. 110 by several scholars, will serve as an example. He certainly knew Matthew and Mark. I am convinced that Papias also knew John: there is no other reasonable explanation for his list of disciples in the order, Andrew, Peter, Philip, and Thomas – precisely the order in which they appear in the Fourth Gospel, an order found nowhere else, though Andrew is singled out in line 14 of the Muratorian Fragment as the apostle who received the revelation that John, 'ex discipulis', should write down 'quartum evangeliorum'.

So when early Christian communities used more than one gospel, how were they differentiated, particularly in the context of worship? What are the possible terms which could have been used to distinguish what we now know as Matthew from Mark? Certainly not βίος ('life'), for which there is no evidence; and not Justin's ἀπομνημονεύματα ('memoirs'), which was not used by any Christian prior to Justin.[59]

As far as I can see, there is only one candidate, εὐαγγέλιον. As is well known, in the first half of the second century it is not always easy to decide whether εὐαγγέλιον refers to oral proclamation or to a written account of the actions and teaching of Jesus. However, we may be confident that εὐαγγέλιον refers to a writing in four passages in the Didache (8.2; 11.3; twice in 15.3-4) which cannot be written off as late second-century redaction; twice in Ignatius' letter to the Smyrnaeans (5.1 and 7.2), and also in II Clement 8.5.[60] Once εὐαγγέλιον began to be used for a writing, it was a natural extension to use this term as a title. What more appropriate way

---

[57] H. Koester, 'From the Kerygma-Gospel to Written Gospels', *NTS* 35 (1989) 361–81, here 373 n. 2.

[58] Cf. H. Koester, 'Kerygma-Gospel', p. 381 n. 1 and Hengel, 'Titles', pp. 74–81.

[59] See Grant, *Earliest Lives* (above, n. 24), pp. 119–20.

[60] For fuller discussion, see above pp. 54–5, and G. N. Stanton, 'Matthew: ΒΙΒΛΟΣ, ΕΥΑΓΓΕΛΙΟΝ, or ΒΙΟΣ?', in F. Van Segbroeck et al., eds., *The Four Gospels 1992*, FS Franz Neirynck, Vol. II (Leuven: Leuven University Press, 1992), pp. 1187–1202. For a different view, see R. H. Gundry, 'ΕΥΑΓΓΕΛΙΟΝ: How Soon a Book?', *JBL* 115 (1996) 321–5.

was there of referring to individual gospels than as εὐαγγέλιον κατά . . .? So one of the roots of the fourfold Gospel was undoubtedly the very early use of the term εὐαγγέλιον to refer to a written gospel, and the strong conviction that there was one Gospel, 'according to' a particular evangelist.

(3) The very early separation of Luke and Acts is another indication of the deep roots of the fourfold Gospel.[61] It is generally accepted that Luke and Acts were originally written on two separate rolls: they could not have been squeezed onto one roll; the short Preface to Acts with its re-dedication to Theophilus was a conventional way of introducing the second roll of a single work. Once Christian scribes began to use the codex early in the second century, it would have been possible for Luke and Acts to have been juxtaposed in the same codex, with or without other writings, but, as far as we know, this never happened.[62] Luke and Acts are separated in the Muratorian Fragment, and in all the lists and catalogues of canonical writings. Irenaeus is the first writer to stress the close relationship between Luke and Acts: he insisted that, if his opponents accepted Luke's Gospel, they should also accept Acts (*Adv. Haer.* III.14.3 and 4).

We are so accustomed to treating Luke and Acts as one single writing in two parts that it is easy to overlook the fact that in the second century Luke's Gospel and Acts circulated separately. Even in later centuries they were not brought together. Two explanations are currently given for the early separation of Luke and Acts. W. A. Strange has recently proposed that, at Luke's death, Acts remained in draft form; it remained in obscurity until published in the third quarter of the second century, following editorial work by both a 'western' and a 'non-western' editor.[63] Even if this is a plausible solution to the textual problems of Acts, I do not think that Acts was unknown until the time of Irenaeus. Neither Irenaeus nor the Muratorian Fragment presses a case for accepting Acts; they both imply that the existence and authority of Acts had long been recognized. Irenaeus' use of Acts in polemic against his opponents would have been self-defeating if Acts had only recently become available, for Irenaeus insists that, unlike

---

[61] For discussion of the relationship of Luke and Acts, see M. C. Parsons and R. I. Pervo, *Rethinking the Unity of Luke and Acts* (Minneapolis: Augsburg Fortress, 1993).

[62] 𝔓53 is a possible exception; see n. 32 above. B. M. Metzger, *The Canon of the New Testament: Its Origin, Development, and Significance* (Oxford: Clarendon, 1987), p. 296, lists a few late examples of Luke coming fourth in a sequence of the four gospels, perhaps from a desire to bring the two books by Luke side by side.

[63] W. A. Strange, *The Problem of the Text of Acts* (Cambridge: Cambridge University Press, 1992), esp. pp. 181–9.

some of the writings used by heretics, the writings the church accepts are ancient.[64]

I think that an alternative explanation is much more likely: the acceptance of Luke into the fourfold Gospel led to its early separation from Acts, probably before Marcion.[65] There was plenty of interest in the second century in the apostles, but even more interest in the sayings and actions of Jesus recorded 'in the Gospel'. Hence Acts seems to have remained somewhat in the shadow of 'the Gospel'.

Taken cumulatively, this evidence suggests that the adoption of the fourfold Gospel may well have taken place in some circles (though not necessarily everywhere) shortly before Justin's day. Before I comment further on the date of the emergence of the fourfold Gospel, I shall refer to explanations which have been advanced for this momentous development within early Christianity.

3.5 HOW AND WHEN?

What were the key factors which led to emergence of the fourfold Gospel? Which form of explanation is preferable, a 'big bang' theory, or a theory of gradual development?

It has often been urged that the fourfold Gospel was adopted in order to counter the rapid growth and success of various groups of heretics, especially gnostics. Of course, the production and use of gospels by gnostics may have encouraged 'the great church' to clarify its position. But if heretics were primarily in view, would it not have been wiser to opt for just one gospel? Why four? When Irenaeus attacked the Valentinians of his day, he had to show that all four gospels supported the theological point he was making: it is hard to see how four gospels gave him a stronger case than one.

The same point is relevant when assessing whether or not the fourfold Gospel was an answer to Marcion.[66] It is hard to see how four gospels assisted the struggle against Marcion. Von Campenhausen's judgement is surely correct: 'That the new Gospel canon was particularly directed against Marcion cannot be deduced from its composition.'[67]

---

[64] See Benoit, *Saint Irénée* (above, n. 7), pp. 122–7 for a fuller discussion.

[65] Similarly, W. R. Farmer and D. M. Farkasfalvy, *The Formation of the New Testament Canon* (New York, 1983), p. 73, though they date the emergence of the fourfold Gospel somewhat later.

[66] See Knox, *Marcion* (above, n. 2); so also Carroll, 'Creation' (above, n. 2).

[67] Von Campenhausen, *Formation*, p. 171 n. 113. Elsewhere von Campenhausen accepts that Marcion was very influential on the emergence of the NT canon; for discussion, see F. Bovon, 'La Structure canonique de l'Evangile et de l'Apôtre', *Cristianesimo nella Storia* 15 (1994) 559–76.

A political explanation has often been advanced. The fourfold Gospel is said to have been a compromise worked out between different regional preferences.[68] However, it is difficult to find any evidence for the second-century equivalent of the European parliament! The older view that individual gospels circulated only in limited geographical areas is no longer tenable:[69] the papyri, both Christian and non-Christian, indicate clearly that there was a great deal of contact between different regions around the Mediterranean.[70]

A very different view is preferable. I am convinced that the emergence of the fourfold Gospel is related to Christian adoption of the codex, for no roll could contain four gospels. This explanation is hardly new: in 1933 F. G. Kenyon noted that the Chester Beatty papyri confirmed that the Christian community was *addicted* to the codex rather than to the roll, and recognized that, when the four gospels were brought into one codex, they were 'marked off as a single unit'.[71] But Kenyon's important observation went largely ignored until C. H. Roberts and T. C. Skeat set out in full the evidence for early Christian use of the codex and showed that Christian scribes borrowed a Roman invention which had not been an immediate success.[72]

The statistics are astonishing: among non-Christian papyri, rolls predominate until early in the fourth century, but Christian papyri are very nearly all fragments of codices. With only one possible exception, every single papyrus copy of the gospels is from a codex.[73]

---

[68] Farmer and Farkasfalvy, *Formation*, emphasize the importance of the decision taken by Irenaeus and Anicetus to agree to disagree over the date of Easter: 'there was no other moment in Church history when it is more likely that the fourfold Gospel canon was, in principle, implicitly agreed upon', p. 72. D. Trobisch also emphasizes the importance of this decision, reported by Eusebius, *HE* v.24.14: *Die Endredaktion des Neuen Testaments. Eine Untersuchung zur Entstehung der christlichen Bibel* (Freiburg: Universitätsverlag; Göttingen: Vandenhoeck & Ruprecht, 1996), pp. 158–9.

[69] So too von Campenhausen, *Formation*, p. 123: 'It is highly questionable whether the idea is correct, that originally each individual Gospel had its own territorial domain.'

[70] See especially E. J. Epp, 'New Testament Papyrus Manuscripts and Letter Carrying in Greco-Roman Times', in B. A. Pearson, ed., *The Future of Early Christianity*, FS H. Koester (Minneapolis: Fortress, 1991), pp. 35–56; E. J. Epp, 'The Papyrus Manuscripts of the New Testament', in B. D. Ehrman and M. W. Holmes, eds., *The Text of the New Testament in Contemporary Research*, FS B. M. Metzger (Grand Rapids: Eerdmans, 1995), pp. 3–21, here pp. 8–10.

[71] Kenyon, *Chester Beatty*, Fasciculus I, pp. 12f.

[72] C. H. Roberts and T. C. Skeat, *The Birth of the Codex* (London: Oxford University Press for the British Academy, 1983).

[73] The exception is 𝔓22 (= P. Oxy. 1228), third-century fragments of John 15, now in Glasgow, with their recto inexplicably blank. It is worth noting that two of the three fragments of the Gospel of Thomas, P. Oxy. 654 and P. Oxy. 655, are from rolls; P. Oxy. 1 is from a papyrus codex. See B. Layton, ed., *Nag Hammadi Codex II, 2–7* (Leiden: Brill, 1989), pp. 96–7.

Why did Christians have such a strong predilection for the codex? Skeat has recently rejected the reasons usually advanced for adoption of the codex and has insisted that the motive 'must have been infinitely more powerful than anything hitherto considered'.[74] Skeat notes that the codex could contain the texts of all four gospels; no roll could do this. He then asks, 'What can have induced the Church so suddenly, and totally, to abandon rolls, and substitute not just codices but a single codex containing all four Gospels?' He accepts that single gospels circulated as codices, but only as 'spin-offs', so to speak, of the four-gospel codex. In his view, the production of the Fourth Gospel about AD 100 caused a crisis in the church: a formal decision was taken to publish the four gospels in a single codex, and as a result the codex became the norm for Christian writings. 'How the decision was reached we have no means of knowing. Clearly there must have been correspondence between the major churches, and perhaps conferences.'[75]

David Trobisch has recently defended a partly similar theory.[76] He claims that the early Christian use of the codex and of *nomina sacra* can be accounted for only by positing deliberate decisions concerning the appropriate format for canonical writings. Trobisch, however, studiously refrains from stating when and where this guideline for the preparation of Christian manuscripts was drawn up.[77]

The strength of the theories advanced by Skeat and Trobisch is that they draw attention to the rapid and universal adoption of the codex for what became in due course canonical writings. However, I am not completely convinced by either theory. Both theories require a much higher level of structure and centralized organization within early second-century Christianity than I think likely.[78] If (as Skeat suggests) the four-gospel codex *preceded* the circulation of single-gospel codices, it must have been adopted soon after the beginning of the second century, for we have in 𝔓52 (usually

---

[74] Skeat, 'Origin', pp. 263–8, here 263.

[75] Skeat, ibid., p. 263, explains that he no longer accepts either of the two theories which he and C. H. Roberts had advanced in *The Birth of the Codex*. For discussion of the various explanations advanced for Christian adoption of the codex, see J. van Haelst, 'Les Origines du codex', in A. Blanchard, ed., *Les Débuts du codex* (Turnhout: Brepols, 1989), pp. 13–36; and S. R. Llewelyn, *New Documents Illustrating Early Christianity*, Vol. VII (Sydney: The Ancient History Documentary Research Centre, Macquarie University, 1994), pp. 249–56. T. C. Skeat's reference to the crisis caused by the publication of the Fourth Gospel recalls E. J. Goodspeed's suggestion that the fourfold Gospel emerged a few years after the appearance of the Fourth Gospel; it was intended to win a wider hearing for the Gospel of John than it would otherwise have received (*Formation*, pp. 35–6).

[76] Trobisch, *Endredaktion*.   [77] Ibid., especially pp. 12 and 124.

[78] I am not convinced by D. Trobisch's attempt (ibid., pp. 67–8) to overturn this generally held view of early second-century Christianity.

dated to c. AD 125) a single-gospel codex. But a date soon after the turn of the century is difficult to square with the ways written gospels and oral gospel traditions were used at that time.

My own view is that Christian scribes first experimented with single-gospel codices by adopting the Roman invention of the use of pocket editions of literary works referred to in AD 84–6 by Martial. In Epigram 1.2 Martial recommends that travellers should carry his poems in copies with small parchment pages which could be held in one hand, presumably parchment codices. Martial even gives his readers the name and address of the 'publisher'.

Early codices, whether Roman or Christian, were quite small in size and therefore much more portable than rolls. Christian scribes preparing writings to be carried by missionaries, messengers, and travellers over long distances would have readily appreciated the advantages of the codex.[79] Their general counter-cultural stance would have made them more willing than their non-Christian counterparts to break with the almost unanimous preference for the roll and to experiment with the unfashionable codex.

No doubt the popularity of the codex in Christian circles was enhanced by its distinctive format. The earliest Christian experiments with the codex took place at a time when Christians were adopting a distinctive identity as a *tertium genus* over against both Judaism and the pagan world. Copying and using the OT Scriptures and their foundation writings in a new format was but one of the ways Christians expressed their sense of 'newness'.[80] Some Christians today still cling to a particular translation and format of the Bible as an identifying mark of their group or theological convictions.

The codex format caught on rapidly in Christian circles.[81] The ability of the codex to hold four gospels seems to have been appreciated at the

[79] See especially M. McCormick, 'The Birth of the Codex and the Apostolic Life-Style', *Scriptorium* 39 (1985) 150–8.

[80] Colette Sirat rejects the claim made by Roberts and Skeat, *Birth*, that there was a Jewish origin for Christian use of the codex. She notes that, in the first centuries of our era, traditional Jewish texts do not make any allusion to the codex: 'Le Livre hébreu dans les premiers siècles de nôtre ère: le témoinage des textes', in A. Blanchard, ed., *Les Débuts du codex*, Bildiologia 9 (Brepols: Turnhout, 1989), pp. 115–24.

[81] Cf. H. Y. Gamble, *Books and Readers in the Early Church: A History of Early Christian Texts* (New Haven and London: Yale University Press, 1995), p. 65: 'To claim the most primitive edition of the Pauline letter collection was put out in a codex and that it was the religious authority of Paul's collected letters that set the standard for the transcription of subsequent Christian literature in codices is not to claim that this marked the first use of the codex in Christian circles. It is possible, perhaps likely, that the codex was first employed in primitive Christianity for collections of texts (*testimonia*) from Jewish scripture.' I accept the latter point, but I am not convinced that it was a collection of the Pauline letters (which Gamble dates in the early second century, 'and probably earlier' (p. 61)) which 'set the standard' for use of the codex. We have far more early codices of individual gospels

very time when four gospels were being brought together in some second-century circles.

When did this happen? All the evidence I have set out in this chapter points to the period shortly before 150. Justin's writings confirm that, in the decade or so after the Bar Cochba rebellion, Christian self-understanding as a *tertium genus* took hold strongly, so perhaps it was during these years that the four-gospel codex and the fourfold Gospel began to become popular. I make this suggestion with some hesitation. Numerous pieces of the jig-saw puzzle are missing; the discovery of only one or two new pieces might well alter the whole picture.

Acceptance of the fourfold Gospel did not mean the end of oral tradition; continuing use of oral traditions did not necessarily mean that written gospels were unknown or of marginal importance. It is a great mistake to suppose that written traditions and oral traditions were mutually exclusive.[82] And it is equally important to note that the emergence of the fourfold Gospel did not instantly suppress either the use of, or the production of, further gospels. To have a set of four authoritative gospels does not mean that one stops reading anything else. In some circles doubts emerged from time to time about one or more of the four gospels; the universal adoption of a four-gospel *canon* took much longer. Above all, we need to recall that, even in Irenaeus' day, when the fourfold Gospel was axiomatic in many circles, the sayings of Jesus possessed an even higher authority.

It will be clear from the preceding paragraphs that I prefer a theory of gradual development to a 'big bang' theory. I envisage the following stages in the emergence of the fourfold Gospel, though of course I recognize that my summary suggests a neat and tidy development, far removed from the reality of continuing debate and of diversity of practice. The codex began to be used for individual gospels soon after the turn of the century, a period when a plurality of gospels was known in many circles. During these decades the term 'Gospel' was used both for oral and for written 'Jesus' traditions. Use of the term 'Gospel' for two or more writings raised the question of their relationship to the *one* Gospel about Jesus Christ. This problem was solved

---

and codices of the four gospels than we do of collections of Paul's letters; the gospels are quoted much more frequently in the second century than are the Pauline epistles. As I have noted above, early Christian use of the LXX in codices must also have encouraged Christians to adopt the codex as a standard format. For further discussion, see Chapter 8 below.

82 See Gamble, *Books and Readers*, pp. 28–30; G. N. Stanton, 'Form Criticism Revisited', in M. D. Hooker and C. J. A. Hickling, eds., *What about the New Testament? FS C. F. Evans* (London: SCM, 1975), pp. 13–27. See also Loveday Alexander, 'The Living Voice: Scepticism towards the Written Word in Early Christian and in Graeco-Roman Texts', in D. J. A. Clines, S. E. Fowl, and S. E. Porter, eds., *The Bible in Three Dimensions* (Sheffield: JSOT, 1990), pp. 221–47.

by use of the title εὐαγγέλιον κατά . . . for individual gospels. The use of
this title facilitated both the acceptance of the fourfold Gospel and the use
of the codex for four gospels. The four-gospel codex strongly encouraged
acceptance of the fourfold Gospel, and vice versa: both are likely to have
taken place for the first time shortly before the middle of the second century.

The fourfold Gospel did not gain immediate acceptance: as I shall recall
in a moment, there were very strong currents running in the opposite direction. Christian insistence that the church had four equally authoritative
stories written by apostles and their followers left doors wide open for both
Jewish and pagan critics. The continuing attraction for many Christians
and 'heretics' of *one* written Gospel (whether or not a harmony), as well
as the jibes of critics, encouraged Irenaeus to mount what seems to have
been the first full theological defence of the fourfold Gospel. The *universal*
acceptance of four gospels – a four gospel *canon* – followed in due course,
but not without further vicissitudes.

3.6 THEOLOGICAL SIGNIFICANCE

The acceptance of the fourfold Gospel does not raise problems for the
historian. On the contrary, the historian is happy to have four sources
available for reconstruction of the actions, words, and intentions of Jesus. Of
course, the historian will want to assess all sources critically, but, in principle,
the more sources the better. However, as soon as the historian considers the
broad sweep of the development of the early Christian movement in the
period before Constantine, it becomes clear that the four canonical gospels
played a greater part in the development of the Christian movement and
of Christian theology than any non-canonical Jesus or gospel traditions.

The fourfold Gospel is of no significance if one wants to make a particular historical reconstruction of the life of Jesus the *sole* focus of religious
concern. For example, if one really believes that nothing more can be said
about Jesus than that he was a Wisdom or a Cynic teacher, then one is opting
for a post-Christian position: in that case, the four evangelists' portraits of
Jesus will be of no more than passing historical interest, to be discarded
along with numerous later faith images of Jesus. But, if one accepts that the
evangelists' attempts to tell the story of Jesus and to spell out his significance
are in some way normative for Christian faith, then the fourfold Gospel is
problematic. Why do Christians need four stories?

The momentous nature of the decision to accept four gospels becomes
clear once we recognize that alternative solutions nearly won the day in
the first and second centuries. Acceptance and use of one gospel was a live

option again and again. When Matthew wrote his gospel, he did not intend to supplement Mark: his incorporation of most of Mark's Gospel is surely an indication that he intended that his gospel should replace Mark's, and that it should become *the* Gospel for Christians of his day. Similarly Luke. Luke's Preface should not be dismissed merely as the evangelist's way of honouring literary convention. There is little doubt that Luke expects that his more complete gospel will displace his predecessors', even though he may not intend to disparage their earlier efforts. Whether or not John knew of the existence of one or more of the synoptic gospels, he seems to have expected that his gospel would win wide acceptance as *the* Gospel.

This pattern continued in the second century. Numerous very different Christian groups used only one gospel. Immediately before his declaration that there can be neither more nor less than four gospels, Irenaeus notes that four groups of heretics, Marcion included, have all fastened on one of the four gospels (*Adv. Haer.* III.11.7). Irenaeus is painting with plenty of rhetoric on his brush at this point; nonetheless, his picture is broadly accurate.

And then there is Tatian, who produced one harmonized gospel out of four, or possibly five, gospels. He was almost certainly not the only person to opt for this solution, and his solution was amazingly successful in some circles for a very long time.

In the first and second centuries there were strong tides moving Christian churches towards acceptance of only one gospel. Acceptance of the fourfold Gospel meant turning back the tidal currents: it carried as a corollary rejection of all the various attempts to opt either for one single gospel, or for a harmony of known gospels. The tide was not turned back in a hurry, but, once it began to turn, there was no going back: we never find manuscript evidence for acceptance of any 'fifth' gospel such as Thomas or Peter alongside one or more of the writings in the fourfold Gospel.[83] The adoption of the four-gospel codex undoubtedly encouraged this whole process.

Was Irenaeus correct to give such a robust extended theological defence of the fourfold Gospel? Was he wise to give it a privileged theological position? Most of us have difficulty in accepting his view that two of the evangelists were apostles, and two were close associates of apostles. However, a careful reading of his writings reveals that his notion of 'apostolic' is acceptably broad, for Irenaeus emphasizes the lines of continuity of the four written

---

[83] So too, J. K. Elliott, 'Manuscripts, the Codex and the Canon', *JSNT* 63 (1996) 107.

gospels with the oral Gospel proclaimed by the apostles; like the apostles, the four gospels all proclaim one God, one Christ; they are held together by one Spirit.

At about the same time, Serapion, bishop of Antioch, made a similar theological judgement. The Gospel of Peter should not be accepted solely because the great apostle's name was attached to it: continuity with the apostolic faith was the criterion by which it should be judged. So too Luther in his insistence that the test of apostolicity was whether or not a book proclaimed Christ. 'That which does not preach Christ is not apostolic, though it be the work of Peter or Paul, and conversely that which does teach Christ is apostolic even though it be written by Judas, Annas, Pilate, Herod.'[84]

Once we understand 'apostolic' in this extended sense, we need not hesitate to affirm Irenaeus' defence of the fourfold Gospel. The other gospels which Irenaeus knew, or which appeared after his day, are clearly beyond the limits of acceptable theological diversity at crucial points. For Irenaeus there were three crucial theological points: the doctrine of one God, the Creator of all; continuity with the Scriptures; and Christology. If we consider all the possible rivals to the four gospels which became canonical, they all fall down on one or more of these theological criteria.

At one point Irenaeus attacks the Valentinians for audaciously accepting 'The Gospel of Truth'. He notes that it is totally unlike the gospels of the apostles, and also that it is a comparatively recent writing (*Adv. Haer.* III.11.9). In modern times some weight has often been attached to this criterion of 'earliness': the four gospels are authoritative for Christian theology because they are the earliest witnesses we have to the actions and teaching of Jesus. Caution is of course necessary, for there are 'non-canonical' traditions which have a good claim to be as early as traditions which found their way into the four 'canonical' gospels. But their importance must not be exaggerated. Even the *Jesus Seminar* accepts as authentic only five of the logia of Thomas which are not found in the canonical four.[85] And, as for complete gospels, are any earlier than the canonical four? Surely J. D. Crossan is exercising a vivid historical imagination when he claims that an early version of the Gospel of Peter was written in the fifties, possibly in Sepphoris.[86]

[84] M. Luther, *Werke* (Erlangen, 1826–57), pp. 63, 156f. I owe this reference to R. H. Bainton in the *Cambridge History of the Bible*, Vol. III, ed. S. L. Greenslade (Cambridge: Cambridge University Press, 1963), p. 7.

[85] See further Stanton, *Gospel Truth?* (above, n. 37), pp. 84–93. [86] See further ibid., pp. 78–82.

In short, a critical Christian theology need not stumble over the fourfold Gospel. But there are corollaries, four of which I shall single out for brief comment. First, the question of genre. If the four gospels are regarded primarily as theological witnesses to Jesus Christ in narrative form, then it makes good sense to retain these four primary witnesses. But, if the four are considered primarily as historical records, then along with Tatian it would surely be preferable to roll up the four into one. I think that it is clear from the brilliant detective work of Tjitze Baarda and William Petersen that Tatian's concerns were primarily historical and included a quest for unity and harmony.[87] By accepting the fourfold Gospel, the early church acknowledged that the gospels are *not histories*; if we follow suit, we are accepting them as witnesses in narrative form, in spite of their discrepancies and contradictions. They belong to the broad genre of βίοι (lives), but they are not βίοι *tout court*; they are four witnesses to the one Gospel.

Secondly, the fourfold Gospel has major implications for Christology. I have drawn attention to the way both the Muratorian Fragment and Irenaeus insisted that, in spite of the different beginnings of the gospels, they were held together by one Spirit. Their comments may have been fuelled by pagan attacks on inconsistencies in the openings of the gospels, but their fascination with the beginnings of the gospels is surely an indication of awareness of the different Christological perspectives which result. This was seen clearly by Theodore of Mopsuestia at the end of the fourth century. He also commented on the different beginnings of the gospels, and noted that in the synoptic gospels teaching on the divinity of Christ was almost entirely lacking: that is why John opened his Gospel with an immediate reference to the divinity of Christ.[88]

Acceptance of the fourfold Gospel carries with it a commitment to the Christological tension between the synoptics and John. The history of Christological discussion right up to the present day reminds us again and again that we ignore this creative tension in perspective, at our peril. The terminology changes – Christology from below and above, implicit and explicit Christology – but the fundamental Christological issue is marked out by the fourfold Gospel: the very different Christological stances of the

---

[87] Baarda, 'ΔΙΑΦΩΝΙΑ – ΣΥΜΦΩΝΙΑ' (above, n. 27); W. L. Petersen, 'Textual Evidence' (above, n. 51), and his *Tatian's Diatessaron: Its Creation, Dissemination, Significance, and History in Scholarship* (Leiden: Brill, 1994).

[88] Theodore of Mopsuestia, *Commentarius in Evangelium Iohannis Apostoli*, Corpus Scriptorum Christianorum Orientalium 116 (Paris and Louvain, 1940). I owe this reference to H. Merkel, *Die Pluralität* (above, n. 26), §36.

synoptics and the Fourth Gospel should not be blurred, but should both be taken with the utmost seriousness.[89]

Thirdly, the fourfold Gospel forces us to reflect on a range of hermeneutical issues. By accepting the fourfold Gospel, we are ignoring the intention of two, or possibly three, of the evangelists, and in a sense we are encouraging the four gospels to interpret one another. These observations do not lead me, at least, to abandon the search for the original intention of the evangelists. But they do remind me that it is the fourfold Gospel which has fed the life of the church for nearly two thousand years, not any one or more single gospels. I personally do not want to give hermeneutical priority to the canonical shape of the gospels over against the original intention of the evangelists: I want to try to take both seriously and critically, along with the ways the gospels have been understood within the continuing Christian tradition.

By accepting that the four are all witnesses to the one Gospel, we are forced to reflect both on the theological convictions which they share and on the points at which they diverge. Why do we prefer one evangelist's portrait or emphasis? What are our theological criteria for making such judgements? Has the continuing scholarly interest in the distinctive features of the individual gospels blinded us to the theological concerns they have in common?

Fourthly, the fourfold Gospel raises liturgical issues, especially for contemporary compilers of lectionaries. Most modern lectionaries treat the gospels as individual writings: one year of lectionary readings is devoted to each gospel. Most churches in the United Kingdom have adopted a three-year cycle in which a whole year is devoted to each of the synoptic gospels, with passages from John's Gospel inserted at appropriate points. Is this compromise satisfactory? I think that it probably is, though extended use of the new pattern may prove otherwise.

I end with my beginning, with Irenaeus. I cannot accept some of the reasons he offers in defence of the fourfold Gospel. But I do accept his theological conviction that the fourfold Gospel is the pillar which sustains the church. This is a static image, so perhaps some may prefer the image which appealed to Hippolytus, Cyprian, Victorinus of Pettau, and, very recently, to Rudolf Schnackenburg: the four gospels are like the rivers of Paradise which flow from the Garden of Eden into the whole known earth at that time

---

[89] On this point, see especially Morgan, 'Hermeneutical Significance' (above, n. 6), pp. 380–6.

(Gen. 2.10-14).[90] The Biblical image of rivers and living, flowing waters was often linked to the gift of the Spirit, as it was by the Fourth Evangelist. So perhaps Irenaeus, with his emphasis on the Spirit who holds together the fourfold Gospel, would have been happy with this later, more dynamic image. After all, for Irenaeus the foundation and pillar of the church is the fourfold Gospel *and* the Spirit of life (στῦλος δὲ καὶ στήριγμα ἐκκλησίας τὸ εὐαγγέλιον καὶ Πνεῦμα ζωῆς, III.11.8).[91]

---

[90] R. Schnackenburg, *Jesus in the Gospels: A Biblical Christology* (Louisville: Westminster John Knox, E. tr. 1995), pp. 324–5. Schnackenburg refers to Gen. 2.10-14, but does not note that this image also appealed to the patristic writers listed above. See Merkel, *Die Widersprüche*, p. 7 n. 1, who gives full references.

[91] I have quoted the Greek text from fragment 11 (Anastasius Sinaita), as edited by Rousseau and Doutreleau, *Irénée* (above, n. 11), pp. 160–2.

CHAPTER 4

Jesus traditions and gospels in Justin Martyr and Irenaeus

The status of Jesus traditions and of the 'canonical' gospels gradually grew in the course of the second century.[1] At the beginning of the century there was widespread respect for 'words of the Lord' and for '*the* Gospel' (whether oral or written) in which Jesus traditions were embedded. By the end of the century the early church seemed to be within a whisker of accepting a 'canon' of four written gospels, no more, no less.

I do not intend to discuss all the developments and factors which led to the sea change which took place during the second century. In order to do so I would need to offer many hostages to fortune, for at crucial points the evidence is disputed, particularly with reference to the first half of the second century. For example, although the Didache has usually been dated to the first decades of the second century, it is now generally accepted that it contains several layers of traditions, the dating of which is problematic. A major challenge has been mounted to the consensus that Ignatius wrote seven letters in the early years of the second century. I do not think that the challenge is likely to be successful, but discussion of it would be a distraction from my primary task. And do we know the date of II Clement?

I shall focus my attention on two second-century giants whose substantial surviving writings can be dated with some confidence, Justin Martyr and Irenaeus. There is general agreement that their writings are important for my topic – and for many others. It will be my contention that some of their evidence for the status and use of Jesus traditions and of gospels has been misconstrued or overlooked in recent discussion. All too often their writings have been subject to what I call 'cherry picking': tasty morsels have been plucked in order to garnish a grand theory, often at the expense of a close reading of the texts. As we shall see, there has been no shortage of grand theories.

---

[1] An earlier version of this chapter was given as a main lecture at the Jubilee Meeting of the Colloquium Biblicum Lovaniense in July 2001. It is published in J.-M. Auwers and H. J. de Jonge, eds., *The Biblical Canons* (Leuven: Peeters, 2003), pp. 351–68.

I shall not attempt to discuss in any detail the text form or the source of the Jesus traditions. It is important to try to establish whether quoted Jesus traditions are from this gospel or that, from oral or from written sources, from a pre- or a post-synoptic harmony. These questions have received plenty of scholarly attention. I shall not avoid these fascinating issues, but I shall concentrate on a different, somewhat neglected, set of questions. What *status* do Justin and Irenaeus give to Jesus traditions and to the gospels? Are they merely respected traditions? Are they cited as authoritative texts? Are they considered to be Scripture? Do they have the same standing in the church as the OT writings? How close are we to the later emergence of the concept of a canon, an agreed list of authoritative writings which cannot be altered?

4.1 JUSTIN MARTYR

Justin's comments on the Septuagint and the alleged Jewish deletions and modifications to the text of what Justin regards as Scripture have often been noted.[2] The hermeneutical principles which underlie Justin's thorough Christianization of the Old Testament have been discussed less frequently, but they are of considerable importance for Christian theology. Both topics are fascinating. However, the key question for this chapter lies elsewhere: where are we to place Justin in the story of the eventual emergence of the NT canon?

Is Justin, as C. H. Cosgrove has claimed, a reactionary figure who stands four square against second-century trends towards regarding apostolic writings as canon?[3] Can we accept Cosgrove's claim that Justin even devalues the authority of the emerging NT canon, limiting himself to the sayings of Jesus, with misgivings about the emerging canonical status of the gospels?[4]

---

[2] We now have available Miroslav Marcovich's much-needed critical editions of the Greek text, *Iustini Martyris Apologiae Pro Christianis,* Patristische Texte und Studien 38 (Berlin: De Gruyter, 1994) and *Iustini Martyris Dialogus cum Tryphone,* Patristische Texte und Studien 47 (Berlin: De Gruyter, 1997). Marcovich regularly proposes additions and corrections to the Parisinus codex, the one surviving manuscript of any importance; this huge codex is dated 11 September 1363. Although Marcovich's own editorial proposals may be a touch too radical for some, they are indicated very clearly in his printed text and can be readily ignored if necessary; details of the editorial emendments made by his predecessors are also indicated. Marcovich's editions provide a solid platform for fresh study of these fascinating writings; nonetheless, they remind us that the text of Justin's writings is in a parlous state.

[3] C. H. Cosgrove, 'Justin Martyr and the Emerging Christian Canon: Observations on the Purpose and Destination of the Dialogue with Trypho', *Vig. Chr.* 36 (1982) 209–32. There are several weaknesses to Cosgrove's case, the most important of which is his failure to consider the evidence of Justin's *Apologies.*

[4] See Cosgrove, 'Justin Martyr', 226–7.

Or does Justin have a very high regard for the sayings of Jesus and the gospels and consider them to be as authoritative as the OT writings?

At first sight Justin's writings seem to offer limited evidence for our quest, for only once does he refer to an individual NT writing by name.[5] However, as in the interpretation of any writing, whether ancient or modern, genre and context must not be ignored. Justin's *Apologies* and his *Dialogue with Trypho* are apologetic writings, which address two very different readerships. Perhaps Justin does hope that his *Apologies* will win the Emperor Marcus Aurelius and the leading Gentile opinion formers of his day over to the Christian 'philosophy'. Perhaps he does hope that Trypho and other Jewish teachers will acknowledge that Jesus is the Messiah promised in Scripture. In my view, however, it is more likely that Justin's extant writings were all intended to provide Christian members of his philosophical school in Rome with apologetic material which they could use in their encounters with both Jews and Gentiles.

In either case, reference to the names of the authors of the NT writings would not have been appropriate. As J. B. Lightfoot noted, 'In works like these, addressed to Heathens and Jews, who attributed no authority to the writings of Apostles and Evangelists, and for whom the names of the writers would have no meaning, we are not surprised that he refers to those writings for the most part anonymously and with reserve.'[6]

Justin's writings provide us with plenty of evidence to assess, though that task is not easy.[7] The *First Apology* was written very shortly after AD 150, the *Dialogue with Trypho* only a few years later in the same decade. However, it is unwise to try to trace development in Justin's thinking. Some sections of the *Dialogue* may well have been written before the *Apology* and inserted into that long, rather rambling account of Justin's conversations with Trypho.[8]

---

[5] The Revelation of John (*Dialogue* 81.4).
[6] *Essays on the Work Entitled Supernatural Religion* (London, 1893), p. 33. I owe this reference to Charles E. Hill, 'Justin and the New Testament Writings', in E. A. Livingstone, ed., *Studia Patristica* 30 (Leuven: Peeters, 1997), p. 43.
[7] E. F. Osborn, *Justin Martyr* (Tübingen: Mohr, 1973), p. 120 notes that in 1877 B. L. Gildersleeve claimed that 'the battle over the question whether Justin's Memoirs of the Apostles are identical with our canonical gospels has lasted nearly a century. Begun by Stroth in 1777, it is safe to say that the fight is going on at this very moment in the powder magazine of some theological review.'
[8] For discussion of Justin's possible use of earlier sources or his own earlier compositions, see O. Skarsaune, *The Proof from Prophecy. A Study in Justin Martyr's Proof-Text Tradition: Text-Type, Provenance, Theological Profile* (Leiden: Brill, 1987), and Luise Abramowski, 'Die "Erinnerungen der Apostel" bei Justin', in P. Stuhlmacher, ed., *Das Evangelium und die Evangelien* (Tübingen: Mohr, 1983), pp. 341–54.

4.1.1 Jesus traditions: 'the words of the Saviour'

The opening chapters of the *First Apology* underline the importance Justin attaches to the teachings of Christ and to their careful transmission (4.7; 6.2; 8.3). In all three passages Justin emphasizes that Christians teach (or hand over, παραδίδωμι) what they have been taught by Christ, whom they 'worship and adore' along with 'the most true God' (6.1). The teachings of Christ are clearly authoritative, but nothing further is said about their status in these chapters.

At the climax of the *Apology*, however, three related passages leave little doubt that the carefully transmitted traditions Justin refers to include the *written* memoirs of the apostles. The prayer following the baptism of 'the one who has been illuminated' asks that Christians show by their deeds that they are 'good citizens and guardians of what has been commanded' (65.5, ἐντέλλομαι). Only those who 'live as Christ handed down' (66.1, παραδίδωμι) are permitted to participate in the baptismal eucharist. The food 'eucharistized' through 'the word of prayer' that is from Jesus Christ is life-giving (66.2). There follows a much-discussed passage to which we shall return: 'For in the memoirs composed by them, called gospels, the *apostles handed down what they had been commanded*: that Jesus took bread and having given thanks said . . . This is my body' (66.3, παρέδωκαν ἐντετάλθαι αὐτοῖς). Justin is adamant that traditions of the sayings and actions of Jesus have been transmitted carefully in the written memoirs by the apostles, and are handed on and carried out by his fellow-Christians. Their ultimate source is Jesus Christ himself. Their authoritative status could hardly be underlined more firmly, even though they are not referred to as 'Scripture'.

In chapter 14 of the *Apology* Justin provides an important full introduction to no fewer than twenty-six sayings of Jesus, organized topically into ten groups.[9] Christians 'pray for their enemies' and try to persuade those who hate them unjustly 'to live according to the good suggestions of Christ' (14.4). Justin then states that he is about to cite some of the teachings given by Christ. He makes two comments on their character.

(a) They are 'short and concise sayings' (βραχεῖς δὲ καὶ σύντομοι παρ' αὐτοῦ λόγοι), for Christ was no sophist. Justin assumes that his addressees will be familiar with long-winded sophists and thus impressed by the

---

[9] A. J. Bellinzoni, *The Sayings of Jesus in the Writings of Justin Martyr*, SNT 17 (Leiden: Brill, 1967), pp. 49–100, examines in detail the text form and source of these sayings. However, he fails to comment on Justin's important introductory remarks in chapter 14.

pithy sayings of Jesus. In an effort to impress Trypho, the sayings of Jesus are also said to be 'short' (βραχέα λόγια) at *Dialogue* 18.1.

(b) Justin claims that the 'commandments' (δογμάτα, 14.4) which are about to be quoted are the word of Christ, and 'his word was the power of God' (14.5, δύναμις θεοῦ ὁ λόγος αὐτοῦ ἦν). This introductory comment is clearly intended to establish the importance and authoritative status of the twenty-six sayings of Jesus which follow in chapters 15–17.

Justin himself opens each set of sayings by announcing its theme; the sayings are then introduced with simple phrases in the aorist tense: 'he said', 'he taught', 'he commanded'. For example, 'Concerning chastity, he said this . . .'; this introduction is followed by four sayings linked only by καί (15.1-4). The fourth set of sayings is introduced by Justin as follows: 'And that we should share with the needy . . . he said these things . . .'; eight sayings linked only twice with καί are juxtaposed (15.10-17).

This pattern is repeated almost identically ten times over. The penultimate paragraph is the single exception (17.1-2). Here Justin insists that Christians pay taxes 'as we have been taught by him' and then sets out a much-abbreviated version of the pronouncement story concerning payment of tribute to Caesar, Mark 12.13-17 and parallels.

The ten sets of Jesus traditions are linked to their present context very loosely. With the partial exception of *Dialogue* 35.3, where Justin cites one set of four sayings concerning false teachers and false prophets, there are no comparable passages in his writings. These ten sets of sayings of Jesus were almost certainly collected and arranged by Justin himself for catechetical purposes in his school in Rome. Their status is underlined by Justin's introduction of them as 'the power of God' and by Justin's repeated claim that his fellow-Christians transmit, and live by, the sayings of Jesus which have been carefully handed on to them. For our present purposes, we may leave it open whether the twenty-six sayings of Jesus quoted in chapters 15–17 have been taken from oral or from written sources.

From the *First Apology* we turn to the *Dialogue*. Here Justin includes explicit statements concerning the sayings of Jesus in his account of his conversion to Christianity, which he dubs 'philosophy safe and simple' (8.1). He tells his Jewish opponent Trypho that at the time of his conversion he experienced a passionate desire for the prophets, and for those men who are the friends of Christ, presumably the apostles. He then expresses the hope that all people should be as keen as he is not to distance themselves from the Saviour's words (μὴ ἀφίστασθαι τῶν τοῦ σωτῆρος λόγων), for they evoke *profound awe* (δέος). Their innate power puts to shame those who turn aside from the right way, while pleasant rest (ἀνάπαυσις) comes to those who carry them out (8.2). Here a version of the 'two ways' ethical tradition is linked to the effect the dynamic sayings of Jesus have.

In his vigorous reply Trypho claims that in his conversion to Christianity Justin has been led astray by false statements and has followed men who are not at all worthy. From the context, the latter can only be 'the friends of Christ', i.e. the apostles. Trypho soon concedes that he has taken some trouble to *read* the admirable and great commands of Christ 'in the so-called Gospel' (10.2), a point Justin repeats at 18.1. At *Dialogue* 88.3, shortly before the thirteen references to 'the memoirs of the apostles' in chapters 100–7, Justin states that 'the apostles of this our Christ' have *written* that the Spirit fluttered down on Jesus at his baptism like a dove. This is clearly a reference to at least two apostles' writings.

So, long before the thirteen references in the *Dialogue* to 'the memoirs of the apostles' are reached in chapters 100–7, the reader can hardly avoid the conclusion that the powerful words of the Saviour may be *read* in the writings of the apostles, the friends of Christ.

This key point emerges again in a particularly dramatic passage in *Dialogue* 113 and 114. Justin states that the words of Jesus are the sharp knives by which Gentile Christians in his own day have experienced the 'second circumcision' (of their hearts). The first physical circumcision is for Jews. The second circumcision, 'which circumcises us from idolatry, and in fact all vice', is carried out 'by the words spoken *by the apostles* of the Corner Stone' (*Dialogue* 113.6-7; 114.4). Given the preceding references to reading and writing, we can be all but certain that written traditions are in mind here. The authoritative status of those traditions could hardly be underlined more strongly.

How does Justin understand the relationship of the sayings of Jesus transmitted through the writings of the apostles to Scripture? In *I Apol.* 61-3, sayings of Jesus are set alongside cited words of Isaiah, with the clear implication that they have the same status. The words of Christ, 'Unless you are born again . . .', are followed almost immediately by a version of Isa. 1.16-20, 'Thus spoke Isaiah the prophet' (61.4-8). The introductory formulae are almost identical: 'Christ said' and 'Isaiah the prophet thus spoke.'

In the next chapter the burning-bush theophany is Christianized: 'our Christ' converses with Moses in the form of fire out of the bush and said, 'Unloose your sandals and come near and hear' (62.3). This is followed by a citation of Isa. 1.3, introduced as words of the prophetic Spirit through Isaiah the prophet (63.1). Justin then cites two sayings of Jesus, introduced as 'Jesus Christ said' and 'Our Lord himself said' (63.3-5).

The first readers of the *Apology* are encouraged to conclude that sayings of Jesus have the same status as the words of Isaiah, though they are left to draw this conclusion for themselves. Justin makes this key point more explicitly in the *Dialogue*. With a rather quaint rhetorical touch, Justin says to his Jewish opponent Trypho, 'Since you have read what our Saviour taught, as you have yourself acknowledged, I think I have not acted in an unseemly fashion by adding some short sayings of his [Christ's] to those found in the prophets' (18.1). The immediate context is significant. In the preceding chapter three passages from Isaiah are linked (52.5; 3.9-11; 5.18-20) as a preface to three sayings of Jesus. The first of the latter sayings is a version of Matt. 21.13, words of Jesus addressed to the money-changers in the temple. Jesus refers to Jer. 7.11 with the words, 'it is written: "My house is a house of prayer, but you have made it a den of robbers."' Justin's version is much closer to Matt. 21.13 than to the LXX (*Dialogue* 17.3), so in all probability Justin has used Matthew's Gospel at this point.

There is a further example of the use of γέγραπται in a quotation from Matthew at *Dialogue* 78.1. Here the quotation of Mic. 5.2 at Matt. 2.5 is referred to. One might have expected Justin to have imitated this NT usage in his own introductions to some of the sayings of Jesus he cites, thus placing them on all fours with the OT passages he quotes so frequently. However, although Justin is familiar with the term γραφή for Scripture (e.g. *Dialogue* 56.12,17), he never uses γέγραπται to introduce either an OT quotation or a saying of Jesus as Scripture.[10]

Nonetheless, it would be a grave mistake to claim that the sayings of Jesus are in any way inferior to Scripture. This emerges very clearly from *Dialogue* 119.6. 'For as he [Abraham] believed the voice of God, and it was imputed to him for righteousness, in like manner we, having believed God's voice spoken through the apostles of Christ, and preached to us through the prophets, have renounced even to death all the things of the world.' Charles Hill comments appropriately: 'Here it is God's own "voice" which has spoken "through" the apostles of Christ, and here Justin explicitly and boldly places this "inspiration" on a par with that of the OT prophets.'[11]

Justin attaches considerable significance to the teachings of Christ. Their authority and power are clear. Justin's readers are left in no doubt that the

---

[10] H. von Campenhausen, *The Formation of the Christian Bible* (Philadelphia: Fortress, E. tr. 1972), p. 170, notes that in the 'later anti-Jewish Dialogue' Justin introduces a dominical saying with the words 'it is written', and suggests cautiously that this is Justin's way of referring to texts which are to be acknowledged as authentic and normative. I do not think that the three uses of γέγραπται in question (49.5; 100.1; 105.6) bear this weight.

[11] Hill, 'Justin and the New Testament Writings', p. 48.

sayings of Jesus have the same standing as the words of the prophets. Justin returns to this point in the closing pages of the *Dialogue*. With an ironical touch he rounds on Trypho: 'If the teaching (διδάγματα) of the prophets *and of Christ* disquiet you, it is better for you to follow God rather than your unintelligent and blind teachers' (134.1). As we have noted above, in several passages Justin remarks that 'the words of the Saviour' have been conveyed in the writings of the apostles. So it is appropriate that we should now consider the status Justin attaches to 'the memoirs of the apostles'.

4.1.2 *The gospels: 'the memoirs of the apostles'*

At the climax of the *First Apology* Justin refers twice to 'the memoirs of the apostles' (τὰ ἀπομνημονεύματα τῶν ἀποστόλων, 66.3; 67.3) in contexts which underline their importance; the phrase is used a further thirteen times in one section of the *Dialogue* (chs. 100–17).

In his account of the origin and significance of the Christian eucharist, Justin quotes Jesus' words of institution as they are recorded in the memoirs written by the apostles 'which are called gospels' (ἃ καλεῖται Εὐαγγέλια, *First Apology* 66.3). The status of the memoirs could hardly be clearer. But is the explanatory reference to the gospels a later addition to the text? This is the only time Justin refers to the noun εὐαγγέλιον in the *Apologies*, so it is not surprising that some scholars have claimed that the clause is a later gloss. We cannot ignore the fact that this is the first time the plural 'gospels' is used in early Christian writings. Even a generation after Justin, Irenaeus only rarely used the phrase 'gospels' in the plural; he much preferred 'the gospel', or 'the Gospel according to . . .'[12]

On the other hand, Justin is in the habit of adding explanatory phrases or clauses, especially (as here) when his putative readers may have been baffled by his terminology.[13] So, with this one exception, Justin may have felt that it was quite unnecessary to explain that 'the memoirs of the apostles' were 'gospels'. A decision is difficult, but I have already given plenty of evidence (and more will follow) to establish that the 'memoirs' were the writings which became known as 'the gospels'.

The second and final reference in the *First Apology* to the memoirs of the apostles occurs in Justin's account of what takes place in his own day in the Sunday gathering of Christians. 'The memoirs of the apostles or the writings

---

[12] See A. Benoit, *Saint Irenée. Introduction à l'étude de sa théologie* (Paris: Presses Universitaires de France, 1960), pp. 103–50.

[13] See further Abramowski, 'Die "Erinnerungen"', p. 323; *I Apology* 65.1; 65.5 and *Dialogue* 10.2 are noted as parallels to this explanatory clause.

of the prophets are read, for as long as time permits' (67.3, μέχρις ἐγχωρεῖ). This is the earliest extant reference to the reading of 'the gospels' in the context of Christian worship. The reading is followed by an exposition given by 'the Ruler' (ὁ προεστώς). There is no lectionary; the only constraint on the length of the passage read is the time available. The 'memoirs of the apostles' are considered to be of equal importance to 'the writings of the prophets'. Indeed, they may even be given a measure of precedence by being referred to before the prophets.[14] The liturgical setting provides further evidence that status of the memoirs was very high indeed.

How many gospels does Justin know? Justin uses the noun εὐαγγέλιον twice in the singular in the *Dialogue*. At 10.2 Trypho is allowed to express admiration for the precepts of Christ recorded 'in the so-called gospel' (ἐν τῷ λεγομένῳ Εὐαγγελίῳ); he has even taken the trouble to read them! Justin introduces his version of Matt. 11.27 = Luke 10.22 with 'it is written in the gospel, saying . . .' (100.2). In both cases, as in several other early Christian writings, the singular is to refer to the 'one gospel' in which sayings of Jesus are written.

The phrase 'the memoirs of the apostles' could be taken to refer to the 'one gospel', but this is most unlikely. We have already noted the explanatory clause in the *First Apology* 66.3, 'the memoirs which are called gospels', and the important comment at *Dialogue* 88.3: '*the apostles* of this our Christ' have *written* that the Spirit fluttered down on Jesus at his baptism like a dove.

Confirmation that in his references to 'the memoirs of the apostles' Justin has in mind more than one written gospel is provided by two of the thirteen references to the memoirs in the *Dialogue*. At 103.8 an explanatory clause follows a reference to the memoirs: 'which, I say, were composed by his apostles and those who followed them'. This comment on the composition of the memoirs implies that they were written by more than one apostle, and more than one follower of an apostle, i.e. Justin accepts at least four gospels, though, unlike Irenaeus, he does not name them or discuss their differences.[15] It is a natural, but not a necessary, inference that Justin has in mind gospels written by the apostles Matthew and John, and by followers

---

[14] Although it has sometimes been suggested that the prophets are Christian prophets, this is unlikely, given Justin's repeated references to, and respect for, the OT prophets. The possibility of choice between a reading from the gospels *or* (ἢ) a reading from the prophets is puzzling. Since this is out of line with later liturgical practice, the text is unlikely to be faulty.

[15] Osborn, *Justin Martyr*, seems to have missed this important passage. He notes that τὰ ἀπομνημονεύματα may have a singular meaning. 'If plurality of authorship were important, some further description of the apostles and their writings could be expected' (p. 124).

of the apostles, Mark and Luke. However, caution is necessary. As we shall see in a moment, it is possible that Justin considered Mark's Gospel to be one of the memoirs of the apostles, i.e. to stem from Peter; and we cannot be confident that Justin had John's Gospel in mind when he penned the phrase 'memoirs composed by his apostles and those who followed them'.

Dialogue 106.3 is more problematic: 'We are told that he [Christ] changed the name of one of the apostles to Peter, and it is written in his memoirs (ἐν τοῖς ἀπομνημονεύμασιν αὐτοῦ) that this took place . . .'. Whose memoirs are referred to here? If we take without emendation the text of the sole witness, the fourteenth-century Parisinus codex, there are two possibilities. The memoirs could be Christ's or Peter's. Justin does not refer elsewhere to the memoirs of one individual; only once does he ever name the author of any earlier Christian writing (the Revelation of John, *Dialogue* 81.4). Nonetheless, both Zahn and Harnack interpreted this sentence as a reference to Peter's memoirs, i.e. to Mark's Gospel, as does Luise Abramowski.[16] Miroslav Marcovich, however, is unimpressed, and proposes that 'of the apostles' (τῶν ἀποστόλων) should be added to the text at this point; this would bring it into line with the phrase used in the next sentence (106.4): 'in the memoirs *of his apostles*', i.e. Christ's apostles. An influential earlier editor of Justin's writings, J. C. Th. von Otto (1847), proposed a similar emendment.

A decision is difficult, especially when we recall the parlous state of the Parisinus codex. Justin's repeated use of the phrase 'memoirs of the apostles' does suggest that emendation may be appropriate. However, the more difficult reading of the Parisinus codex is undoubtedly preferable. It is the context which confirms that Justin is here referring to Peter's memoirs, i.e. Mark's Gospel. In the same very complex sentence in which he refers to the change of Peter's name, Justin refers to the change of names of the sons of Zebedee to 'Boanerges, which is sons of thunder' (106.3), a phrase found at Mark 3.17, but not in the parallel passages in Matthew and Luke.

There is a strong cumulative argument for Justin's acceptance of at least four gospels. Although the gospels are not named individually, there is no doubt that Justin used Matthew's and Luke's Gospels extensively, and Mark to a more limited extent. But what about John's Gospel? This is a controversial question, which can be referred to only briefly here.[17] There

---

[16] Abramowski, 'Die "Erinnerungen"', pp. 334–5.
[17] For bibliography see J. W. Pryor, 'Justin Martyr and the Fourth Gospel', *The Second Century* 9 (1992) 153–69, esp. 153 n. 1.

is only one quotation to be considered, *I Apol.* 61.4-5: 'Christ also said: "Unless you are born again, you will not enter the kingdom of heaven"; for it is clear to all that "it is impossible for those who have once been born to enter into their mothers' wombs".'[18] This is a free rendering of John 3.4-5, not out of line with the way Jesus traditions are quoted elsewhere in Justin's writings.[19] The phrase 'kingdom of heaven' (as in the similar tradition at Matt. 18.3) is found in several manuscripts of John 3.3 (including the first hand of Sinaiticus) as well as in numerous patristic witnesses.[20] Justin may have known the text of John 3.3 in this form, or he may have harmonized John's and Matthew's phraseology, as others certainly did.

In addition to this free quotation, there are numerous allusions to passages in the Fourth Gospel, to say nothing of the probability that Justin knew and developed the evangelist's Logos doctrine.[21] In 1943 J. N. Sanders noted twenty-three possible allusions to John's Gospel; others have compiled their own similar lists.[22] There is a strong cumulative case, though this raises two obvious problems. The more clearly one discerns the influence of John's Gospel, the more difficult it is to explain why Justin quotes it only once. And, as we noted above, Justin refers to the sayings of Jesus as 'short and concise', hardly a natural way to refer to Jesus traditions in John's Gospel.

J. W. Pryor has recently argued that, while Justin knows the Fourth Gospel, there is no evidence that he includes it among 'the memoirs of the apostles'. I do not think that we can rule out so firmly the possibility that Justin's reference to memoirs written by 'apostles and those who followed them' includes the Fourth Gospel. I prefer to leave this as an open question.

[18] Καὶ γὰρ ὁ Χριστὸς εἶπεν· Ἂν μὴ ἀναγεννηθῆτε, οὐ μὴ εἰσέλθητε εἰς τὴν Βασιλείαν τῶν οὐρανῶν. Ὅτι δὲ καὶ ἀδύνατον εἰς τὰς μήτρας τῶν τεκουσῶν τοὺς ἅπαξ γεννωμένους ἐμβῆναι, φανερὸν πᾶσίν ἐστι.
[19] See J. W. Pryor's full discussion, with good bibliography, 'Justin Martyr', pp. 163–6. Pryor accepts that *I Apology* 61.4-5 stems from John 3.3-5, but 'it is not a case of direct borrowing by Justin himself, for the saying of Jesus does bear the marks of having been changed under the influence of Matthew 18.3' (p. 166). Osborn, *Justin Martyr*, p. 138, notes that Justin's theology is not openly derived from the Fourth Gospel. 'The influence is shown on particular points and not on the shape of the whole.'
[20] For details see esp. A. Huck and H. Greeven, eds., *Synopse der drei ersten Evangelien* (Tübingen: Mohr, 1981), ad loc.
[21] See M. J. Edwards, 'Justin's Logos and the Word of God', *JECS* 3 (1995) 261–80. Edwards claims that the roots of Justin's Logos are in the Biblical tradition. Justin's acquaintance with the Fourth Gospel is left open.
[22] J. N. Sanders, *The Fourth Gospel in the Early Church* (Cambridge: Cambridge University Press, 1943), pp. 27–32. Osborn, *Justin Martyr*, p. 137, lists some twenty 'coincidences of thought and expression'. Pryor, 'Justin Martyr', pp. 158–9, adds some further examples of allusions to Sanders's list, but notes that some are more convincing than others.

While Justin does know a handful of traditions which did not find their way into the canonical gospels,[23] there is no evidence that he knew or used an apocryphal gospel.[24] Did he know, or compose, a harmony of several gospels? Helmut Koester has recently claimed that the sayings Justin included in his catechism were already harmonized in his *Vorlage*. In composing this source, Justin or his 'school' did not intend to construct a catechism, but was composing the *one* inclusive new gospel which would make its predecessors, Matthew and Luke (and possibly Mark), obsolete.[25] Although Koester's theory has won some support,[26] the limited evidence he cites can be explained more plausibly along other lines.

It is much more likely that sayings of Jesus from the synoptic gospels were harmonized for inclusion in the topically organized sets of sayings mentioned above. While some of Justin's harmonized traditions do seem to have been used in his pupil Tatian's more thorough-going harmony,[27] there is no evidence to support the view that Justin intended to *replace* the synoptic gospels. As we have seen, Justin's own comments confirm that he had a very high regard for gospels 'written by the apostles and their followers' (*Dialogue* 103.8). So his *preference* for one single harmonized gospel is inherently unlikely. There is no reason at all why Justin should not have composed harmonized collections of sayings of Jesus for catechetical purposes and have used them alongside written gospels. Indeed, in my view, he almost certainly did just that.

Justin's high regard for *written* gospels should by now be clear. Two considerations provide further support. (a) In several passages Justin refers to 'reading'. I have already noted that Justin's opponent Trypho is twice said to have *read* appreciatively the sayings of Jesus 'in the gospel' (*Dialogue* 10.2; 18.1). In *II Apology* Justin's opponent Crescens is accused of 'running us down without having *read* the teachings of Christ . . . or if he has *read*

---

[23] The most notable are the references to the birth of Jesus in a cave (*Dialogue* 78.5); to the fire kindled at the baptism of Jesus (*Dialogue* 88.3); and to an *agraphon* at *Dialogue* 47.5: 'Our Lord Jesus Christ said: "In whatsoever I overtake you, in that I will also judge you."' On the latter, see A. J. Bellinzoni, 'The Source of the Agraphon in Justin's Dialogue with Trypho 47.5', *Vig. Chr.* 17 (1963) 65–70.

[24] See especially Osborn, *Justin Martyr*, pp. 129–30; similarly, T. K. Heckel, *Vom Evangelium des Markus zum viergestaltigen Evangelium* (Tübingen, Mohr, 1999), p. 326.

[25] Helmut Koester, 'The Text of the Synoptic Gospels in the Second Century', in W. L. Petersen, ed., *Gospel Traditions in the Second Century* (Notre Dame and London: University of Notre Dame Press, 1989), pp. 28–33.

[26] A. J. Bellinzoni, 'The Gospel of Matthew in the Second Century', *SC* 9 (1992) 197–258, esp. 239–42. Miroslav Marcovich, *Iustini Martyris Apologiae*, p. 29, refers approvingly to Koester's theory, but does not discuss it.

[27] See W. L. Petersen, 'Textual Evidence of Tatian's Dependence upon Justin's APOMNHMONEY-MATA', *NTS* 36 (1990) 512–34.

them, he has not understood them'. In his own summary of Luke 24.25-6 and 44-6 and Acts 1.8-9 Justin notes that the risen Jesus 'taught the disciples to *read* the prophecies in which all these things were predicted as coming to pass' (*I Apology* 54.12, καὶ ταῖς προφητείαις ἐντυχεῖν).[28] Luke's narrative implies oral teaching – indeed, it would have been difficult to *read* scrolls while walking on the road to Emmaus. At this point, as in numerous other passages, Justin's narrative is very 'bookish'.

(b) But what of the term 'memoirs' (ἀπομνημονεύματα)? Does this square with the above observations concerning the 'bookish' character of Justin's writings? Although the term can refer to mere 'notes', it has now been established by Niels Hyldahl that in Justin's writings the term has clear literary connotations. Hyldahl quotes Martin Dibelius approvingly: 'An apologetic tendency is operative which is lifting up Christendom into the region of culture. By means of the title "Memoirs" the Gospel books would be classified as literature proper.' Hyldahl notes that Socrates has such a distinctive place in Justin's writings that it was natural for him to allude to Xenophon's *Memorabilia* concerning Socrates in his choice of the term ἀπομνημονεύματα.[29]

While it is easy to see why Justin would want to underline the literary credentials of the gospels for apologetic purposes, we need not conclude that he was exaggerating his case. I have recently argued that the Oxyrhynchus papyri published in 1997 and 1998 suggest that, by the second half of the second century, much earlier than has been usually assumed, the literary qualities of the gospels and their authoritative status for the life and faith of the church were widely recognized. The often-repeated claim that the gospels were considered at first to be utilitarian handbooks written, by and large, in a 'reformed documentary' style now needs to be modified, and we need to remember that we do have a handful of second-century codices with literary texts.[30]

For Justin, 'the words of the Saviour' were transmitted by the apostles in written 'upmarket' memoirs which were known as gospels, though of course he may well have known sayings of Jesus in other written or oral forms. A close reading of all the evidence confirms the high regard in which Justin held both the sayings of Jesus and the 'memoirs of the apostles'. While it

---

[28] Justin uses ἐντυγχάνω as 'read' in a number of passages; see, for example, *I Apology* 14.1; 26.8; 42.1; 44.12,13; 45.6; *II Apology* 3.6, 8; 15.3.

[29] Niels Hyldahl, 'Hesesipps Hypomnemata', *ST* 14 (1960) 70–113. The quotation from Dibelius is from his *From Tradition to Gospels* (London, Ivor Nicholson and E. Watson, tr. 1934), p. 40. See especially Luise Abramowski's full discussion, 'Die "Erinnerungen"'.

[30] See Chapter 9 in this volume.

is true that Justin does not refer explicitly either to the sayings or to the memoirs as 'Scripture', he comes within a whisker of doing so. Like the 'Scriptural' prophets, the 'memoirs' are read at length and expounded in the liturgical Sunday gatherings of Christians.

4.2 IRENAEUS

Irenaeus wrote his *Adversus Haereses* about AD 180, barely a generation after Justin composed his *Apologies* and *Dialogue*. Irenaeus knows Justin's writings,[31] and may even have met him in Rome. Although both writers hold the gospels and especially the words of Jesus in high regard, there are important differences. Whereas Justin made limited use of John's Gospel, Irenaeus has no hesitation in accepting its authority. Indeed, it is arguable that this gospel influenced Irenaeus' theological thought more deeply than any other writing.

Justin seems to have known four gospels, though he never names any of the evangelists and in only one passage does he show even the slightest interest in the plurality of the gospels.[32] Irenaeus is more specific: two gospels were written by named apostles or disciples (Matthew and John) and two by their followers (Mark and Luke) (*Adv. Haer.* III.10.1; 10.6; 11.1). His lengthy and sophisticated defence of the fourfold Gospel takes us far beyond Justin. His line of argument strongly suggests that he is not making a case for a recent innovation, but underpinning what he and others had long accepted, i.e. that the church had been given one Gospel in fourfold form – four authoritative writings, no more, no less.

Both writers give the same status to the gospels as they do to the OT writings. Although Justin is familiar with the term γραφή for Scripture (e.g. *Dialogue* 56.12,17), he never uses this term to refer to a gospel, nor does he himself use 'it is written' (γέγραπται) to introduce either an OT quotation or a saying of Jesus as Scripture. Irenaeus, however, does refer to the gospels explicitly as 'Scripture': 'since all the Scriptures, both the prophets and the Gospels proclaim this' ('cum itaque universae Scripturae, et prophetiae et Euangelii . . . praedicent', *Adv Haer.* II.27.2). At the end of Book II, he announces that in his next book he will support his argument from 'divine Scripture'; in Book III there are very many more references

---

[31] The extent of this knowledge merits further investigation. For discussion of the similar use of Matt. 7.15 by Justin and Irenaeus, see D. J. Bingham, *Irenaeus's Use of Matthew's Gospel in Adversus Haereses* (Leuven: Peeters, 1998), pp. 27–32.
[32] *Dialogue* 103.8. See above, pp. 100–01.

to the gospels than to the OT, so there is a clear implication that they are 'Scripture'.

Nonetheless, Irenaeus remains somewhat coy about referring to the gospels as Scripture. Only once does he introduce a saying of Jesus with 'Scripture says', and even in this case Matt. 13.18 is alluded to rather than quoted (IV.41.2). In a handful of places he introduces a verse from the gospels with 'it is written'; see, for example, II.22.3; IV.20.6. For Irenaeus 'Scripture' is first and foremost the OT, though it is quite clear that the gospels and sayings of Jesus enjoy the same level of authority as the OT.[33]

We noted above that Justin is adamant that traditions of the sayings and actions of Jesus have been transmitted carefully in the written gospels by the apostles, and are handed on and carried out by his fellow Christians. In the introductory sections of the *First Apology* Justin emphasizes the careful transmission of tradition by using repeatedly the verb παραδίδωμι. The same points are made even more strongly by Irenaeus. In his introduction to Book III, where he is concerned above all with the status of the Gospel in fourfold form, he stresses that the oral proclamation of the Gospel by the apostles was 'later handed down to us in the Scriptures' (III.1.1, 'in Scripturis nobis tradiderunt'; ἐν γραφαῖς παρέδωκαν ἡμῖν).[34] Irenaeus then refers briefly to the origin and authorship of the individual gospels. His comment on Mark, the disciple and interpreter of Peter, echoes the phraseology just quoted: 'he handed down to us in written form the things proclaimed by Peter' ('ipse quae a Petro adnuntiata per scripta nobis tradidit' (III.1.1).[35]

At the close of his extended comments on the origin and authority of the gospels, Irenaeus summarizes his key points. The Gospel has been transmitted in written form by the apostles; since God made all things in due proportion and adaptation, it was fit also that the outward aspect of the Gospel should be well arranged and harmonized (III.11.12, 'oportebat et speciem Euangelii bene compositam et bene compaginatam esse'). In this closing section Irenaeus states three times over that the gospels can be neither more nor fewer in number than they are (III.11.8.1, 'neque autem plura numero quam haec sunt neque rursus pauciora capit esse Euangelia'; cf. 11.9.1 and 11.9.12, where almost identical terminology is used).

[33] For these comments on Irenaeus' use of 'Scripture' I am indebted to Benoit, *Saint Irenée*, pp. 120–2.
[34] I have cited the Latin text and Greek retroversion from *Sources chrétiennes* 211, ed. A. Rousseau and L. Doutreleau (Paris: Cerf, 1974).
[35] At this point we have Eusebius' version of the original Greek: καὶ αὐτὸς τὰ ὑπὸ Πέτρου κηρυσσό- μενα ἐγγράφως ἡμῖν παραδέδωκεν (*HE* v.8.3).

'No more, no less' almost becomes a slogan for Irenaeus. His terminology is so closely related to a 'canon formula' widely known in antiquity that it is most surprising that Irenaeus does not draw on it.[36] As W. C. van Unnik noted, the 'canon formula', 'neither add nor take away', has deep roots in both Biblical and Greek thought.[37] Irenaeus knows the concepts in the same order, 'no more, no less'.

From Aristotle onwards, a 'canonical' work was defined as one to which nothing could be added and from which nothing could be subtracted *without harming its aesthetic unity*. Aristotle states that 'neither add nor take away' is a proverbial expression.[38] The 'canon formula' was a well-known slogan in the Hellenistic world in the realm of *aesthetics*. Irenaeus places a great deal of weight on the aesthetic unity of the fourfold Gospel, so that his failure to quote the slogan is baffling, especially as Eusebius refers to it.[39]

Justin emphasizes the importance and power of the words of Jesus. As we noted above, several passages confirm that he is concerned primarily with their written form rather than with continuing oral tradition. Justin does not state that 'the words of the Saviour' are available anywhere but in 'the memoirs of the apostles'. I am convinced that this is also the case with Irenaeus, though here I am somewhat out of line with the current consensus. Hans von Campenhausen claims that Irenaeus does not think of the gospels as sources for the words of Jesus. Their purpose is simply to provide documentary evidence of the teaching of 'that apostle' who wrote down the gospel; the words of the Lord are treated on their own, without reference to the gospels.[40] Y.-M. Blanchard has recently gone much further down this path: 'ainsi, au temps d'Irénée, la mémoire vivante des logia du Seigneur paraît constituer le canal privilégié de la Tradition chrétienne'.[41] According to Blanchard, the gospels are of secondary importance; pride of place among the four is given to Luke.[42]

---

[36] See, however, iv.33.8: 'neque additamentum, neque ablationem recipiens'.
[37] W. C. van Unnik, 'De la règle Μήτε προσθεῖναι μήτε ἀφελεῖν', *Vig. Chr.* 3 (1949) 1–36. See also Christoph Dohmen and Manfred Oeming, *Biblischer Kanon, warum und wozu?: eine Kanontheologie* (Freiburg: Herder, 1992), especially pp. 78–89; John Barton, *The Spirit and the Letter: Studies in the Biblical Canon* (London: SPCK, 1997), pp. 133–4.
[38] Aristotle, *EN* II.1106b.
[39] At *HE* v.16.3 Eusebius cites an anonymous letter which refers to the formula with reference to the 'canon' of the NT.
[40] Von Campenhausen, *Formation*, pp. 191 and 202. John Barton summarizes approvingly von Campenhausen's position in his *The Spirit and the Letter*, pp. 82–4.
[41] Y.-M. Blanchard, *Aux sources du canon, le Témoignage d'Irénée*, Cogitatio Fidei 174 (Paris: Cerf, 1993), p. 221.
[42] Ibid., pp. 206 and 229.

Irenaeus does attach special importance to the sayings of Jesus, but it is a Christological, not a hermeneutical, priority.[43] Irenaeus does not single out the words of Jesus as a 'canon within the canon'. He sees the gospels as the records of the teaching of Jesus. This is nowhere clearer than in the Preface to Book III: 'The Lord of all gave to his apostles the power to proclaim the Gospel, and from them we have known the truth, that is to say the teaching of the Son of God. And it is to them that the Lord said: "Anyone who hears you hears me." Irenaeus devotes Book IV to the 'words of the Lord', but at IV.6.I there is a further clear indication that they are not to be thought of in isolation from their written form in the gospels.[44] Irenaeus cites Matt. 11.27 = Luke 10.22, and then comments: 'Thus has Matthew set it down, and Luke similarly, and also Mark; for John omits this passage.' He is, of course, mistaken about Mark, but that is beside the point. In several passages in Book IV the narrative context of the cited 'words of the Lord' in one of the gospels (usually Matthew) is retained; in other passages the deeds of Jesus are referred to or summarized.[45]

It would be rash to claim that Irenaeus does not know oral traditions of the sayings of Jesus. But his vigorous exposition of the fourfold form of the Gospel leaves little room for continuing oral tradition. If one were to ask either Justin or Irenaeus where one could find the sayings of Jesus, the answer would surely be, 'in the writings of the apostles and their followers'.

Justin and Irenaeus both hold the sayings of Jesus and the gospels in high regard, and on a level with the OT Scriptures. In this respect the similarities between the two second-century giants are as important as the differences. Although Irenaeus takes several more steps towards acceptance of a 'canon' of four written gospels than does Justin, the great teacher of the new 'philosophy of Christ' paves the way. I have emphasized more strongly than most the importance of *written* Jesus traditions for both Justin and Irenaeus. There is an obvious corollary: we may have allowed Papias' preference for 'the living voice' over 'the written word' to influence too strongly our reading of both Justin and Irenaeus.

The physical appearance of early Christian writings at the time in question is regularly overlooked in discussions of their status. I have argued elsewhere that the emergence of the four-gospel canon is related to the dissemination of the four gospels in codex form. Justin may well have had

---

[43] See especially the Preface to Book IV, and IV.1.1. See also Bingham, *Irenaeus's Use of Matthew's Gospel in Adversus Haereses*, pp. 97–8.

[44] Not surprisingly, Blanchard, *Aux sources du canon*, fails to discuss this passage.

[45] For the former, see, for example, IV.12.4-5; 10.1; 29.1. For the latter: IV.8.2.

a four-gospel codex in his catechetical school in Rome by about AD 150. As long ago as 1933, F. G. Kenyon suggested that Irenaeus may have been accustomed to the sight of codices which contained all four gospels. The evidence for this conclusion is now much stronger than it was seventy years ago.[46] Today, when we hear vociferous claims on behalf of the Gospels of Peter and Thomas, we need to recall that there is no manuscript evidence for the acceptance of any 'fifth' gospel alongside one or more of the writings of the fourfold Gospel. Codex and canon go hand in hand, but that is another story.

In discussions of the emergence of the canon, whether of the OT or the NT writings, definitions are all important, and the devil is in the detail. Even though Irenaeus does not use the term 'canon' in its now customary sense, his insistence that the one Gospel proclaimed by the apostles is found in four written gospels, no more, no less, implies a 'closed' gospel canon. If our definition of 'gospel canon' includes reference to an agreed list of widely accepted authoritative writings, then it did not exist at the end of the second century. Irenaeus was a towering figure, but we must not assume that his views on the fourfold Gospel were accepted universally. Justin Martyr influenced Irenaeus strongly, but Justin's pupil Tatian, whose *Diatessaron* almost won the day, took a very different path.[47]

---

[46] See Chapter 8, pp. 165–7 below.
[47] After I had completed this chapter my attention was drawn to the following: W. A. Lohr, 'Kanons-geschichtliche Beobachtungen zum Verhältnis von mundlicher und schriftlicher Tradition im zweiten Jahrhundert', *ZNW* 85 (1995) 234–58.

CHAPTER 5

The law of Christ and the Gospel

There are some baffling phrases hidden in early Christian writings which are worth careful examination.[1] The phrase 'the law of Christ' is one such. Although it is used only once in the New Testament (Gal. 6.2), it teases exegetes, it raises central questions of theological method, and it still forces us to ask awkward questions.[2] Was this phrase part of Paul's Gospel? And should it be part of Christian proclamation today?

In his influential commentary, H. D. Betz insists that Gal. 6.2, and indeed all the ethical directives in Gal. 5.13-6.10, are not directly derived from the Gospel that Paul preached.[3] Richard Hays has argued, surely correctly, that this disjunction of *kerygma* from conduct arises from an over-emphasis on individualistic soteriological elements at the expense of the corporate dimension in Paul's theological thought.[4] Paul's encouragement to the Galatian Christians to 'fulfil the law of Christ' (Gal. 6.2) was surely part of the Gospel message he wished to convey to the Galatian churches and no mere ethical addendum.

But that leaves us with a further set of questions. Why did Paul not make good theological capital out of the phrase in his other letters? Did the apostle decide that the phrase was too ambiguous or too prone to misunderstanding to merit further use? If so, should we follow his lead and drop it from contemporary theological reflection and from liturgies? Is this a phrase which has 'punched above its weight' for far too long?

---

[1] An earlier version of this chapter was given as a paper in a series of special seminars in Cambridge which formed part of the celebrations in 2002 of the 500th anniversary of the establishment of the Lady Margaret's Professorship. It was published in D. F. Ford and G. N. Stanton, *Scripture and Theology: Reading Texts, Seeking Wisdom* (London: SCM, 2003), pp. 169–84.

[2] See especially R. B. Hays, 'Christology and Ethics in Galatians: The Law of Christ', *CBQ* 49 (1987) 268–90; M. Winger, 'The Law of Christ', *NTS* 46 (2000) 537–46. Winger claims that the phrase 'the law of Christ' is more likely to mislead than to instruct. Paul 'probably thought it clearer than it has turned out to be; every writer has that experience' (p. 545).

[3] H. D. Betz, *Galatians*, Hermeneia Commentary (Philadelphia: Fortress, 1979), p. 292.

[4] Hays, 'Christology and Ethics', pp. 270–2.

On the other hand, we may decide that statistics can mislead. Paul may have used the phrase only once, but we should not forget that he also referred to the Lord's Supper in only one of his letters. As we shall see, there is a handful of related phrases and themes in Paul's letters and elsewhere in the New Testament. And in several early second-century writings similar phrases are prominent. Although the phrase often suffered benign neglect in later centuries,[5] from time to time this gem has been dusted down and polished, and sometimes partly recut.

'The law of Christ' has played at least one major role on the stage of history. John Fisher, the first holder of the Lady Margaret's Professorship of Divinity at Cambridge, used the phrase at a turning point in his dispute with King Henry VIII. When Henry began to seek a divorce from Catherine of Aragon in 1527, Fisher soon became the Queen's foremost defender. In 1531 he wrote the mitigating words by which the clergy in Convocation qualified their earlier acceptance of the King as their Supreme Head on earth. The clergy acknowledged the King only 'as far as the law of Christ allows' ('quantum per legem Christi licet'). This move set in motion a train of events, one of which was the beheading of John Fisher in 1535. Why did Fisher appeal to 'the law of Christ' at such a tense time? What did he understand by this phrase?

The phrase had not been part of Thomas Aquinas' vocabulary; he preferred 'the new law'. And, although John Fisher had close contact with Erasmus, he doesn't seem to have been influenced by Erasmus in his choice of this phrase. For in none of the five editions of the *Annotationes* does Erasmus say a single word about 'the law of Christ' in his comments on Gal. 6.2.[6] Perhaps Fisher chose the phrase because it was vague and ill-defined, but sounded good.[7] Or perhaps Fisher picked up the phrase quite deliberately from Gal. 6.2. If the latter, then I would love to know how he interpreted Paul's baffling words!

Martin Luther commented powerfully on the phrase in his 1519 and 1535 commentaries on Gal. 6.2, but it played no more than a very minor role in his expositions of the two uses of the law or in the later controversies

[5] Bernard Häring's *The Law of Christ* (3 vols., Cork: Mercier, 1963) is only a partial exception. In spite of its title, the phrase 'the law of Christ' is not discussed in this very traditional Roman Catholic moral theology until pp. 252–63. Häring seems to take the phrase to refer to the ethical teaching of the NT as a whole and to be synonymous with Thomas Aquinas' frequently used phrase, 'the new law'. I am grateful to my colleague Dr Markus Bockmuehl for this reference and for a number of helpful comments on an earlier draft of this chapter.
[6] See Anne Reeve, ed., *Erasmus's Annotations on the NT. Galatians to the Apocalypse: Facsimile of the Final Latin Text with All Earlier Variants* (Leiden: Brill, 1993).
[7] So my colleague Dr Richard Rex in a written communication dated 30 January 2002. See his *The Theology of John Fisher* (Cambridge: Cambridge University Press, 1991).

over the 'tertium usus legis'. Neither John Calvin nor Karl Barth found any
theological use for the phrase. And, since very few contemporary systematic
theologians bother to wrestle with exegesis, we shall be surprised to find
much interest in the phrase in their writings.

As we shall see, over the centuries, whenever 'the law of Christ' has found
favour, it has been understood in several different ways. Which of those
interpretations, if any, can still play a part in the Christian Gospel today?

I shall start with Paul's use of the phrase at Gal. 6.2. What was Paul's
intention when he first used the phrase? Should his understanding determine any continuing theological use today? I shall then turn to this phrase's
closest relatives elsewhere in the NT and in early Christian writings. Do
the second-century uses of the phrase help us theologically? 'The law of
Christ' raises perennial questions for Biblical scholars and for theologians,
and for those who want to wear both hats.

In this chapter I hope to show that there are themes associated with this
phrase which can still be put to good use as part of the Christian Gospel.
We may continue to use the well-known intercessory prayer based on
Gal. 6.2: 'Help us so to bear the burdens of others that we may fulfil
the law of Christ.' But if we do so, we shall need to be clear what we are
doing when we attempt to bear the burdens of others.

5.1 FULFILLING THE LAW OF CHRIST: GAL. 6.2

Here is the thirty-first of Paul's references in Galatians to νόμος, law. In
nearly all the preceding instances the reference is to *the* law, i.e. the law
of Moses.[8] So it is most unlikely that, without alerting his listeners, Paul
changes tack and refers to the teaching of Jesus as 'law', or to 'showing love
for others' (i.e. bearing the burdens of others) as 'law'.

Ever since Gal. 2.16, 'law' has been pounding relentlessly in the Galatians'
ears with a negative beat. However, at 4.21b, 5.14, and 6.2 Paul's tone
changes dramatically: νόμος is used in a positive sense in all three verses.
The reference at 5.14 to fulfilling the law in loving one's neighbour is
particularly striking; it paves the way for 6.2, for in both verses verbs from
the same root are used. Although 'Christ' and 'law' have regularly stood in
stark contrast earlier in the letter, at 6.2 they are brought together in an ear-
catching but baffling phrase. Since 'fulfilling the law' at 5.14 clearly refers
to the law of Moses, the use of the similar verb at 6.2 strongly suggests that
'law' here also refers to the law of Moses, and not to a norm or principle.

[8] J. L. Martyn, *Galatians*, Anchor Bible Commentary (New York: Doubleday, 1997), p. 555.

'Carry one another's burdens', urges Paul, 'and in this way you will fulfil the law of Christ.'[9] The careful listener to this letter being read aloud in the Galatian churches can hardly have failed to miss Paul's insistence that Christ himself 'bore the burdens of others' and so provided an example for the Galatian Christians. Paul's expansions of his opening 'grace and peace' formula in his letters often foreshadow several of the letters' main theological themes. This is certainly the case in Galatians. At Gal. 1.4 Paul notes that Christ 'gave himself for our sins'. Christ's self-giving love forms the climax of the richest section of the letter, Gal. 2.15-20: 'the Son of God loved me and gave himself for me'. Christ has fulfilled the law himself in his self-giving in love for others.[10]

So in Galatians we have *one* answer to the question: what is the law of Christ? *In Gal. 6.2 it is the law of Moses interpreted by Christ, with the 'love commandment' and 'carrying the burdens of others' as its essence; it is fulfilled by Christ in his own self-giving love.*[11]

Several further comments are in order. (1) With their positive references to law, Gal. 4.21b, 5.14, and 6.2 stand in counterpoise to Paul's other references to the law of Moses in Galatians. Taken together, these verses confirm that, in spite of the numerous negative comments on the law elsewhere in this letter, Paul did not repudiate the law of Moses, as some of his later followers (most notably Marcion) and some of his opponents (see Acts 21.28) wrongly supposed.

(2) The immediate context emphasizes that those who live by the Spirit are not free to gratify the desires of the flesh (5.16).[12] However, Paul does not spell out the precise ways in which the law of Moses is to be retained now that believers in Christ have been set free from the present evil age (1.4). No one will be right-wised by God on the basis of carrying out the law of Moses (2.16), but the law is not to be ignored or discarded, for it is not opposed to the promises of God (3.21).

---

[9] Dr Michael Thompson has drawn my attention to the partial parallel at Rom. 15.1-3, where encouragement to bear (βαστάζειν) the failings of the weak is linked to the example of Christ.

[10] Winger, 'The Law of Christ', p. 538, protests that, in order to find a reference to the example of the self-giving love of Christ at Gal. 6.2, Hays must reach 'back all the way to 2.20'. But he fails to note the importance of 1.4, and sweeps aside 3.13 and 4.4-5 too readily.

[11] Cf. John Barclay's explanation, *Obeying the Truth* (Edinburgh: T. & T. Clark, 1988), p. 134: the law of Christ is 'the Law as it has been taken in hand by Christ himself'; and also J. L. Martyn's comment on the phrase (*Galatians*, ad loc.): 'the law as it has fallen into the hands of Christ'.

[12] Winger, 'The Law of Christ', helpfully emphasizes the importance of Gal. 5.16-25 for the interpretation of 6.2. He claims that, for Paul, 'those who live according to the Spirit follow the law of Christ – or better, as Paul says, they bring it to realization' (p. 544). However, I am not convinced that Paul uses 'law' at Gal. 6.2 'in a somewhat looser sense, not as identifying any specific, legal instruction, but as referring to the way Christ exercises his lordship over those called by him'.

Paul continued to mull over this antinomy. The apostle takes a further step in Rom. 13. 8-10. 'Love is the fulfilling of the law', to be sure, but this axiom does not mean that the commandments concerning adultery, murder, theft, and covetousness may be ignored. This passage seems to have encouraged the later strong Christian conviction that the ten commandments are the core of the Mosaic law; they (and, for some, they alone) have abiding significance for Christians.

(3) The encouragement to 'bear one another's burdens' is almost certainly taken from the Socratic tradition and the Greek doctrines about 'friendship'.[13] A well-known maxim is transposed by Paul into a new key. We should welcome Paul's appropriation of the conventional ethical teaching of his day at several points in Galatians 5 and 6, and especially in the lists of virtues and vices at Gal. 5.19-23. For, in so doing, Paul has given us an example to follow. Why should we not appropriate some of the insights of the moral philosophers of our day and set them in a firmly constructed theological framework, as Paul himself does?

I do not think that Paul is picking up a slogan used by the agitators in Galatia and throwing it back in their face. Nor do I think that Paul is being merely playful, as has been suggested. In the preceding argument of the letter Paul has carefully prepared his listeners and readers for his dramatic use of the phrase at 6.2. His failure to spell out its meaning more fully may indicate that the Galatian house churches had already been well drilled by Paul in its meaning. This is an interesting possibility, which has been overlooked in the voluminous literature. In his letters Paul does use a series of key 'short-hand' phrases whose content his recipients could readily fill out for themselves.[14] 'The law of Christ' may be one such phrase.

Not long after writing Galatians, Paul wrote I Corinthians. In a highly rhetorical paragraph in chapter 9 Paul comments on his missionary strategy. In v.20 he explains that when preaching to Jews he was prepared to exercise a measure of self-renunciation. In v.21 he comments on his strategy when preaching to Gentiles: 'I identified as one outside Mosaic jurisdiction with those outside it.' A rider is added immediately: 'Of course, I am not outside God's law (ἄνομος θεοῦ), but I am ἔννομος Χριστοῦ.' The latter phrase is often translated, 'I am under the law of Christ', which is adequate, though it suggests that the Greek here is the same as in Gal. 6.2. Given the subtle play on words in I Cor. 9.20 and 21, it was hardly an option for Paul

---

[13] Betz, *Galatians*, p. 549.
[14] See especially Margaret Mitchell, 'Rhetorical Shorthand in Pauline Argumentation: the Functions of "the Gospel" in the Corinthian Correspondence', in L. A. Jervis and P. Richardson, eds., *Gospel in Paul, FS R. N. Longenecker* (Sheffield: JSOT Press, 1994), pp. 63–88. See also pp. 49–52 above.

to repeat the phrase used in Galatians, ὁ νόμος τοῦ Χριστοῦ. In fact, as far as we know, the apostle never reused that phrase.

What did Paul mean by ἔννομος Χριστοῦ? 'I am under Christ's jurisdiction' catches the sense. The preceding chapters of I Corinthians suggest that the phrase may include commitment to sayings of Jesus, but to limit it in that way would miss its Christological thrust.

Paul's use of the phrase 'the law of faith' at Rom. 3.27 has teased many a commentator. Although many claim that Paul here uses νόμος to mean 'principle' or 'rule', it is most unlikely that Paul jumps without warning, from using νόμος to refer to the law of Moses, to the more general sense of 'principle', and in any case the context will not allow this reading. We must take our cue from v.31, the final step in Paul's argument. 'Do we overthrow the Torah on the basis of faith in Jesus?' By no means: we uphold the law. So 'the law of faith' is the law discerned and obeyed on the basis of faith in Jesus. In other words, this phrase is a first cousin of ὁ νόμος τοῦ Χριστοῦ.[15]

5.2   SIMILAR PHRASES OUTSIDE THE PAULINE CORPUS

At Jas. 1.25, 2.8, and 12 the writer qualifies νόμος three times. His other uses of νόμος refer to the law of Moses or to one of its specific commandments. So it is probable that 'the perfect law of freedom', 'the royal law', and 'the law of liberty' are almost synonymous references to the law understood from a Christian perspective; in the context of this letter, that means the teaching of Jesus.[16] In other words, we are not far from 'the law of Christ'. This is especially clear at Jas. 2.8: 'You are doing well if you are carrying out the royal law according to the Scripture, "Love your neighbour as yourself."' There is a clear implication that the love commandment lies at the heart of the law (cf. Matt. 22.34-40).

What is implicit in James is much more explicit in Matthew's Gospel. The evangelist has taken great care over the composition of his five discourses because he values the sayings of Jesus so highly. The sayings of Jesus are to be prominent in the missionary proclamation and catechetical instruction of the 'new people' (28.18-20). The closing verses of the Sermon on the Mount emphasize strongly the importance of hearing and acting on the

---

[15] Perhaps Rom. 8.2 is also a first cousin of Gal. 6.2: in Christ Jesus the law (of Moses) becomes life-giving (cf. 7.10 and 14a) and of the Spirit.

[16] So also Sophie Laws, *The Epistle of James*, Black's NT Commentaries (London: A. & C. Black, 1980), p. 110: 'It is probable that when James quotes Lev 19.18 as *scripture* he does so in the knowledge that this scripture has received the added authority of Jesus' use.'

words of Jesus (7.24-7). For Matthew 'the will of the heavenly Father' is equated with carrying out *the sayings of Jesus* (7.21, cf. Luke 6.46).

Matthew's Gospel provided the 'new people' with a set of authoritative traditions to be set alongside the law and the prophets. The evangelist does not spell out as clearly as his modern interpreters would like the precise relationship between 'new' and 'old'. Matthew's Jesus does not repudiate the law: its continuing importance is affirmed very strongly (5.17-19). The love commandment is singled out by Jesus as expressing the very essence of Scripture (7.12; 22.37-9), but in no way does this contradict the law, any more than do the so-called antitheses in 5.21-48. Matthew hints – but no more – that the sayings of Jesus are the criterion for the interpretation of the law, but his primary emphasis is on the ways the sayings of Jesus strengthen and fulfil the law and the prophets.

In Matthew, as elsewhere in the NT, Christology and ethics are linked inextricably. The full significance of the teaching of Jesus can only be discerned in the light of the conviction that Jesus is 'God with us' (Matt. 1.23). With his coming, in fulfilment of Isa. 9.1, 'light has dawned' (4.16). The Sermon on the Mount is proclamation of the good news of God's kingly rule (4.17, 22). It is both gift and demand; it is not a new set of rules and regulations.

Matthew does not use the phrase 'the law of Christ', but he would not have been unhappy with it. For Matthew, the person and words of Jesus are the criterion by which the law is to be interpreted. Although some exegetes argue that the teaching of Jesus is also in view at Gal. 6.2, in my opinion they are mistaken. However, in spite of differences, Matthew and Paul agree that 'the law of Christ' has as its focal point the love commandment and has a Christological reference. Both notions were to be important in later theological exposition of our phrase.

The writer of I John insists at 2.3 that we know God if we keep God's commandments. The phraseology recalls Sirach 29.1 and Matt. 19.17, and we are only one step from Tobit 14.9, Acts 15.5, and James 2.10, where the verb τηρεῖν is used of keeping the law of Moses. Three verses later the writer's train of thought turns to Christ: whoever says, 'I abide in him' ought to walk just as Christ walked (I John 2.6). He then refers to the old commandment which his readers have had from the beginning, the 'word' that they have heard. What is it? It is of course Christ's command, 'love one another'. In short, the writer implies that the love commandment is the focal point of God's commandments, i.e. the law of Moses. There is certainly no suggestion that the commandment to love is not found in the OT, for at 3.11-12 Cain is attacked for failing to love his brother Abel.

Although νόμος is not used in the Johannine letters, we are not far from the thought that 'the law of Christ', and in particular the commandment to love one another, is the lens through which God's commandments should be read and obeyed.

A similar pattern of thought is found in II John 6-10. God's commandments and Christ's command to love one another are juxtaposed and all but fused together. But this letter adds a note not found explicitly in I John: Christ's teaching is referred to twice over (verses 9 and 10), and it is fairly clear that this teaching extends beyond the love commandment.

The preceding paragraphs have confirmed that there is a strikingly similar pattern to be observed in several NT writings – a generally overlooked show of unity amidst diversity. There are almost certainly no direct literary relationships between Paul, James, Matthew, and the writers of the Johannine letters. Yet in all four strands of earliest Christianity we find a continuing commitment to the law of Moses alongside an insistence that it should be understood from a new perspective. That new perspective is not sketched out fully, but in every case it includes a Christological element, and either the sayings of Jesus or the love commandment, or both.

This theological pattern can be traced down through the centuries whenever our theological gem 'the law of Christ' is dusted down. Sometimes Christology is more prominent, sometimes the teaching of Jesus, sometimes the love commandment. I shall now give the merest sketch to back up that contention.

5.3 SECOND-CENTURY WRITERS

In the early decades of the second century the *Shepherd of Hermas* takes an interesting step beyond NT writers. The Son of God is the lawgiver: he has given to the people the law given to him by the Father (*Sim.* 5.6, 3; ch. 59). The Son of God is himself 'the law of God' given to the whole world (*Sim.* 8.3, 2-3; ch. 69).

Christ is also called 'the law' three times in the *Kerygma Petri*, which dates from the same period. Alas, all we have from this treatise is a handful of quotations in later writers, especially Clement of Alexandria. Christians worship God in the manner neither of the Greeks nor of the Jews. 'We worship God through Christ in a new way.' 'For we have found in the Scriptures, how the Lord says: "Behold, I make with you a new covenant, not as I made (one) with your fathers in Mt Horeb." A new one he made with us. For what has reference to the Greeks and Jews is old. But we are Christians, who as a third race worship him in a new way.'[17] Here we have early evidence for a very radical sense of self-understanding on the part of Christians. Scripture is not abandoned, but Christ himself has become 'the law'.

A fuller exposition of the same theme is found in Justin Martyr's *Dialogue with Trypho*, written c. AD 160, possibly in dependence on the *Kerygma Petri*.[18] For Justin, Christ is himself given by God as the final and eternal law (*Dialogue* 11.2, twice), and the new law (11.4, ὁ καινὸς νόμος).[19] Justin elaborates his point in a striking credal passage in 43.1: by the will of the Father, Christ was born Son of God by means of the Virgin; he was proclaimed by the prophets as about to come 'as an everlasting law and a new covenant for the whole world'. Justin insists that the law given by God to Moses at Mt Horeb is antiquated and belongs to Trypho and his fellow-Jews alone, whereas Christ, the new law, was given to all people (11.2). Justin does not believe for one moment that the law of Moses has been abolished, though he does have difficulty spelling out precisely how Christians should use it, as, of course, did Paul himself.

Justin also understands 'the law of Christ' in a different sense. His Jewish opponent Trypho issues a strong challenge: Justin and his fellow-Christians claim to worship God, but fail to make their lives different from those of Gentiles in that they keep neither the feasts nor the sabbaths, nor do they have circumcision, nor do they carry out God's commandments (10.3). In short, Christians are law-less. As a key part of his extended response, Justin refers to Christ as *the new lawgiver* (ὁ καινὸς νομοθέτης, 12.2 and 14.3), through whom 'the poor have the Gospel preached to them, and the blind receive their sight' (cf. Matt. 11.6 = Luke 7.22). The sayings of Jesus are understood here as the gift of the new lawgiver. For Justin the teaching of Jesus embedded in the gospels is 'the law of Christ'.[20]

So, for Hermas and for Justin, Christ is himself both the new law and the new lawgiver, but without the implication that the law of Moses is to be abandoned. The Epistle of Barnabas comes perilously close to the

[17] For the texts and bibliography, see J. K. Elliott, *The Apocryphal New Testament* (Oxford: Clarendon, 1993), pp. 20–3; more fully, W. Schneemelcher, ed., *New Testament Apocrypha*, Vol. II (Cambridge: Clarke, 1992), pp. 34–41.

[18] So O. Skarsaune, *The Proof from Prophecy. A Study in Justin Martyr's Proof-Text Tradition: Text-Type, Provenance, Theological Profile* (Leiden: Brill, 1987), pp. 72–3.

[19] The most accessible translation is by A. Lukyn Williams, *Justin Martyr: The Dialogue with Trypho* (London: SPCK, 1930).

[20] For a fuller discussion, see Chapter 4. Although Justin does not refer explicitly to Paul or to his letters, at numerous points he betrays knowledge of them. So it is possible that his understanding of Christ as the new lawgiver has been influenced by Gal. 6.2.

latter notion: the Lord has abolished sacrifices, new moons, and sabbaths so that 'the new law of our Lord Jesus Christ which is free from the yoke of compulsion might have its offering, one not made by man' (2.6). For Barnabas the Mosaic law has mistakenly been interpreted literally rather than spiritually as intended (10.2, 9).

5.4   THE TEACHING OF JESUS AS 'THE LAW OF CHRIST'

Justin Martyr's notion of Christ as the 'new lawgiver' became all pervasive in the later tradition of the church. I shall now refer briefly to a handful of examples. First of all, the magnificent thirteenth-century statue of Christ the lawgiver from the south side of Chartres Cathedral in France. Here Christ is depicted holding up one arm in blessing. His other hand is offering a beautifully bound codex, which I take to be the gospels. In other words, Christ is offering his own teaching as a 'new law'. Protestants underestimate the powerful influence a statue such as this had on the continuing Christian tradition.

In many parish churches in England to this day two panels painted with Scripture texts hang behind the altar: the ten commandments on the left, and the Lord's prayer on the right. This practice goes back to the late sixteenth century, with even deeper roots in the medieval period. The setting up of these panels is related to the catechism in the 1552 Book of Common Prayer. Every person brought before the bishop for confirmation was expected to be able to recite the ten commandments and the Lord's prayer, as well as the brief explanations of both texts in the catechism. Perhaps the panels often acted as a crib for those with short memories!

The impact of this practice on the life of the church is clear. The ten commandments are singled out as the essence of the law of Moses, while the Lord's prayer is assumed to provide the essence of the 'law of Christ'. The theological instincts which lie behind the erection of those two panels of texts are profound, and in my view profoundly correct.

Given the strength of the tradition I have just sketched, it is no surprise to discover that Gal. 6.2 has often been taken as a reference by Paul to the importance he attached to the teaching of Jesus. There have been several influential modern supporters of this interpretation. In his ICC commentary on Galatians, E. D. Burton wrote: 'this is one of the few passages in which the apostle refers to teaching of Jesus transmitted to him through the Twelve or their companions'.[21] Burton, however, failed to list the Jesus traditions which might have been in the apostle's mind.

C. H. Dodd was more specific, arguing in 1951 and 1953 that Gal. 6.1-5 was an adaptation of Jesus' teaching at Matt. 23.4 and 18.15-16.[22] At about the same time Dodd's pupil W. D. Davies was equally adamant. 'When he [Paul] used the phrase νόμος τοῦ Χριστοῦ (the law of Christ) he meant that the actual words of Jesus were for him a New Torah.'[23] More recently, R. N. Longenecker has defended a more sophisticated version of the same interpretation. He takes 'the law of Christ' to refer to those 'prescriptive principles stemming from the heart of the gospel (usually embodied in the example and teachings of Jesus), which are meant to be applied to specific situations by the direction and enablement of the Holy Spirit, being always motivated and conditioned by love'.[24]

The difficulty with this general line of interpretation is that Paul alludes very rarely to sayings of Jesus, and refers explicitly to them even less often.[25] There is limited evidence in I Corinthians and in Romans 12-14, but even less evidence in Galatians.[26] When the phraseology of Gal. 6.1-5 is compared closely with the synoptic tradition, there are only two words in common, βάρη (burdens) and φορτίον (load), and even they are not used in similar contexts.

In my view, interpreters of Gal. 6.2 who claim that the words of Jesus are 'the law of Christ' are reading Paul through Matthean eyes. Their reading may not do justice to Paul, but it does resonate with a long and strong

---

[21] E. D. Burton, *The Epistle to the Galatians*, ICC (Edinburgh: T. & T. Clark, 1921).

[22] John Barclay, *Obeying the Truth* (Edinburgh: T. & T. Clark, 1988), p. 129 n. 70, astutely notes that in 1935 C. H. Dodd had denied that Gal. 6.2 could mean the 'Torah of Jesus', but had changed his position by 1951 in his *Gospel and Law* (Cambridge: Cambridge University Press), pp. 64–83. See also C. H. Dodd's important article '"Εννομος Χριστοῦ', reprinted in his *More New Testament Studies* (Manchester: Manchester University Press, 1968), pp. 134–8.

[23] In his *Paul and Rabbinic Judaism* (London: SPCK, 1948), p. 144, Davies went somewhat further than Dodd in claiming that there was rabbinic evidence (albeit somewhat limited) to suggest that in the new age there would be a new 'law of the Messiah'. See especially W. D. Davies, *The Setting of the Sermon on the Mount* (Cambridge: Cambridge University Press, 1963), pp. 109–90. H. Schlier also insisted that the 'law of Christ' is 'die Tora des Messias Jesus', *Die Brief an die Galater*, KEK, 12th edn (Göttingen: Vandenhoeck & Ruprecht, 1961), p. 272. As there are major problems over the dating and interpretation of the handful of rabbinic passages Davies and Schlier cite, their case has won little scholarly support. See especially R. J. Banks, *Jesus and the Law in the Synoptic Tradition* (Cambridge: Cambridge University Press, 1975), pp. 65–81.

[24] See especially R. N. Longenecker, *Galatians*, Word Biblical Commentary (Dallas: Word, 1990), pp. 275–6.

[25] For a cautious assessment, see D. C. Allison, 'The Pauline Epistles and the Synoptic Gospels: The Pattern of the Parallels', *NTS* 28 (1982) 1–32.

[26] For Romans see especially M. B. Thompson, *Clothed with Christ: The Example and Teaching of Jesus in Romans 12.1-15.3* (Sheffield: Sheffield Academic Press, 1991).

tradition which should not be rejected without further ado. We turn now
to a further interpretation of 'the law of Christ' with an equally impressive
pedigree, even though it too does not do full justice to Paul's intention in
Gal. 6.2.

5.5   LEX CHRISTI, LEX AMORIS

In his first commentary on Galatians (1519), Luther wrote several powerful
and perceptive paragraphs on Gal. 6.2, which he describes as 'a very beautiful and thoroughly golden maxim: Love is the law of Christ'. In his 1535
commentary on Gal. 6.2, Luther goes even further. 'The Law of Christ is
the law of love', he writes three times over. 'After redeeming and regenerat-
ing us and constituting us as His church, Christ did not give us any new
law except the law of mutual love (John 13.34-5).' 'To love does not mean,
as the sophists imagine, to wish someone else well, but to bear someone
else's burdens, that is, to bear what is burdensome to you and what you
would rather not bear.'

Two centuries after Luther, J. A. Bengel echoed Luther's interpretation
in a typically pithy comment on Gal. 6.2 in his influential *Gnomon Novi
Testamenti* (1742): 'Lex Christi, lex amoris' ('the law of Christ is the law of
love').

The same interpretation is set out much more fully in V. P. Furnish's
standard textbook *The Love Command in the New Testament*[27] and supported by many other writers. It is probably the consensus interpretation
of Gal. 6.2 at present.

Who would want to deny the importance of love in Paul's ethical
thinking? At Gal. 5.14 love is said to sum up the whole law. Love heads
the list of the fruits of the Spirit at Gal. 5.22, a list which ends with the
ironic comment, 'there is no law against such things'. Nonetheless, I am
not convinced that this interpretation does full justice to Paul's intention
in Gal. 6.2, for if the 'law of Christ' is taken to mean no more than 'the law
of love', Paul's careful counterpoise with 'the law of Moses' is missed, as is
his emphasis on Christ's own example of self-giving love.

5.6   THEOLOGICAL REFLECTIONS

In Gal. 6.2 and I Cor. 9.21 Paul's Christological emphasis is clear, as is the
love commandment, but there is little or no trace of the teachings of Jesus
as constituting the law of Christ. If we are reflecting on the current value of

[27] V. P. Furnish, *The Love Command in the New Testament* (London: SCM, 1968), pp. 59–65.

'the law of Christ' for the Christian Gospel today, why should we privilege Paul's usage?

Quite independently of Paul, we find James, Matthew, and the writer of the Johannine letters using *the concept*, even if they do not use the actual phrase. As with Paul, there is a continuing commitment to the law of Moses as interpreted by Christ. But there is also the addition of a much clearer emphasis on the teaching of Jesus and a less explicit Christological note.

Early in the second century, notable theological steps were taken. In the writings of Hermas, the *Kerygma Petri*, and Justin Martyr, there is a strong emphasis on Christ himself as the new law. Arguably one of Paul's notions is taken much further, even though it is difficult to trace direct use of Paul's letters. In Hermas and Justin, Christ is not only the new law; he is himself the new lawgiver.

The later Christian tradition develops one or other of the strands of thought found in the NT and in early Christian writings, but without adding significant or new understandings. As far as I am aware, the phrase 'the law of Christ' is suffering benign neglect in contemporary theological writing. However, I hope that I have shown that, if we consider Christian writings up to the middle of the second century and do not confine ourselves to Paul or to canonical writings, we are not going to be bereft of matters for continuing theological reflection. Indeed, we have an agenda.

(1) Christology and ethics must not be separated.

(2) The 'law of Christ' or whatever alternative or synonymous phrase we choose must not be allowed to imply abandonment of the law of Moses. In particular, if we use the phrase 'new law', we must do so with care, for 'new' can easily imply that we are discarding the 'old'. The terms 'new covenant' or 'new testament' are analogies. They may be used, but there are lurking dangers. In saying this, I am well aware that there are unresolved issues concerning Christian theological interpretation of the Old Testament or the Hebrew Scriptures, if you prefer. But I am heartened by the number of Biblical scholars who are now wrestling with these very issues.

(3) The radical, disturbing teaching of Jesus recorded by the evangelists is of continuing importance, with the love commandment as its focal point.

(4) In Galatians (and elsewhere) Paul juxtaposes the wisdom of Scripture (the love commandment of Lev. 19.18 at Gal. 5.14) and baptizes into Christ the conventional ethical wisdom of the day (bear one another's burdens at Gal. 6.2). Why shouldn't we do likewise?

(5) Our explorations have warned us yet again not to allow particular strands of the later Christian tradition to determine our Biblical exegesis. On the other hand, we have seen that later interpretation and development of a Biblical tradition may stimulate theological reflection in unexpected directions.

All this seems to me to be a useful starting agenda for a theological ethics in which Scripture is taken seriously. I am not advocating a return to the old model whereby the Biblical scholar hands over to the systematic theologian his or her results, to be used according to whim. Rather, I am urging that there should be a continuing dialogue between close attention to Biblical text, the effects of the text (for good or ill) through the centuries, and contemporary theological reflection.

When we have engaged in this dialogue, we may find that the phrase 'the law of Christ' is too prone to misunderstanding or one-sided interpretation to be of further use. But the themes associated with this phrase through the centuries will continue to enrich our theological reflection on the Gospel.

PART II

Jesus

CHAPTER 6

Jesus of Nazareth: a magician and a false prophet who deceived God's people?

The relationship of Jesus to first-century Judaism continues to be discussed vigorously.[1] This continuing debate was sparked off initially by the publication of Hermann Samuel Reimarus's *Wolfenbüttel Fragments* between 1774 and 1778.[2] In deliberately provocative comments, Reimarus insisted that Jesus did not intend to abolish the Jewish religion and to introduce a new one in its place. The intention of Jesus, Reimarus claimed, was reversed completely after his death by both the actions and the teaching of the apostles. With their abandonment of the law, 'Judaism was laid in its grave.'[3]

In an equally influential publication two generations later, David Friedrich Strauss noted that a radical account of the origins of Christianity along these lines had been propounded by 'the enemies of Christianity in its ecclesiastical form', and that it had been done 'most concisely of all in the *Wolfenbüttel Fragments*', i.e. by Reimarus.[4] Although Strauss was sympathetic to many of Reimarus's claims, he knew that any presentation of Jesus as a faithful Jew was built on a one-sided reading of the evidence. Strauss emphasized that there was clear strong evidence within the gospels to support the opposite viewpoint: Jesus was at odds with the religious leaders of his day.[5]

---

[1] Earlier versions of this chapter were given as the Thatcher Lecture at the Uniting Theological College in Sydney on 18 July 1991, and as a lecture or seminar paper at the Universities of Otago (New Zealand), Leiden (the Netherlands), Lancaster, Leeds, Belfast, and Aberdeen. This chapter is a revised version of my contribution to the I. H. Marshall Festschrift, Joel B. Green and Max Turner, eds., *Jesus of Nazareth: Lord and Christ* (Grand Rapids: Eerdmans, 1994), pp. 164–80.

[2] Reimarus died in 1768. The *Fragments* were published anonymously by G. E. Lessing. The identity of the author did not become generally known until 1814.

[3] Reimarus, *Fragments*, 1.19, ed. C. H. Talbert (Philadelphia: Fortress, 1970), p. 101. In a note at this point Talbert insists that 'this entire argument is an oversimplification by Reimarus'.

[4] *The Life of Jesus Critically Examined*, §67. I have cited the edition by P. C. Hodgson (London: SCM, 1973), p. 298; this is George Eliot's translation of the fourth German edition.

[5] Ibid., pp. 297–300 and 599–602.

Reimarus and Strauss both still have plenty of supporters, and many mediating positions are defended. After one hundred and fifty years of discussion, the relationship of Jesus to Judaism remains a contentious issue, as a cluster of influential book titles confirms: *Jesus the Jew; Jesus and Judaism; Jesus and the Transformation of Judaism; Jesus within Judaism.*[6] Although our knowledge of first-century Judaism has increased enormously in recent decades, the variety of views still on offer is bewildering in its rich profusion.

An impasse has been reached. This is partly because at key points there are crucial gaps in our knowledge. For example, we cannot be certain just what were the conventions of various religious groups on the fine points of sabbath observance in, say, Capernaum in AD 30.

And in addition, the relevant evidence which has survived is difficult to interpret. Almost all of it has come down to us from a partisan point of view. Whether we are examining the evidence of Josephus, or of the rabbis, or of the New Testament evangelists, this fact has to be taken very seriously indeed.

However, I do not think that these difficulties should deter critical inquiry. I am convinced that discussion of the relationship of Jesus to contemporary Judaism can be advanced as effectively by opening up unconventional lines of inquiry as it can be by rehearsing familiar arguments. In this chapter I shall plot a path which has been neglected in most recent discussion.

I shall examine the most widely attested ancient criticism of Jesus of Nazareth: he was a magician and a false prophet who deceived God's people.[7] The barbed criticisms from the opponents of any striking individual are often as revealing as the fulsome praise of close associates, so we do well to take seriously the small number of negative comments about Jesus which have come down to us from antiquity.[8]

I shall start with criticisms of Jesus which are found in Jewish, Christian, and pagan circles in the middle of the second century. I shall then discuss

---

[6] G. Vermes, *Jesus the Jew* (London: Collins, 1973); E. P. Sanders, *Jesus and Judaism* (London: SCM, 1985); J. Riches, *Jesus and the Transformation of Judaism* (London: Darton, Longman & Todd, 1980); J. H. Charlesworth, *Jesus within Judaism* (London: SPCK, 1989). In *The Historical Jesus: The Life of a Mediterranean Jewish Peasant* (Edinburgh: T. & T. Clark, 1991), J. D. Crossan paints on an even larger canvas and portrays Jesus as a Mediterranean peasant, a Jewish Cynic. Quotations from the Cynic letters and Epictetus are given greater prominence than (for example) the Qumran writings. In effect, Crossan downplays the Jewishness of Jesus. See my review in *Theology* 95 (1992) 452–3.

[7] For a fine discussion of the allegation that Jesus was an 'illegitimate son', see S. McKnight, 'Calling Jesus *Mamzer*', *Journal for the Study of the Historical Jesus* 1 (2003) 73–103. See also B. D. Chilton, 'Jésus, le *mamzer* (Mt 1.18)', *NTS* 46 (2000) 222–7.

[8] It is worth noting that no ancient opponent of early Christianity ever denied that Jesus existed. This is the Achilles' heel of attempts by a few modern scholars such as G. A. Wells to deny that Jesus existed.

earlier forms of this stock polemic in the writings of Josephus, and then the four evangelists, before turning, finally, to traditions which go back to the lifetime of Jesus. It is often helpful in studies of earliest Christianity to work back from later, clearer evidence to more problematic earlier evidence. Of course there is a risk of anachronism. But sometimes risks have to be taken: later traditions may well suggest new questions and new ways of looking at much-disputed issues.

Accusations of magic and of false prophecy/deception are very closely related to one another in ancient polemic. In many polemical traditions in which only one of the two terms occurs, the other is usually implied. There is a third, closely related concept which is prominent in polemic in antiquity: the apparent success of the magician and the false prophet/deceiver is regularly ascribed by opponents to some form of demonic possession. Readers familiar with elementary mathematics will quickly appreciate that I have in mind three overlapping circles in a Venn diagram.

I shall try to show that the accusations that Jesus was a magician and a false prophet who deceived God's people were well known in the middle of the second century in both Christian and Jewish circles; they became part of the stock rabbinic polemic against Jesus. These jibes were probably known to Josephus about AD 90; they were known to, and countered by, the evangelists; they were almost certainly used by some of Jesus' adversaries in his own lifetime. If this final point can be established, there are important implications for our appreciation of the relationship of Jesus to the Judaism of his day.

6.1 JUSTIN MARTYR, RABBINIC TRADITIONS, JOSEPHUS

In the middle of his extended debate with his Jewish adversary Trypho, Justin claims that the healing miracles of Jesus were the fulfilment of the messianic prophecies of Isa. 35.1-7. The miracles of Jesus were intended to elicit recognition of him as Messiah, but many who saw them drew the opposite conclusion: 'they said it was a display of magic art, for they even dared to say that he was a magician and a deceiver of the people (μάγος καὶ λαοπλάνος)', *Dialogue* 69.7. From the context in the *Dialogue*, there is no doubt that the term 'deceiver' is being used against the background of Deut. 13.5 in the special sense of a false prophet who leads God's people astray.[9]

---

[9] The notion of 'deception' is widespread in ancient polemic of all kinds, where it is not necessarily linked to false prophecy. False prophecy, however, always involves deception.

The title of this chapter is taken from this double polemical accusation in *Dialogue* 69.7. Justin clearly believes that it was prevalent in the lifetime of Jesus. Was he correct in this judgement? Or do his comments simply reflect Jewish–Christian controversies in the middle decades of the second century? It is not easy to answer these questions – and a great deal is at stake.

To label someone a 'magician' and/or a 'deceiver' ('false prophet') in antiquity was an attempt to marginalize a person who was perceived to be a threat to the dominant social order. If we can show that these terms, with their roots in Deuteronomy 13 and 18, were used by contemporary opponents of Jesus, an important corollary will follow: the teachings and actions of Jesus must have been considered by some of his contemporaries to be deeply offensive.

The extent to which Justin's *Dialogue* reflects genuine discussion and controversy between Christians and Jews has been keenly debated. The *Dialogue* is highly stylized, and it is far from being a dispassionate verbatim account of a debate between Justin and Trypho. There is at least some truth in Harnack's view that Justin's dialogue with Trypho was in fact the monologue of a victor.[10] However, there is little doubt that the double accusation against Jesus which is recorded in *Dialogue* 69.7, 'magician and deceiver of God's people', was being used in Jewish anti-Christian polemic in the middle of the second century, for it is also found in two related rabbinic traditions.[11]

In *b. Sanh.* 43a an anonymous tradition is introduced with the formula, 'It is said', an indication that it is a *baraitha*, an old tradition:

On the eve of Passover Yeshu was hanged. For forty days before the execution took place, a herald went forth and cried, He is going forth to be stoned because *he has practised sorcery and enticed and led Israel astray*. Anyone who can say anything in his favour, let him come forward and plead on his behalf. But since nothing was brought forward in his favour, he was hanged on the eve of Passover! Ulla retorted: Do you suppose that he was one for whom a defence could be made? Was he not *a deceiver*, concerning whom scripture says [Deut 13.8], Neither shalt thou spare neither shalt thou conceal him? With Yeshu however it was different, for he was connected with the government.

[10] A. Harnack, *Judentum und Judenchristentum in Justins Dialog mit Tryphon* (Leipzig, 1930).
[11] For a fuller discussion than is possible here, see D. R. Catchpole, *The Trial of Jesus* (Leiden: Brill, 1971), pp. 1–71; J. L. Martyn, *History and Theology in the Fourth Gospel*, 2nd edn (Nashville: Abingdon, 1979), pp. 73–81; W. Horbury, 'The Benediction of the *Minim* and Early Jewish–Christian Controversy', *JTS* 33 (1982) 19–61; J. Maier, *Jesus von Nazareth in der talmudischen Überlieferung* (Darmstadt: Wissenschaftliche Buchgesellschaft, 1978); G. Twelftree, 'Jesus in Jewish Traditions', in D. Wenham, ed., *Gospel Perspectives: The Jesus Traditions Outside the Gospels*, Vol. v (Sheffield: JSOT Press, 1985), pp. 289–342.

The pronouncement of the herald, 'forty days before the execution took place', confirms that this is no casual polemical comment, but a *formal legal accusation* against Jesus.[12] The two verbs 'entice' and 'lead astray' have the same direct object, Israel, and are closely related in meaning, as are the corresponding nouns in the related passage in *Mishnah Sanhedrin* 7.10-11. Although the comment attributed to Ulla (a late third-century rabbi) may be a later elaboration of this polemical tradition, the reference to Deuteronomy 13 confirms that 'entice' and 'lead astray' amount to a charge of false prophecy, for in that *locus classicus* these three terms are very closely related.

In *b. Sanh.* 107b the same double accusation is found in the same order:

One day he [R. Joshua] was reciting the Shema when Jesus came before him. He intended to receive him and made a sign to him. He (Jesus) thinking it was to repel him, went, put up a brick and worshipped it.[13]

'Repent', said he [R. Joshua] to him. He replied, 'I have thus learned from thee: He who sins and causes others to sin is not afforded the means of repentance.' And a Master has said, 'Jesus the Nazarene *practised magic and led Israel astray*.

These two rabbinic traditions are very difficult to interpret in detail, and even more difficult to date with any confidence. Were it not for the close correspondence between these traditions and Justin's *Dialogue* 69.7, it would be tempting to dismiss them as third-century (or even later) Jewish anti-Christian polemic. However, the semi-technical terminology used in Justin Martyr's Greek is almost as close as one could reasonably expect to the Hebrew of the rabbinic traditions.[14] Equally important, the order in which the accusations are cited is the same. In Deuteronomy the discussion of enticement to apostasy and false prophecy in chapter 13 which is referred to in *b. Sanh.* 43a *precedes* detailed reference to various forms of magic and sorcery in chapter 18.[15] The order of the discussion in Deuteronomy is followed in *Mishnah Sanhedrin* 10-11 (where there is no reference to Jesus), but it is reversed in Jewish polemic against Jesus both in Justin's *Dialogue* and

[12] Maier, *Jesus von Nazareth in der talmudischen Überlieferung*, has claimed that *b. Sanh.* 43a did not originally refer to Jesus: that identification was made only in post-Talmudic redaction. W. Horbury, however, has argued strongly that the sentences 'on Passover Eve they hanged Jesus' and 'Jesus the Nazarene . . . practised sorcery and deceived and led astray Israel' may be older than their immediate context: *JTS* 33 (1982) 19–61 (57).
[13] See especially E. Bammel, 'Jesus and "Setting up a Brick"', in his *Judaica: Kleine Schriften I* (Tübingen: Mohr, 1986), pp. 204–8.
[14] See especially Martyn, *History and Theology*, p. 79 n. 110.
[15] In Deuteronomy 18 rejection of magic in verses 9–14 is followed immediately by the promise of the 'prophet like Moses' and discussion of true and false prophecy in verses 15–22. However, the latter passage does not seem to be in view in either of the two rabbinic traditions quoted above.

in *b. Sanh.* 107b and 43a. Since direct dependence is very unlikely, the similar wording and the correspondence in order strongly suggest independent use of a stock polemical tradition.

If this double accusation echoed polemical passages in the New Testament gospels, the close correspondence in terminology and in order might be coincidental. But this is not the case. Jesus is not called ὁ μάγος ('magician') in the New Testament. Although the πλάνος ('deceiver') accusation occurs explicitly (as we shall see) in redactional passages in the gospels, there are no grounds for suspecting literary dependence. So the jibes against Jesus which are found both in Justin's writings and in rabbinic traditions have not been taken directly from the canonical gospels. They put us in touch with an independent negative assessment of Jesus which appears to have been widespread by the middle of the second century, and probably much earlier.

There is a further example of this double accusation in the *Acts of Thomas*, a third-century writing which almost certainly incorporates earlier traditions. In a strongly polemical passage in chapter 96, Charisius rounds on his wife Mygdonia: 'I have heard that that *magician and deceiver* (ὁ μάγος ἐκεῖνος καὶ πλάνος) teaches that a man should not live with his own wife.' He said to her again, 'be not led astray by deceitful and vain words nor by the works of magic'. The phrase 'magician and deceiver' recalls Justin's *Dialogue* 69.7 and the rabbinic allegations against Jesus. The same phrase is used in chapter 102, and again (though in separate sentences) in chapters 106–7.[16]

These passages in the *Acts of Thomas* are very different from the examples of this allegation which have been referred to above. Here there is hardly a trace of Christian–Jewish polemic or apologetic, and, with the exception of chapter 48 (where Jesus is referred to with the single accusation, 'deceiver', πλάνος), they are made against the apostle Thomas, not against Jesus. But there is no doubt at all that Thomas is an *alter ego* of Jesus.[17] The use of the phrase 'magician and deceiver' (μάγος καὶ πλάνος) can hardly be a coincidence. In the *Acts of Thomas* a 'stock' Jewish criticism of Jesus has survived

---

[16] The English translation is taken from E. Hennecke, *New Testament Apocrypha*, Vol. ii, ed. R. Wilson (London: Lutterworth, 1965). The Greek text is from *Acta Apostolorum Apocrypha*, ii/2, ed. M. Bonnet (Leipzig, 1903; repr. Hildesheim, 1959). The reference in chapter 48 to Jesus as ὁ πλάνος is noted, but without discussion, by Martyn, *History and Theology*, p. 79 n. 110, and by A. Strobel, *Die Stunde der Wahrheit* (Tübingen: Mohr, 1980), p. 90, but they do not refer to chs. 96 or 106–7. A. F. J. Klijn, *The Acts of Thomas* (Leiden: Brill, 1962), p. 271, includes a note on the 'sorcerer' accusation which is made against Thomas in numerous passages, but does not comment on the πλάνος accusation or on the combination of μάγος and πλάνος noted above.

[17] See, for example, chapters 2, 11, and 45.

in a very different setting. This confirms that it was a widespread and well-known polemical accusation.

A further example of this double accusation is found in the *Testimonium Flavianum*, the paragraph about Jesus in Josephus, *Antiquities* XVIII.3. In its present form it cannot have been written by the Jewish historian c. AD 93–4, for several phrases are undeniably Christian assessments of the significance of Jesus. The key question, debated since the sixteenth century, is whether the whole five-sentence paragraph is a later Christian interpolation, or whether a Christian scribe has added a few phrases (and perhaps altered a few words) in a 'neutral' or mildly hostile account of Jesus which was originally written by Josephus himself.[18]

Over the last decade or so, several influential voices have supported the latter view.[19] I believe that this is much the more likely solution. For our present purposes the second sentence is the most important. In the Loeb edition of the writings of Josephus, L. H. Feldman translates it as follows: 'For he [Jesus] was one who wrought surprising feats and was a teacher of such people as accept the truth gladly. He won over many Jews and many of the Greeks.' Translations along these lines are found in several books on Jesus and the gospels; they offer a neutral or even mildly *positive* assessment of Jesus. I believe that they are unduly influenced by the view that the whole pericope is a later Christian addition. Without any emendation of the text, the key Greek words can be translated more plausibly to give an ambivalent or even a mildly *hostile* assessment of Jesus, i.e. one which can be attributed to Josephus with much greater confidence.

Let us start with the final verb, ἐπηγάγετο, translated by Feldman as 'he won over', and by J. P. Meier as 'he gained a following among'. R. Eisler emended the verb to ἀπηγάγετο, and translated it as 'seduce'.[20] If this proposal is adopted, we are close to Justin's λαοπλάνος ('deceiver of the people') and the related rabbinic terms discussed above.

---

[18] See now James Carleton Paget's important detailed discussion, 'Some Observations on Josephus and Christianity', *JTS* 52 (2001) 539–624.

[19] See especially E. Bammel, 'Zum Testimonium Flavianum (Jos Ant 18, 63-64)', in O. Betz, K. Haacker, and M. Hengel, eds., *Josephus-Studien, FS O. Michel* (Göttingen: Vandenhoeck & Ruprecht, 1974), pp. 9–22, reprinted in his *Judaica*, pp. 177–89. For a perceptive assessment of the literature, see J. P. Meier, 'Jesus in Josephus: A Modest Proposal', *CBQ* 52 (1990) 76-103. Meier argues that, with the extraction of the three most obviously Christian statements, the *Testimonium* yields the original or 'core' text Josephus wrote, with no need to rewrite any words or phrases in the core. I believe that this solution is correct, but I do not accept all Meier's translations of what is admittedly difficult and ambiguous Greek. Meier does not discuss the relationship of the original text of the paragraph to the other assessments of Jesus with which I am concerned in this chapter.

[20] R. Eisler, *The Messiah Jesus and John the Baptist* (London, 1931), pp. 61–2.

But there is no need to emend the verb. The Bauer–Danker lexicon gives 'to cause a state or condition to be or occur', 'to bring on' as the meaning of ἐπάγω, and notes that it usually has the sense 'bring something bad upon someone'.[21] Hence ἐπηγάγετο in the *Testimonium* can be understood as 'brought trouble to', or even 'seduced, led astray'.[22] In other words, the verb ἐπάγομαι is only a little less close to πλανάω than is ἀπάγομαι.

The preceding two phrases in the *Testimonium* are equally important for our present concerns. The translation of the first is not problematic: the phrase refers to Jesus as 'one who did surprising (or unexpected) deeds'. Depending on one's perspective, this could refer negatively to a magician, or positively to a miracle worker.

Meier translates the next phrase as 'a teacher of people who receive the truth with pleasure', but in a note accepts (correctly) that it could imply simple-minded enthusiasm, even self-delusion.[23] A decision depends on whether Josephus paints his portrait of Jesus from a mildly hostile or from a 'neutral' perspective. I believe that the former is much more likely, though a full defence is not possible here.[24]

In short, in the *Testimonium* Jesus is said to have been a miracle worker / magician who impressed rather gullible people, and led many Jews (and many Greeks) astray. Although the terminology in the terse assessment of Jesus in the *Testimonium* differs from that used in the anti-Christian Jewish polemic quoted by Justin, and in the rabbinic traditions discussed above, there is notable agreement.

In all these summary assessments of Jesus, his actions and his words are linked closely; they are referred to in the same order, and in broadly similar ways, as those of a 'magician' and a 'false prophet' who led God's people astray. I do not think that these similarities can be mere coincidence. From these passages, which are all independent of one another, we may conclude that there was a stable form of anti-Jesus polemic which may date from the

[21] Josephus, *Life* 18 is a good example of the verb in this sense. 'Win over' is attested in Thucydides and Polybius (see Liddell, Scott, and Jones, *Lexicon*) and Chrysostom (see Lampe, *Patristic Greek Lexicon*), but the verb is rarely used with this positive sense.
[22] E. Bammel notes that *significatio seditionis* is possible for ἐπάγομαι; 'Zum Testimonium Flavianum', *Judaica*, pp. 179–81. J. P. Meier acknowledges that this is 'a possible though not necessary meaning of the verb', but does not give supporting references or reasons for rejecting this translation: 'Jesus in Josephus', p. 88 n. 33. M. Smith, *Jesus the Magician* (London: Victor Gollancz, 1978), p. 178 translates 'lead astray' and claims that this sense is implied by the Greek text.
[23] 'Jesus in Josephus', p. 84 and n. 19.
[24] See especially Bammel, 'Zum Testimonium Flavianum', *Judaica*, pp. 177–89. Bammel's article is perceptive and generally persuasive, though I am not convinced by his proposed conjectural emendation of ἀγαπήσαντες το ἀπατήσαντες.

time of Josephus towards the end of the first century. In the final section of this chapter we shall consider its earlier roots.

6.2   MAGIC, FALSE PROPHECY, DEMONIC POSSESSION

So far we have considered examples of the *double* polemical accusation that Jesus was a magician and a false prophet / deceiver. Both accusations are also found singly. Since, as we shall see in a moment, these charges are closely related to one another, use of one or other polemical term often carries with it an implication of the other.

The single accusation that Jesus was a sorcerer is found in several passages. In *I. Apol.* 30 Justin refers to the claim by his opponents that the miracles of Jesus were done by the use of magical arts. This accusation is also made repeatedly by Celsus, writing at about the same time as Justin, usually when he is citing the polemic of a Jew.[25]

The single accusation that Jesus was a false prophet / deceiver is found even more widely. In chapter 108 of his *Dialogue*, Justin claims that Jewish leaders 'appointed chosen men and sent them into all the civilized world, proclaiming that "a certain godless and lawless sect has been raised by one Jesus of Galilee, a deceiver (πλάνος)"'. A Christian redaction of *The Testament of Levi*, which may well date from the same time as Justin and Celsus, alleges that those who plotted to kill Jesus categorized him as a deceiver (πλάνος) (*T. Levi* 16.3).[26] As we shall see in the final section of this chapter, this line of polemic is also found in the gospels.

The following passages confirm the close relationship in antiquity between 'magician', 'impostor' (μάγος, γόης) and 'false prophet / deceiver' (ψευδοπροφήτης / πλάνος).

(1) At Acts 13.6-12 Luke records that Barnabas and Paul met a certain magician, a Jewish false prophet named Bar-Jesus, also known as Elymas (τινὰ ψευδοπροφήτην μάγον, verse 6). Luke carefully contrasts Paul, who has been filled with the Holy Spirit, with Elymas, who is a son of the devil and full of deceit and villainy (verses 9–10). In this passage 'magician' and 'false prophet' are almost synonymous; not quite synonymous, however, for otherwise one or other term would be redundant.

---

[25] See *Contra Celsum* 1.6, 28, 68, 71; 11.32, 48-9. On Celsus' Jew, see Bammel, 'Der Jude des Celsus', in his *Judaica*, pp. 265–83.

[26] For a fuller discussion of these passages, see G. N. Stanton, 'Aspects of Early Christian–Jewish Polemic and Apologetic' *NTS* 31 (1985) 377–82, included in *A Gospel for a New People: Studies in Matthew* (Edinburgh: T. & T. Clark, 1992), pp. 232–55. See also *The Apocryphon of John* 1.1; Origen, *Contra Celsum* 11.1; Chrysostom, *Sermons against Judaizers*, v.5.8-9.

(2) In Philo, *Spec. Leg.* 1.315, 'prophet' and 'impostor' (προφήτης and γόης) are contrasted, probably with the discussion of false prophecy in Deuteronomy 13 in mind:

If anyone cloaking himself under the name and guise of a prophet and claiming himself to be possessed by inspiration lead us on to the worship of the gods recognised in the different cities, we ought not to listen to him and be deceived by the name of a prophet. For such a one is no prophet, but an impostor (γόης), since his oracles and pronouncements are falsehoods invented by himself.

In this passage γόης is used in the general sense of 'impostor', 'charlatan'; 'sorcery' is probably, but not necessarily, in view. However, 'false prophecy' and 'sorcery' are associated explicitly in *Vit. Mos.* 1.277, where Philo contrasts the technique of the magician (μάγος) with the 'prophetic spirit' (πνεῦμα προφηπκόν): 'there fell upon him [Balaam] the truly prophetic spirit which banished utterly from his soul his art of wizardry'; Balaam then delivers a prophetic oracle.[27]

(3) In Josephus, *Ant.* 20.169-72; *Bell.* 2.261-3 (cf. Acts 21.38), we read of an unnamed Egyptian who designated himself as a prophet (προφήτης) and promised a legitimating miracle: at his command, Jerusalem's walls would fall down. Josephus, however, scornfully labels him as a 'false prophet' and 'sorcerer' (ψευδοπροφήτης and γόης).[28]

In *Ant.* 20.97 Josephus refers to a certain sorcerer (γόης) called Theudas, who persuaded a large number of people to follow him to the river Jordan; 'he stated that he was a prophet and that at his command the river would be parted and would provide him with an easy passage'. Josephus clearly believes that Theudas was a false prophet whose promised miracle was a typical ploy of a γόης.

(4) This close relationship between 'magic' and 'false prophecy' is by no means confined to Hellenistic Jewish and early Christian writers. A second century AD papyrus notes that, in the eyes of his opponent, the prophet of Apollo is a 'hungry γόης'.[29] In Philostratus, *Life* 5.12 we read that Apollonius does not prophesy on the basis of 'sorcery' (γοητεία), but on that of divine revelation. Lucian of Samosata, *Peregrinus* 13 attacks opponents as 'false prophets who are really charlatans and sorcerers'. And

---

[27] See G. Delling, art. μάγος in *TDNT* IV, p. 358. In most of the passages with which I am concerned, there is no significant difference between μάγος and γόης.

[28] See also the descriptions of individual rebels in Josephus, *Ant.* 20.97-8; 18.1-10 (and 20.102); and summary passages in *Ant.* 20.167f.; *Bell.* 2.259. For discussion, see D. Aune, 'Magic in Early Christianity', *ANRW* II.23.2, ed. W. Haase (Berlin: de Gruyter, 1980), pp. 1540–1, here p. 1528.

[29] For details, see BDAG, sub γόης.

in an intriguing magical papyrus which is difficult to date (*PGM* 5.110), we read, 'I am Moses your prophet.'[30]

These passages (which are by no means exhaustive) confirm the close relationship between 'magic' and 'false prophecy'. In ancient polemic, reference to one or other term often implies the other.[31] From the evidence set out above, it is clear that the allegations that Jesus was a magician and that he was a false prophet who deceived God's people are closely related. They are found in tandem (and, strikingly, in the same order), and also singly in a wide range of writings. The strength of the evidence from the middle of the second century is most impressive. The *Testimonium Flavianum* suggests that the polemic has deeper roots in the first century.

Before we explore the origin of what became stock polemic against Jesus and early Christianity, it will be important to show that there is a third, closely related line of polemic in writings from our period. The examples which follow show that, in ancient polemic, opponents often allege that both the 'magician' and the 'false prophet' are able to act as they do as the result of their close relationship to the devil or to demons.

(1) At the beginning of chapter 69 of Justin's *Dialogue* with Trypho, the chapter which I have taken as my starting point in this chapter, Justin notes that both the deeds of the magicians in Egypt and the words of the false prophets in the time of Elijah were the work of the devil. This linking of magic, false prophecy, and the work of the devil is significant. It is found in several passages in Justin and in a wide range of ancient polemical writings.

A further important example of the close relationship of these three concepts occurs at the opening of the *Dialogue*. When Justin recounts his conversion experience to his Jewish dialogue partner Trypho, he attaches great weight to the witness of the Old Testament prophets. The fulfilment of their prophecies compels agreement with what they have spoken:

And also on account of the miracles which they did, they were entitled to belief, for they both glorified the Maker of all things as God and Father, and proclaimed the Christ sent from Him, as His Son, a thing which the false prophets who are

---

[30] I owe this reference to Anitra Bingham Kolenkow, who quotes the passage in full: 'Relationships between Miracle and Prophecy in the Graeco-Roman World and Early Christianity', *ANRW* ii.23.2, ed. W. Haase (Berlin: de Gruyter, 1980), p. 1488.

[31] In *Jesus the Magician*, p. 79, Morton Smith goes further and states that 'false prophet' and 'magician' were often used almost as synonyms. However, in his Appendix B, 'Jesus vs. the Prophets', he downplays evidence which suggests that Jesus saw himself and was seen by others as a prophet. P. Samain has also stressed the close relationship between 'impostor' and 'magician': 'L'Accusation de magie contre le Christ dans les évangiles', *ETL* 15 (1938) 449–90. I have not been able to consult this article; see the summary in Aune, 'Magic in Early Christianity', pp. 1540–1.

filled with the seducing and unclean spirit never did nor even do, but dare to work miracles of a sort to amaze men, and give glory to the spirits of error and demons. (*Dialogue* 7.3)[32]

(2) About fifteen years after Justin wrote his *Dialogue* (c. AD 160), the pagan philosopher Celsus mounted the oldest surviving literary attack on Christianity, known to us only from Origen's reply, *Contra Celsum*. In a number of passages Celsus quotes approvingly the objections of a Jew. At a key point Celsus' Jew challenges Jesus: 'Come let us believe that these miracles were really done by you'. He then refers to the works of sorcerers who profess to do wonderful miracles and asks, 'Since these men do these wonders, ought we to think them sons of God? Or ought we to say that they are the practices of wicked men possessed by an evil daemon?'[33]

There is no doubt or even hesitation on the part of Celsus' Jew about miracles. The key question is whether the 'wonderful miracles' of Jesus were the result of demonic possession or of a special relationship to God.

(3) In his *Panarion* 48.1-13 Epiphanius quotes at length an anti-Montanist source. This includes a warning that disciples of the prophetess Maximilla (associated with Montanus) may well be shown to be false prophets inspired not by the Holy Spirit, but by demonic error, and to have duped their hearers.

(4) Within the New Testament there are several examples of the close relationship between false prophecy, magic, and demonic possession which was widely accepted in antiquity.

(a) In a Q tradition (Matt. 11.7-19 = Luke 7.24-35) John the Baptist is accepted by Jesus as a prophet, indeed more than a prophet. Yet John is written off by 'this generation' as a false prophet, with the jibe, 'he has a demon'.

(b) Luke's carefully drawn contrast in Acts 13.6-12 between Paul and Bar-Jesus / Elymas (noted above) is striking. Paul has been filled with the Holy Spirit, but Elymas is a son of the devil and full of deceit and villainy (verses 9–10). Whereas the true prophet acts and speaks as a result of being filled with the Spirit, the magician and false prophet Bar-Jesus / Elymas is in league with the devil.

---

[32] With some minor modifications I have quoted A. L. Williams's translation: *Justin Martyr: The Dialogue with Trypho* (London: SPCK, 1930). For a further example from Justin, see *I Apol.* 26 and 56: Menander, a Samaritan and a disciple of Simon Magus, 'was possessed by the demons. He deceived many at Antioch by magic arts.' (ch. 26).

[33] *Contra Celsum* 1.68. I have quoted the translation by H. Chadwick, *Contra Celsum* (Cambridge: Cambridge University Press, 1953). See also *Contra Celsum* II.49, where Celsus' Jew uses a similar line of argument: Jesus referred to miracle workers whom he clearly regarded as wicked men and sorcerers (Matt. 24.23-7 and 7.22-3), so why should one conclude that the miracles of Jesus are those of a god, while those who employ similar miracles are sorcerers?

(c) In I John 4:1 false prophets do not confess that Jesus is from God, for they are inspired by the spirit of the antichrist.

(d) In Rev. 2.20-5 the false prophetess Jezebel's outrageous actions and deeds are linked to her teaching 'the deep things of Satan'.

(e) In Rev. 13.11 we meet the second beast, who is referred to as a 'false prophet' three times (16.13; 19.20; 20.10). John Sweet astutely notes that its 'great signs' and 'fire from heaven' (13.13) parody the activity of the Pentecostal Spirit and the true prophets.[34] The false prophet's signs deceive (πλανάω) those who had received the mark of the beast (13.14 and 19.20). In Rev. 16.13-14 three foul spirits like frogs issue from the mouth of the false prophet (and the dragon and the beast); all three are demonic spirits who perform signs. In other words, the 'signs' of the false prophet are the result of demonic possession.

In the first and second centuries AD, three closely related concepts are found in polemical traditions which attack Jesus and a wide range of other individuals. General accusations of deception are often given sharper focus by reference to false prophecy. In Jewish polemic which echoes Deuteronomy 13, this is nearly always the case: the 'deceiver' is a 'false prophet' who leads God's people astray.

Although γόης is used in the more general sense of 'rogue' or 'impostor', where the individual concerned has laid claim to legitimating miracles (and this is the norm, rather than the exception), the label γόης implies sorcery, as, of course, does μάγος.[35]

The claim that an opponent was possessed by demons or in some other way was closely related to the demonic world was easy to make and difficult to refute. As we have seen, it was often used in conjunction with allegations of sorcery and false prophecy. These three labels, which are so prominent in ancient polemic, have a specific social setting. They are used to marginalize and undermine the influence of individuals whose claims and behaviour are perceived to pose a threat to the stability of the dominant social order. In short, the polemic is a form of social control.[36] With these considerations in mind, we turn now to the gospels.

---

[34] John Sweet, *Revelation*, Pelican Commentaries (London: SCM, 1979), p. 214.
[35] In the writings to which I have referred, with the exception of Matt. 2.1-16, μάγος always has a pejorative sense.
[36] For a helpful discussion of the social setting of magic, see Aune, 'Magic in Early Christianity', pp. 1510–16. Part of L. T. Johnson's article, 'The New Testament's Anti-Jewish Slander and the Conventions of Ancient Polemic', *JBL* 108 (1989) 419–41, is relevant at this point. See also Bruce J. Malina and Jerome H. Neyrey, *Calling Jesus Names: The Social Value of Labels in Matthew* (Sonoma, Calif.: Polebridge, 1988), esp. pp. 35–42.

6.3 THE EVANGELISTS

Before considering the possibility that already in his own lifetime Jesus
was labelled by his opponents as a magician and a false prophet, we must
examine evidence which stems from the hands of the evangelists. This
procedure is in line with the method of 'working backwards' from later,
clearer evidence to earlier, more problematic evidence, which I have used
in earlier sections of this chapter. I take this method to be axiomatic for all
critical inquiry into the teaching and actions of Jesus.[37]

In the central chapters of John's Gospel we are able to overhear the
disputes between the Johannine community and the local synagogue in
the evangelist's own day. In chapter 7 there are three references to division
among the people on account of Jesus (7.12, 25-7, 40). In 7.12 some who are
antagonistic to Jesus claim that he is leading the people astray. At the climax
of the chapter, the officers who were sent by the chief priests and Pharisees to
arrest Jesus returned empty-handed, only to be asked why they had failed to
bring Jesus with them (verse 45). The officers answered, 'No man ever spoke
like this man!' (verse 46). Their positive response to Jesus is immediately
undermined by the taunt, 'Are you led astray, you also?' (verse 47).

In both 7.12 and 7.47 reference to 'leading astray' (πλανάω) is to
a formal allegation, with roots in the discussion of false prophecy and
apostasy in Deuteronomy 13. In John 4.19 and 9.17 acknowledgement of
Jesus as a prophet is shown to be an acceptable, if partial, response to
Jesus. So it is no surprise to find reference to Jesus as a *false* prophet in 7.12
and 7.47 and, by implication, in 7.52. There is little doubt that the jibe is
related to the polemic Justin refers to in *Dialogue* 69.7 and 108.2, and to
the allegations found in the rabbinic traditions quoted above. In both 7.12
and 7.47 the claim that Jesus leads the people astray is used to ridicule
sympathetic responses to Jesus. This may well have been the context in
which this jibe was used in the evangelist's day. The evangelist refers to
this and to other allegations against Jesus because he is confident that his
gospel as a whole is an adequate response.

The claim that Jesus is a magician is not referred to explicitly in
the Fourth Gospel. Perhaps this is not surprising, given the absence of
references to exorcism in this gospel and the fact that exorcism is unques-
tionably the best-attested form of magic among Jews before Bar Kokhba.[38]

---

[37] I have tried to use this method consistently in my book, *The Gospels and Jesus*.
[38] So P. S. Alexander, 'Incantations and Books of Magic', in E. Schürer, *The History of the Jewish People in the Age of Jesus Christ* III.1, ed. G. Vermes, F. Millar, and M. Goodman (Edinburgh: T. & T. Clark, 1986), §32.VII, pp. 342–79, here p. 342.

Although John 8.48, which contains the allegation that Jesus has a demon, has sometimes been said to be related to the charge that he was a magician,[39] this is unlikely. We noted above that allegations of demonic possession were associated with charges both of sorcery and of false prophecy. Since the latter is so clearly in view in John 7, and since in the immediate context it is the (prophetic) words of Jesus which are being attacked by his opponents, false prophecy rather than sorcery probably lies behind John 8.48.

John 10.19-21 is all of a piece.[40] As in John 7.12 and 47, following a division among the people, a hostile allegation is used to discredit those who make a sympathetic response to Jesus. Jesus is said to have a demon and therefore to be mad. 'So why listen to him as the prophet like Moses (*to him you shall listen*, Deut. 18.15)?' Others insist that the sayings of Jesus are not those of one who has a demon. And then, unexpectedly for modern readers, they say, 'Can a demon open the eyes of the blind?' Although this final question might be taken as a rebuttal of an accusation that Jesus is a magician, once again (as in John 8.48) false prophecy is more likely to be in view. As we noted above, demon possession is often said to confirm false prophecy as well as sorcery. And there are some Jewish traditions in which the prophet like Moses is expected to perform signs.[41] This hope is reflected in John 6.14; 7.31; 9.16-17 and, we may add, 10.21.

In view of the role which accusations of demonic possession (and similar charges) play in ancient polemic, it is perhaps not surprising that both parties to the ferocious disputes which lie behind the central chapters of the Fourth Gospel use this taunt. In John 8.44 'the Jews' are said to be 'of their father the devil', while in 8.48, 52, and 10.20 Jesus is alleged to have a demon. The evangelist is confident that his readers will know where the truth lies.

In Luke 23 there are three references to Jesus leading the people astray. In verse 2 the verb is διαστρέφω, in verse 5 ἀνασείω, and in verse 14 ἀποστρέφω. These clauses are certainly not taken from Matthew or from John; in all probability they come from Luke's own redaction of Marcan traditions rather than from pre-Lucan material. From Luke's perspective, such charges were mischievous if not unexpected; they were all of a piece

---

[39] J. L. Martyn, *History and Theology in the Fourth Gospel*, 2nd edn (Nashville: Abingdon, 1979), p. 77, notes in passing that this is a possibility. See also R. Bultmann, *The Gospel of John* (E. tr. Oxford: Blackwell, 1971), p. 299 n. 4.

[40] The importance of these verses has been regularly overlooked in the standard commentaries and recent major books on the Fourth Gospel.

[41] See Martyn, *History and Theology in the Fourth Gospel*, pp. 106–12, with references both to primary sources and to secondary literature.

with the false allegations brought against Stephen and Paul.[42] These three verses in Luke 23 strongly suggest that Luke was aware of what became the standard polemical claim that Jesus was a false prophet who led the people astray. This is made more probable by the comment in the next chapter, made by two followers of Jesus on the road to Emmaus: they acknowledge Jesus as a prophet mighty in deed and word (24.19). So in the finale of his story the evangelist poses the stark alternative: was Jesus the expected messianic prophet who would redeem Israel (24.19, 21, 26) or was he a false prophet who was deceiving God's people?

Matthew's Gospel reflects the double allegation that Jesus was a magician and a false prophet who deceived God's people. The threefold accusation that the exorcisms of Jesus have been carried out 'by the prince of demons' (9.34; 10.25; 12.24, 27) is a way of alleging that Jesus is a magician. As we noted above, exorcism is the best-attested form of magic among Jews before Bar Kokhba.[43] The first two of Matthew's three references to this accusation, 9.34 and 10.25, come from the evangelist's own hand. The third, 12.24, 27, is taken from Mark 3.22 and from Q (= Luke 11.19); Matthew has redacted his traditions at this point. So the evangelist Matthew clearly has a special interest in this allegation: he is anxious to acknowledge it and to refute it.

At the climax of Matthew 12 the tables are turned on the scribes and the Pharisees: they are part of a generation which is possessed by seven evil spirits (12.43-5). They are demon possessed, not Jesus. As in the Fourth Gospel, both sides in this bitter dispute between Christians and Jews trade the same taunt.[44] The threefold accusation that the exorcisms of Jesus have been carried out by dint of collusion with Beelzebul, the prince of demons, is carefully balanced by a threefold insistence that Jesus acts 'by the Spirit of God' (ἐν πνεύματι θεοῦ; 12.18, 28, 31-2).

The final words attributed to the Jewish leaders in Matthew refer to the second half of the double allegation with which we are concerned. In 27.63-4 Jesus is referred to as 'that deceiver' (ἐκεῖνος ὁ πλάνος) and his life is summed up as 'deception' (πλάνη). Once again the Pharisees are singled out as the arch-opponents. They have been conspicuously absent from Matthew's story line since the end of chapter 23, but in 27.62-6 they join the chief priests (whose presence is demanded by the preceding narratives) in petitioning Pilate. The whole pericope is thoroughly Matthean, so here

[42] See G. N. Stanton, 'Stephen in Lucan Perspective', in E. A. Livingstone, ed., *Studia Biblica III* (Sheffield: JSOT Press, 1980), pp. 345–60.
[43] In Acts 19.11-20 Luke almost equates exorcism and magic. See also Josephus, *Ant.* VIII.45-9; Justin, *Dialogue* 85.3; Origen, *Contra Celsum* 1.68.
[44] For a fuller discussion of these passages, see Stanton, *A Gospel for a New People*, pp. 173–9.

we have further evidence of the evangelist's own special interest in a hostile assessment of Jesus.[45]

This time Matthew does not reply directly to the polemic. He takes great pains to convince the reader that the resurrection of Jesus from the tomb in which he was buried was not the 'final deception', but he simply lets the Jewish leaders' critical comments stand. Presumably he is convinced that readers of his gospel will readily agree that the claim of the Jewish leaders that Jesus is a 'deceiver' is monstrous; perhaps the closing verses of the gospel (28.18-20) were intended to prove the point.

And so to our earliest gospel, Mark. Chapter 3.19b–35 is a classic example of the evangelist's 'sandwich technique' of intercalation. The evangelist's own redactional hand is evident at several points.[46] The response of Jesus to the strong attack launched by the scribes from Jerusalem (verses 22–30) is inserted into the response of Jesus to the only marginally less hostile comments of his family (verses 19b–21 and 31–5). The criticisms are strikingly similar. The family of Jesus accepts the validity of the crowd's conviction that Jesus was mad – and in antiquity madness was generally ascribed to possession by an evil spirit. The scribes from Jerusalem bring a double charge: Jesus is possessed by Beelzebul (verse 22a); by the prince of demons he casts out demons (verse 22b).

As in the other examples of Mark's distinctive sandwich technique, the intercalated tradition and the framework into which it is inserted interpret and reinforce one another. In this case the evangelist is acutely aware of the jibe that Jesus is a demon-possessed magician, and responds to it vigorously by means of the sayings of Jesus in verses 23b–29 and in verses 33–5. The fact that what I take to be the same jibe is repeated four times in this passage is striking (verse 21 family / crowd; verse 22 *bis* the scribes; verse 30 the evangelist's redactional repetition of the scribes' attack).

The allegation that Jesus was a magician and that he was a false prophet was known at the time the evangelists wrote. Matthew knew the double form of the accusation. John (certainly) and Luke (very probably) were aware that Jewish opponents of Christian claims alleged that Jesus was a false prophet who led God's people astray. Mark is stung by the strength of the claim that Jesus' actions, and in particular his exorcisms, were the result of demon-possession.

---

[45] For details of Matthean vocabulary and style in this pericope, see R. H. Gundry, *Matthew: A Commentary on his Literary and Theological Art* (Grand Rapids: Eerdmans, 1982), pp. 540–1.

[46] See the fine discussion in S. C. Barton, *Discipleship and Family Ties in Mark and Matthew* (Cambridge: Cambridge University Press, 1994), pp. 68–86.

The passages from the gospels discussed in this section all bear the stamp of the individual evangelists. They confirm that the evangelists were all aware of polemical allegations against Jesus and sought to counter them. The four evangelists all wrote in the 70s and 80s, at a time of mutual incomprehension, keen rivalry, and sour disputes between Christians and Jews. So it is no surprise to find in all four gospels charges and counter-charges concerning the significance of the actions and teaching of Jesus.

<h2 style="text-align:center">6.4 JESUS</h2>

We have now traced anti-Jesus polemic back from the latter half of the second century AD to the time when the four gospels were written, in the 70s and 80s of the first century. Does this polemic have earlier roots in the lifetime of Jesus? I shall argue that there are sound reasons for concluding that even in his own lifetime Jesus was labelled 'a magician' by his opponents, and very probably 'a false prophet' who led God's people astray.

First of all we shall return to the double criticism of the scribes from Jerusalem in Mark 3.22: 'He has Beelzebul, and by the ruler of demons he casts out demons.' The opponents of Jesus represent the dominant social order which he is threatening.[47] Although the reference to Jerusalem may be a redactional note from Mark himself, the scribes were probably identified as opponents of Jesus in the pre-Marcan tradition.

The same jibe is recorded independently in a Q tradition: 'It is only by Beelzebul, the ruler of the demons, that this fellow casts out the demons.'[48] In Matthew's version (12.24) of the Q tradition it is said to stem from the Pharisees, and, in Luke's (11.15), from some of the crowd. The varied attribution of the criticism is striking. This is a stock taunt thought to have been thrown at Jesus by more than one group of opponents.

The content of the jibe is stable: in both Mark and in Q the exorcisms of Jesus are said to be carried out as a result of Jesus' association with Beelzebul, the prince of demons. We noted above that exorcism was the best-attested form of magic among Jews in the first century and that magicians were regularly said to be demon-possessed. Hence there is little doubt that both

---

[47] A. F. Segal's comments are instructive: *Rebecca's Children: Judaism and Christianity in the Roman World* (Cambridge: Harvard University Press, 1986), pp. 144–5: 'The logic from the scribes' perspective is that if Jesus were from God, he could not oppose the ideas of the legitimate authorities of Judea. Since he does oppose them, his power must have other sources.'

[48] In most recent reconstructions of Q, Matt. 12.24 = Luke 11.15 is accepted as a Q tradition. See especially David Catchpole, *The Quest for Q* (Edinburgh: T. & T. Clark, 1993), pp. 48–50; also J. Kloppenborg, *Q Parallels: Synopsis, Critical Notes & Concordance* (Sonoma, Calif.: Polebridge, 1988), pp. 90–2.

the Marcan and the Q traditions are tantamount to a charge that Jesus was a magician.

In his healing miracles and exorcisms Jesus undoubtedly used techniques which would have been perceived by contemporaries to be magical.[49] Since few scholars have any reservations about the authenticity of these two traditions,[50] it is highly likely that Jesus was written off by his opponents as a magician, and thus as a social deviant.

Not surprisingly, already within both the Q tradition and the form of the tradition known to Mark (as well as in the completed gospels) there are responses to this charge. Followers of Jesus would not have transmitted such a hostile assessment of him unless a firm refutation of the allegation were juxtaposed.

The Q pericope contrasts sharply two ways of assessing the exorcising activity of Jesus: is Jesus in league with the prince of demons, or are his actions the result of his relationship to God? Jesus himself claims that his exorcisms were carried out 'by the finger of God', as signs of the breaking in of God's kingly rule (Matt. 12.28 = Luke 11.20).

In later polemic the same issue arises, but without specific reference to this passage. At *I Apol.* 30 Justin notes that critics claim that the miracles of Jesus were done by magic arts, rather than as a result of Jesus' relationship to God as his Son. Celsus' Jew argues similarly: on account of his miraculous powers, Jesus gave himself the title God, but in fact they were the result of magical powers gained in Egypt (*Contra Celsum* 1.28). Celsus' Jew closes his remarks addressed to Jesus with the claim that the miracles were the actions of one 'hated by God and of a wicked sorcerer' (*Contra Celsum* 1.71); in this way the claim of Christians that Jesus stands in a special relationship to God is undermined.

As we have noted above, Mark himself has shaped considerably the traditions he links together in 3.19b–35. In a redactional comment in verse 30 he points out that the saying of Jesus concerning blasphemy against the Holy Spirit (3.28-9) applies to those who claimed that Jesus was possessed by Beelzebul, and that he casts out demons by the prince of demons (3.22). R. A. Guelich has perceptively summed up the key point Mark is making: 'To attribute the work of the Spirit through Jesus to demonic forces is the ultimate calumny for which there is no forgiveness.'[51] Once again, as in the

---

[49] See Aune, 'Magic in Early Christianity', pp. 1523–9; Smith, *Jesus the Magician*, (above, n. 22) pp. 94–139.

[50] These traditions critical of Jesus would have been an embarrassment to his followers, and so are most unlikely to have been invented. For discussion of the criterion of embarrassment, see Stanton, *The Gospels and Jesus*, pp. 174–7.

[51] R. A. Guelich, *Mark*, Word Biblical Commentary (Dallas: Word, 1989), p. 180.

Q Beelzebul traditions, there are two opposing assessments of the actions of Jesus: are they to be ascribed to demonic possession or to divine agency?

It is more difficult to establish that in his own lifetime Jesus was considered by some to be a false prophet who led Israel astray. In the gospels there is no specific allegation along these lines. However, cumulative evidence makes this a strong probability.

(1) As we have seen above, Matthew and John, and probably Luke, were aware of this polemical charge. There is no reason to suppose that it first arose at the time they wrote, for tension between Jews who accepted Christian claims about Jesus and those who rejected them did not arise overnight in the 80s.

(2) Given that Jesus was alleged by some to be a magician, and given the close links between the 'magician' and 'false prophet' allegations to which I drew attention above, it is highly likely that Jesus was said by some to be a false prophet.

(3) John the Baptist was said to have a demon (Q: Matt. 11.18 = Luke 7.33). Since neither the synoptic evangelists nor Josephus (*Antiquities* 18.116-19) attribute miracle-working powers to John,[52] the polemical jibe recorded in Q labels him as a demon-possessed false prophet. Since John and Jesus were associated closely, Jesus was almost certainly also marginalized by some with the same accusation.

(4) Although the evangelists do not emphasize that Jesus was a prophet, in two sayings, Mark 6.4 and Luke 13.33, Jesus refers to himself as a prophet. A number of other sayings and several of his actions confirm that he saw himself as a prophet.[53] Thus it would be surprising if some opponents did not dub him a false prophet, perhaps even with Deuteronomy 13 in mind.[54]

I have argued that the double allegation found in Justin's *Dialogue* 69.7 and in the rabbinic traditions quoted above has deep roots. In his own lifetime Jesus was said by some to be a demon-possessed magician. It is probable, but not certain, that he was also said to be a demon-possessed false prophet.

Several corollaries follow. It is generally accepted that in the first and second centuries followers of Jesus and Jews who did not accept their claims

---

[52] Cf. John 10.41. Mark 6.14 is an apparent exception, but on any view this is a puzzling verse.

[53] I have summarized and discussed the evidence briefly in *The Gospels and Jesus*, pp. 194–9. See especially D. E. Aune, *Prophecy in Early Christianity and the Ancient Mediterranean World* (Grand Rapids: Eerdmans, 1983), pp. 153–89.

[54] Strobel, *Die Stunde der Wahrheit* (above, n. 16), goes much further and argues that this accusation was in fact central in the Sanhedrin trial.

were at odds about Christology and the law. It is less frequently appreciated that both the actions and the teaching of Jesus were also a source of tension and dispute: they were assessed very differently by his later followers and opponents.

The allegations of the contemporary opponents of Jesus confirm that he was seen by many to be a disruptive threat to social and religious order. His claims to act and speak on the basis of a special relationship to God were rightly perceived to be radical. For some who heard the teaching and saw the actions of Jesus, those claims were so radical and so unacceptable that they had to be undermined by an alternative explanation of their source.

There is no reason to doubt that both the actions and the teaching of Jesus brought him into conflict from time to time with the religious authorities of the day. In that social setting, allegations of false prophecy and sorcery thrive. As we noted above, they are used to marginalize and undermine the influence of individuals whose claims and behaviour are perceived to pose a threat to the stability of the dominant social order.

It is often urged that reconstructions of the life and teaching of Jesus must account for his crucifixion on a Roman cross. If, for example, Jesus merely echoed the conventional teaching and piety of his day, then it is difficult to account for his downfall. In my judgement, the historian must also account for the 'aftermath' of Jesus of Nazareth, i.e. for the stubborn fact that, in the very conservative religious and social climate of the post-Easter decades, followers of Jesus made profound claims about him and took radical steps in his name. The claim advanced in this chapter that Jesus was perceived in his own lifetime to be a demon-possessed magician / sorcerer and a false prophet who deceived God's people coheres well both with his downfall and with the 'aftermath'. Both the teaching and the actions of Jesus drew criticism. Were his exorcisms and healing miracles signs that God's kingly rule was breaking into history, or were they the result of his collusion with the prince of demons? Was Jesus a prophet sent by God, or was he a false prophet who was deceiving Israel? The polemical traditions confirm that, as Jesus moved around Galilean villages, his relationship to God was a central issue.[55]

---

[55] For fuller discussion of the points made in the final five paragraphs, see Stanton, *The Gospels and Jesus*, pp. 292–9.

CHAPTER 7

Early objections to the resurrection of Jesus

Recent studies of early Christian traditions about the resurrection of Jesus have generally overlooked the objections which were raised by opponents of Christianity in the first and second centuries. This is somewhat surprising. Historians know how important it is to consider evidence or arguments which are an embarrassment to the eventual 'winners'. Astute theologians always listen carefully to the voices of 'outsiders'.[1]

There are three reasons for taking this rather off-beat approach. (1) Criticisms of early Christian claims concerning the resurrection of Jesus give us some limited insights into the variety of ancient attitudes to life after death. (2) They help us to appreciate more keenly the ways Christian proclamation of the resurrection was understood or misunderstood by both Jews and pagans. (3) By paying attention to early criticisms we may be able to trace more readily the points at which early Christian traditions about the resurrection have been shaped by apologetic concerns.

The potential value of this approach will be clear. So why have the voices of the critics not been heard? They have been ignored mainly because it is undeniably difficult to uncover the critics' views. We have much more extensive evidence for early polemical comments on the actions and teaching of Jesus.[2] However, by casting the net widely I believe that it is possible to make a number of observations which are relevant to inquiries into the setting, development, and reception of early resurrection traditions, observations which stimulate further theological reflection today.

Since it is often helpful in studies of earliest Christianity to work back from later, clearer evidence to more problematic earlier evidence, I shall start with objections to the resurrection of Jesus made in the second half of

---

[1] This chapter is a revised version of my contribution to a *Festschrift* edited by Stephen Barton and Graham Stanton, *Resurrection* (London: SPCK, 1994), pp. 79–94, in honour of my former colleague at King's College London, Leslie Houlden, who always goes out of his way to listen to those whose viewpoints differ from his own.
[2] See Chapter 6 above.

the second century and work back, where appropriate, to New Testament evidence. I am starting outside the canon for the further reason that it is all too easy to use the New Testament texts as a mirror to find opponents and rivals under every canonical bed. Evidence from outside the canon may help us to avoid some of the pitfalls of mirror-reading.[3]

7.1 THE PAGAN CELSUS AND A JEW

The first pagan comments on earliest Christianity come from the early decades of the second century. Although Suetonius, Tacitus, Pliny, Epictetus, Hadrian (in his imperial rescript), and Fronto provide invaluable insights into the ways Christians were perceived by pagans, they do not help our quest for objections to the resurrection of Jesus. They tell us that the odd behaviour of Christians raised many eyebrows, but they say little or nothing about what Christians believed or taught.

In the second half of the second century, however, some pagan writers do comment on Christian beliefs.[4] Lucian of Samosata noted that Christians associated with Peregrinus (a Christian convert who died about AD 165) 'were poor souls who convinced themselves that they would all be immortal and live forever, on account of which they think lightly of death'. Galen of Pergamum also commented on the contempt Christians showed for death. Lucian and Galen both remind us that belief in life after death (whether resurrection or immortality) was by no means universal in the pagan world of their day and that Christians were known for their distinctive hopes for the future. However, neither writer refers explicitly to the resurrection of Jesus.

For the first extended pagan objections to the resurrection of Jesus we must turn to Celsus' thorough-going attack on Christianity, which was was written between 177 and 180. Some seventy years later, Origen recognized that Celsus' trenchant voice could be neither silenced nor ignored. So he took the trouble to write a lengthy reply. Fortunately, Origen's reply includes quotations from as much as 70 per cent of Celsus' now lost book.

Celsus' wide-ranging attack includes comments on the resurrection of Jesus, and on Christian beliefs in life after death. In the first sections of his book the Platonist philosopher repeatedly quotes the views of a Jew. In

---

[3] See John Barclay, 'Mirror-Reading a Polemical Letter: Galatians as a Test Case', *JSNT* 31 (1987) 73–93.

[4] For the texts and comments, see S. Benko, 'Pagan Criticism of Christianity during the First Two Centuries', *ANRW* II.23.2, ed. W. Haase (Berlin: de Gruyter, 1980), pp. 1055–1118; R. L. Wilken, *The Christians as the Romans Saw them* (New Haven and London: Yale University Press, 1984); and Molly Whittaker, *Jews and Christians: Graeco-Roman Views* (Cambridge: Cambridge University Press, 1984).

response, Origen insists that Celsus' Jew is an 'imaginary character . . . who addresses childish remarks to Jesus', and claims that the views attributed to him are not consistent with those of a Jew (*Contra Celsum* 1.28).[5]

However, there are good grounds for concluding that on this issue even the learned Origen has nodded. Some of the critical comments attributed to Celsus' Jew concerning the birth, actions, and teaching of Jesus are also found in polemical Jewish traditions and, independently, in other early Christian writings.[6] Celsus has clearly drawn on earlier Jewish traditions: it is impossible to say just how early they are, but their value as evidence for the views of Jewish opponents of Jesus and his followers can hardly be overestimated.

In some passages it is not always possible to decide whether Celsus is setting out his own objections to Christianity, or those of the Jewish opponent whom he quotes. However, close attention to the text discloses that Celsus and the Jew have quite different views on life after death and also on the resurrection of Jesus. As in Luke–Acts – I shall discuss the evidence below – it is possible to distinguish between pagan and Jewish objections.

Celsus claims that a dead man cannot be immortal (II.16) and that Christians worship a corpse (VII.68): for the pagan philosopher the very notion of resurrection is absurd (V.14; VI.29), though he is willing to discuss the possibility of some form of immortality (V.14; cf. IV.56). Celsus insists that 'the fact that hope of the resurrection of the dead is not shared by some Jews [presumably Sadducees] and some Christians [presumably gnostics] shows its utter repulsiveness, and that it is both revolting and impossible' (V.14). However, he does not relate this observation to the resurrection of Jesus. Hence it it not surprising to find that he does not discuss the resurrection of Jesus at length: he leaves extended criticism to the Jew whom he quotes.[7] In contrast to Celsus himself, however, the Jew insists that 'Jews hope to be resurrected in the body and to have everlasting life' (II.77), a view which Origen accepts and expounds at some length (V.14-26).

At a later point in his attack on Christianity, long after he has stopped quoting a Jew, Celsus returns to the evidence for the resurrection of Jesus and mentions in passing the presence of *women* at the empty tomb, not one hysterical woman, as in the objection of the Jew (cf. II.55 and V.52). Rather

---

[5] Quotations are from Henry Chadwick, *Origen: Contra Celsum* (Cambridge: Cambridge University Press, 1953).

[6] See G. N. Stanton, *A Gospel for a New People: Studies in Matthew* (Edinburgh: T. & T. Clark, 1992), pp. 171–2, 185–9.

[7] See E. Bammel, 'Der Jude des Celsus', in his collected essays, *Judaica: Kleine Schriften I* (Tübingen: Mohr, 1986), pp. 265–83. Bammel concludes that, since the comments of Celsus' Jew come from the time of the apostolic fathers and the later writers of the NT, they are of unsurpassed value.

surprisingly, Celsus himself makes nothing of the fact that Christian claims rest on the evidence of women. Instead he points out scornfully that the alleged Son of God 'was not able to open the tomb, but needed someone else to move the stone' (v.52). This is an objection which Celsus' Jew is unlikely to have made; in a Jewish context, 'Son of God' did not necessarily denote divinity.

In short, the pagan Celsus and his Jewish ally raise rather different objections to the resurrection of Jesus. Celsus uses the Jew's specific objections to supplement his own scornful comments on the whole notion of post-mortem resurrection.

Pagan parallels to the resurrection of Jesus are discussed in a particularly interesting passage in II.55-8. At this point Celsus' Jew is addressing Jews who believe in Jesus. He claims that six Greek legends provide parallels to the resurrection of Jesus. 'Do you think that the stories of these others really are the legends which they appear to be, and yet that the ending of your tragedy is to be regarded as noble and convincing?' The implication is that Christian Jews believe that the resurrection of Jesus cannot be put on a par with other stories about individuals brought back to life. But nothing is made of this.

Origen's own defence is striking: whereas the heroes in the Greek legends disappeared secretly and then returned to the men they had left, 'Jesus was crucified before all the Jews and his body put to death in the sight of their people.' However, he then goes on to claim that there are important Biblical parallels: the raising to life of the young boys by Elijah (I Kgs 17.21-2) and Elisha (II Kgs 4.34-5). The resurrection of Jesus, he insists, was more remarkable because of the greater benefits it brought to mankind.

No doubt this latter comment is valid, but Origen misses a far more important point: the young boys to whom he refers, along with Jairus' daughter, the widow's son at Nain, and Lazarus, were restored to this life. The evangelists, for all their differences in emphasis, did not claim that the body of Jesus was resuscitated only to die again at a later point. Perhaps in their refusal to appeal to parallels to the resurrection of Jesus, the Christian Jews addressed by Celsus' Jew saw this more clearly than either Origen or Celsus. One hopes so.

Celsus' Jew advances vigorously the theory that the followers of Jesus 'saw' their recently crucified leader in a dream or hallucination. Origen's response is not very persuasive: 'Celsus's idea of a vision in the daytime is not convincing when the people were in no way mentally disturbed and were not suffering from delirium or melancholy. Because Celsus foresaw this objection he said that the woman was hysterical; but there is no evidence of this in the scriptural account' (II.60).

This discussion reminds us of the ultimate futility of trying to seek proof one way or the other. 'Vision' or 'hallucination', how can one decide? Surely the matter can be settled only on the basis of wider considerations, which are theological rather than historical or psychological.

Three of Celsus' objections elicit a similar theological response from Origen. Celsus claims that, if Jesus really wanted to show forth divine power, he ought to have appeared to those who maltreated him, to the man who condemned him, and 'to everyone everywhere' (II.63, 67). In reply to this threefold challenge, Origen insists that, when Jesus was sent into the world, he did not merely make himself known; he also concealed himself (II.67). Similarly (with reference to the baptism as well as the resurrection appearances), 'the divine voice is such that it is heard only by those whom the speaker wishes to hear it' (II.72). Perhaps the sharpest objection raised by Celsus' Jew is his jibe, 'Where is the risen Jesus, that we may see and believe?' In response, Origen turns the tables on his Jewish opponent and asks for proof that Israel is God's 'portion' (II.77). Origen's riposte is terse and to the point: God's self-disclosure to Israel was not openly accessible to all and sundry on a permanent basis, and its reality cannot be proven. So too with the appearances of the risen Jesus.

A theological thread runs through these responses to Celsus that is as important for current theological reflection as it was in the middle of the third century. Origen sees clearly that, although some of Celsus' objections were based on misunderstandings and others were mischievous, he himself could not offer clear-cut historical proof of the resurrection of Jesus (see especially II.77): God is not at the beck and call of men and women.

Origen knows full well that proof of the historicity of an incident in the gospels is difficult and in some cases impossible (I.42). He knows that he cannot sidestep allegations that the text of the gospels has been tampered with (II.27) and that the resurrection narratives contain discrepancies (V.55-6). He repudiates 'mere irrational faith', and insists that readers of the gospels need an open mind and considerable study. 'If I may say so', he writes, 'readers need to enter into the mind of the writers to find out with what spiritual meaning each event was recorded.' Is this the way faith and reason should be held together in discussion of the resurrection narratives? Is there still a place for discerning 'spiritual meaning' by Origen's own method of allegorical interpretation? If so, what criteria will guard against 'irrational faith'?

Nearly all the objections to the resurrection of Jesus which have been raised since the Enlightenment were anticipated by the pagan Celsus, or by the Jew whom he quotes. There is only one notable exception, the theory that the disciples stole the body of Jesus from the tomb.[8] Most of the objections to the resurrection of Jesus which are pressed by Celsus' Jew are likely to have been made long before Celsus wrote, between AD 166 and 170. Their importance for serious discussion of New Testament resurrection traditions cannot be overestimated. Some of Origen's replies carry little or no persuasive power today, but some are (or should be) still on the agenda of current theological discussion.

7.2   TRYPHO THE JEW

Just over a decade before Celsus launched his attack on Christianity, Justin Martyr wrote his *Dialogue* with the Jew Trypho. Four passages are of particular interest.

(1) Justin and Trypho, just like Origen and Celsus (and, as we shall see shortly, Luke's Paul and his Jewish opponents), can agree that there will be a resurrection of the righteous (45.2-3).

(2) Justin, just like Celsus, knows that there are some so-called Christians (presumably gnostics) who say that there is no resurrection of the dead. He is confident that Trypho will agree that Sadducees (and some other Jewish groups) who deny the resurrection should not be considered true Jews (80.3-4). We shall see below that Luke also sees hope for resurrection from the dead as a line of continuity between Judaism and Christianity.

(3) In one passage a Christian credal summary is put into the mouth of Trypho. 'You say many blasphemous things', says Trypho, 'thinking to persuade us that this man who was crucified has been with Moses and Aaron, and has spoken to them in a pillar of a cloud, that he then became man and was crucified, and has ascended into heaven, and comes again on earth, and is to be worshipped' (*Dialogue* 38.1). Just as in several New Testament passages (e.g. Phil. 2.5-11; I Tim. 3.16; Eph. 4.7-10; Rom. 10.5-8), this 'creed' moves directly from the crucifixion to the exaltation of Jesus without referring to resurrection.

(4) I noted above that the only major objection to the resurrection of Jesus which is not mentioned by Celsus is the claim that the disciples stole

---

[8] In 1.51 Origen mentions, but only in passing and not in response to an objection raised by Celsus, Matthew's attempt to rule out the claim that the disciples stole the body of Jesus (28.13-14). Origen even claims that the soldiers who guarded the tomb and were later bribed were *eyewitnesses* of the resurrection, as in the Gospel of Peter 9–10!

the body of Jesus. By a curious irony, this is the only Jewish criticism of Christian claims about the resurrection which Justin does mention. Justin claims that on hearing that Christ had risen from the dead, Jewish leaders

appointed chosen men and sent them into all the civilized world, proclaiming that 'a certain godless and lawless sect has been raised by one Jesus of Galilee, a deceiver, whom we crucified, but his disciples stole him by night from the tomb, where he had been laid after being unnailed from the cross, and they deceive men, saying that he is risen from the dead and has ascended into heaven'. (*Dialogue* 108)[9]

Some of the phraseology of this alleged anti-Christian Jewish propaganda comes from Justin himself, some of it possibly from Matt. 28.13, 15. However, there are good reasons for supposing that Justin may here be drawing on an earlier source, for these Jewish allegations and not simply on New Testament passages. (1) At this point at least, Justin is not setting up Trypho as a straw man who lists Jewish objections in order to allow Justin to refute them one by one, for Justin does not respond to them anywhere in the *Dialogue*. (2) The reference to Christianity as a 'sect' is striking and unique in Justin: he uses the term elsewhere to refer to factions *within* Judaism (62.3; 80.4) and *within* Christianity (35.3; 51.2), but not to Christianity *per se*. (3) The reference to Christianity as a godless and lawless sect raised by Jesus does not come from the gospels, nor does the reference to the *disciples* as deceivers.

While it is impossible to confirm that a Jewish counter-mission of this kind took place, there is nothing inherently improbable in the reference to Jewish messengers being sent 'into all the civilized world'.[10] Justin is probably drawing on (as well as filling out himself) early Jewish allegations. Certainly *Dialogue* 108 sets out what Justin *felt* to be the heart of Jewish arguments against the resurrection of Jesus. This chapter confirms that Christians were aware of, and sensitive to, Jewish claims that the disciples stole the body of Jesus from the tomb. But, unlike the evangelist Matthew, Justin does not bother to refute this obvious objection to Christian claims. Perhaps he felt that it was so absurd that refutation was unnecessary.

In some versions of the Jewish polemical traditions known as the *Toledoth Jeshu*, there is an interesting variant on the theory that the body of Jesus

[9] Justin refers to this 'counter-mission' near the opening of the *Dialogue* (ch. 17), but at that point he gives only a summary of its contents, without mentioning the objection to the resurrection; there is an even briefer reference in ch. 117.
[10] Following formal declaration in Jerusalem of observation of the new moon, messengers were sent to the diaspora. My former research student Dr Eileen Poh has drawn my attention to references to letters on other matters which were sent to the diaspora: Jer. 29. 4-23; 2 Baruch 78-87; 2 Macc. 1.1-10a; 10b–2.18; Esther 9.20-32.

was stolen from the tomb. The body of Jesus is stolen, not by his disciples as in Matthew and in Justin, but by his opponents: they drag the body through the streets of Tiberias.[11] These traditions almost certainly stem from a time after the conversion of the Emperor Constantine: by then Jews and Christians were no longer rivals, and Jews were all too aware of the heavy hand of Christian oppression. This form of anti-Christian polemic falsifies Christian claims at a stroke; there is no need for the elaborate ruses Matthew alleges were adopted by 'the Pharisees' and by 'the chief priests and elders' (27.62-6; 28.11-15).

The fact that the passage quoted above from *Dialogue* 108 is the only reference to Jewish objections to the resurrection of Jesus and that there is no debate between Justin and Trypho on this topic is striking. Why do Justin and Trypho share convictions about a general resurrection of the dead (*Dialogue* 45.2-3), but fail to discuss the resurrection of Jesus? For them both, Christology and the law are more important issues. Their central dispute concerning Jesus of Nazareth is not his resurrection, but whether or not Jesus fulfils Scripture; as we shall see in a moment, this was also Luke's view.

As in other Jewish polemic from this period, the claim that Jesus was a magician and a deceiver who led Israel astray is much more prominent than objections to the resurrection of Jesus. Perhaps the latter was not an easy issue to debate. After all, many Jews accepted that one day God would raise the (righteous) dead: how could one decide whether or not this general resurrection had been anticipated in the case of Jesus? As in Justin's *Dialogue*, debate could be neatly sidestepped by the claim that the disciples had stolen the body of Jesus.

7.3 GENTILE AND JEWISH RESPONSES IN ACTS

I turn now from Justin to an earlier Christian apologist. Luke is aware of rather different negative reactions to Christian proclamation of the resurrection of Jesus. I shall start with his presentation of Gentile objections to the resurrection of Jesus.

Paul ends his speech to the 'Athenians' in the Council of the Areopagus with the claim that God has raised from the dead the man whom he has designated to judge the world (Acts 17.31). Paul's listeners do not comment on his proclamation of God the Creator who does not live in shrines made

---

[11] See E. Bammel, 'The *Titulus*', in Ernst Bammel and C. F. D. Moule, *Jesus and the Politics of his Day* (Cambridge: Cambridge University Press, 1984), pp. 361–2.

by human hands, but some of them scoff at his reference to resurrection from the dead (17.32). From Luke's point of view, Gentiles find the notion of resurrection quite incomprehensible.

Here Luke is echoing widely held views. The prevailing Greek attitude towards resurrection is summed up by Aeschylus, *Eumenides* 647-8. On the occasion of the founding of the court of the Areopagus in Athens, the god Apollo observes, 'Once a person is slain and the dust has drunk up his blood, there is no resurrection (ἀνάστασις)'.

There may be a further reference in Acts 17.18 to a negative response in Athens to Paul's proclamation of the resurrection, but I am not as confident about this as most translators and commentators. Luke opens his account of Paul's visit to Athens by noting that he argued in the marketplace every day with passers-by, some of whom were Epicurean and Stoic philosophers. As is often the case in Acts, there is a division of opinion. Some said, 'What does this babbler want to say?' Others said, 'He seems to be a proclaimer of foreign divinities.' In most editions of the Greek text and in modern translations Luke then explains in an aside to the reader that these critical comments were responses to Paul's proclamation of 'the good news about Jesus and the resurrection' (17.18).

Many scholars now accept that in this lengthy verse Luke claims that the Athenians totally misunderstood Paul's proclamation of Jesus and the resurrection (*anastasis*) as a reference to two divinities, 'Jesus and Anastasis'. This ingenious explanation has an impressive pedigree, which goes back to Chrysostom; it is supported by the NEB's translation in 17.18, 'Jesus and Resurrection'.[12] But the explanation is unlikely, for it implies in an un-Lucan way either that Paul was a completely ineffective communicator, or that his listeners were stupid. In addition, in Codex Bezae (supported by the old Latin codex Gigas) there is important, though often overlooked, evidence for omission of the whole aside at the end of verse 18: a very early copyist may have noted Luke's failure to indicate the content of Paul's initial proclamation to the Athenians, and inserted the aside on the assumption (based on 17.32) that Paul must have preached about 'Jesus and the resurrection' and been totally misunderstood.[13]

---

[12] REB is a little less confident; 'Jesus and *the* Resurrection'. NRSV and NIV have 'Jesus and the resurrection'.

[13] Since Codex Bezae (and the so-called western text) includes a large number of additional words and phrases in Acts (often as explanatory comments), in some of the small number of places where this codex offers a shorter reading it may well retain the original wording. It is less easy to account for later omission of the phrase than for a later addition. W. A. Strange, *The Problem of the Text of Acts* (Cambridge: Cambridge University Press, 1992), pp. 188–9, suggests that addition of the explanatory clause at the end of Acts 17.18 may have been the clarification of a copyist who was concerned that

In the second passage in Acts which refers to Gentile reaction to Christian proclamation of the resurrection, the Roman governor Festus informs Agrippa that he had been surprised by the accusations the chief priests and elders of the Jews had brought against Paul. 'They merely had certain points of disagreement with him about their religion, and about someone called Jesus, a dead man whom Paul alleged to be alive' (Acts 25.19, REB). Festus quickly concedes that he is out of his depth in such discussions.

Luke then draws a careful contrast between Gentile and Jewish responses to proclamation of the resurrection. When Paul defends himself before Agrippa, he assumes that the Jewish king will not find it incredible that God should raise the dead (26.8). He then claims that in his preaching he asserts nothing beyond what was foretold by the prophets and by Moses: 'that the Messiah would suffer and that, as the first to rise from the dead, he would proclaim light both to the Jewish people and to the Gentiles' (26.22-3). At mention of the resurrection of the Messiah, it is not the Jewish king Agrippa but the Roman governor Festus who intervenes: 'Paul, you are raving; too much study is driving you mad.' Paul does not attempt to enlighten Festus on the subject of the Messiahship of Jesus and the resurrection. Instead, he draws Agrippa into the discussion and repeats his claim that, since Agrippa is a Jew, he is well versed in these matters (26.24-6).

This passage is the final reference to the resurrection in Acts. In it Luke sets out clearly his belief that, while Gentiles are completely baffled by Christian proclamation of the resurrection of Jesus, at least some Jews responded (or should have responded) much more sympathetically.

This latter point is developed by Luke in a rather subtle way which is well worth exploring, for it raises important theological issues. Luke first isolates Sadducean denial of the resurrection of the dead as a minority Jewish opinion (Acts 4.1-4; 5.17; 23.6). Luke believes that other Jews, including the Pharisees, do not have a fundamental objection to Christian claims concerning the resurrection of the dead. Hence, so the argument runs, they ought not to dismiss Christian claims concerning the resurrection of Jesus.

In the account of the trial of Paul by the Sanhedrin (Acts 23.1-10), Paul emphasizes that he is himself a Pharisee, a son of Pharisees, and then singles out 'the hope and resurrection of the dead' as the central issue at stake. The Sanhedrin is divided. Luke reminds the reader that the Sadducees say that there is no resurrection and then notes that 'some scribes of the

the reference to Paul preaching strange δαιμονία should not become the growth point for Gnostic speculation.

Pharisees' defend Paul: 'we find nothing wrong with this man' (23.9). They even concede the possibility that the appearance of Christ to Paul outside Damascus was a reality: a spirit or angel has spoken to him.[14]

A similar point is made in Paul's defence before Agrippa (26.2-23). Luke's Paul refers once again to his membership of the 'sect' of the Pharisees. An important switch from the singular to the plural in verse 8 (missed by many translators) indicates that Paul is addressing not merely Agrippa, but Jews generally: they should not think it incredible that God raises the dead! From the context it is clear that the resurrection of Jesus is in view. The line of argument is bold, to say the least. Luke's Paul is claiming that, on the basis of Jewish (especially Pharisaic) beliefs about the resurrection from the dead, the resurrection of Jesus is not at all problematic. In Luke's view, 'resurrection' is one of the lines of continuity between Judaism and Christianity.[15]

This reading is consistent with the earlier chapters of Acts. In numerous passages Luke records the objections Jews raised to Stephen's and Paul's preaching. Although the resurrection of Jesus is prominent in the preceding 'sermons' (or, better, 'speeches'), with the exception of Sadducees and their allies, objections are not raised by Jewish opponents.

However, in two passages Luke makes a key theological point, which he could hardly have expected non-Christian Jews to accept: the resurrection of Jesus is the first example of the resurrection of the dead. In rather terse Greek at Acts 4.2, Luke insists that the resurrection had come to pass in the person of Jesus.[16] He repeats the point in his final reference to the resurrection: Paul proclaims to Agrippa 'that the Messiah must suffer, and that, by being the first (πρῶτος) to rise from the dead', he would proclaim light 'both to our people and to the Gentiles' (26.23). Luke believes that as a Jew Agrippa will not find the notion of resurrection from the dead absurd (26.8). However, the claim that 'Jesus is the *first* to rise from the dead' must be asserted vigorously, for it will not find a ready welcome.

---

[14] So E. Haenchen, *The Acts of the Apostles* (Oxford: Blackwell, 1971), pp. 638–9.

[15] Cf. ibid., p. 659: 'The new faith . . . is not a treason to the old. The hope of resurrection is the bond which holds the two together. That the Sadducees do not believe in the resurrection means only that it is a question within the Jewish faith in which Rome need not interfere.'

[16] So also ibid., p. 214. C. K. Barrett is not persuaded: 'That the resurrection of Jesus was the firstfruits of the final resurrection is a NT thought, but it is not clear that Luke entertained it.' *Acts*, Vol. 1, ICC (Edinburgh: T. & T. Clark, 1994), p. 220. However, in his comments on 4.2, Barrett fails to note 26.23. In his comments on the latter verse he allows that the interpretation offered above is plausible. NRSV echoes the terse Greek: 'they were proclaiming that in Jesus there is the resurrection of the dead'. REB attempts to unpack the Greek and almost misses the point: 'they were proclaiming the resurrection from the dead by teaching the people about Jesus'.

Luke sets the resurrection of Jesus into an eschatological framework which is distinctively Christian. In addition to the two passages just mentioned, the four passages which refer to the hope of Israel make this clear. In 23.6 ('the hope and the resurrection of the dead'); 24.15f.; 26.6f.; and 28.20 Luke's Paul insists that the resurrection of Jesus should be seen as the climax of the messianic hopes of Israel.[17]

For Luke the resurrection of Jesus is the fulfilment 'of what the prophets and Moses said would take place' (Acts 26.23). The same points had already been made strongly in Luke's Gospel: 24.21, 26-7, 32, 44-6. Perhaps somewhat optimistically, Luke believes that most Jews will not have fundamental objections to the resurrection of Jesus. What separates most Jews and most Christians from one another is not the historical evidence for the resurrection of Jesus, but whether or not Jesus fulfils the messianic hopes of Israel. To the surprise of many Christians, the contemporary Jewish theologian Pinchas Lapide defends a similar position. He openly accepts the resurrection of Jesus as a historical event and as an act of God. But for Lapide, as for Luke, it is the Messiahship of Jesus which marks the division between Christianity and Judaism.[18]

7.4   OTHER FIRST-CENTURY OBJECTIONS

In the light of the preceding discussion, several further New Testament passages need to be reconsidered, though in each case the dangers of mirror-reading, to which I drew attention above, should be borne in mind. I noted above that Celsus presses the objection that, if Jesus had really wanted to show forth divine power, he ought to have appeared to those who put him to death, and to everyone everywhere (ii.63, 67). Perhaps similar objections lie behind Acts 10.40-2. Luke's 'answer' to the objection that the risen Jesus was not seen by the whole people is striking: the chosen witnesses to whom Jesus had appeared were commanded to proclaim him to the people.

John 14.18-22 may also reflect similar consternation over the resurrection appearances. In these verses it is not clear whether resurrection appearances or the parousia (or both) are in view. In verse 22, however, the question of the 'other' Judas certainly refers to the resurrection appearances: 'how is it that that you intend to disclose yourself to us, and not to the world?'. From the immediate context, John's answer to this possible objection is that

---

[17] On these passages, see K. Haacker, 'Das Bekenntnis des Paulus zur Hoffnung Israels nach der Apostelgeschichte des Lukas', *NTS* 31 (1985) 437 51.

[18] Pinchas Lapide, *The Resurrection of Jesus* (London: SPCK, 1984).

Jesus will disclose himself to those who love him and keep his commands (verse 21).[19]

In Mark 15.44-5 we read that 'Pilate wondered if he were already dead; and, summoning the centurion, he asked him whether he had been dead for some time. When he learned from the centurion that he was dead, he granted the body to Joseph.' These verses may also be related to an early objection to the resurrection of Jesus. Although Matthew and Luke follow Mark closely in this pericope, these two verses are not found in either gospel. So I think it is probable that these two verses were added very early to the version of Mark used by Matthew and by Luke. They were intended to underline the reality of the death of Jesus and so rule out a claim that Jesus had not really died on the cross, but had revived in the cool tomb. If this explanation is accepted, the 'swoon' theory, like most modern objections to the resurrection of Jesus, may have been anticipated in antiquity.

By now some readers of this chapter will have recalled the objection mentioned by Paul at I Cor. 15.12: 'If . . . we proclaim that Christ was raised from the dead, how can some of you say there is no resurrection of the dead?' I do not think that this verse reflects any doubt on the part of the Corinthians about the resurrection of Jesus: there is no hint either in the immediate context or elsewhere in I Corinthians that this was the case. For reasons which we need not discuss here, some Christians in Corinth denied that believers could or should look forward to a *general* resurrection.

The early objections to the resurrection of Jesus remind us of the varied views of both Jews and pagans on post-mortem existence. It is not very surprising that some of the New Testament resurrection traditions have been shaped in the light of a range of apologetic concerns. More surprising, however, are the ways in which the evangelists and those who earlier transmitted resurrection traditions offered hostages to fortune. In most of the traditions, discovery of the empty tomb is bewildering and does not lead to faith. The risen Jesus appears only to a small number of his followers – and their doubts are not excised from the traditions. Several obvious objections are not countered: resurrection traditions are transmitted and proclaimed, doubts and all.

Early objections to the resurrection hardly ever seem to have been made in isolation from negative assessments of the teaching and the actions of Jesus.[20] Opponents and followers alike saw that claims about the

---

[19] I am grateful to the Revd Roger Larkinson for pointing out to me the possible relevance of this passage for my approach.

[20] For the latter, see Chapter 6 above.

resurrection of Jesus raised the same issues as his actions and his teaching: for opponents, the whole story was riddled with trickery and deceit; for followers the story was God's story.

An even more important issue emerges from this study of early objections to the resurrection of Jesus. For some early opponents of Christianity, the theological claims about the Risen Jesus which were made by his followers raised far more fundamental issues than did allegedly implausible details in the resurrection traditions. The opponents who saw this still deserve to be listened to.

PART III

The gospels and papyri codices

CHAPTER 8

Why were early Christians addicted to the codex?

The transition from the roll format to the codex-book format in the early centuries of the Christian era was at least as revolutionary as its two later counterparts. Who doubts the importance of Johannes Gutenberg's mid-fifteenth-century invention of printing by using movable type? Or the late twentieth-century emergence of a CD-ROM only 12 cm in diameter yet able to hold a very large book in digital form?

In this chapter I shall refer to new evidence and try to account for early Christian 'addiction' to the codex along partly fresh lines. But I cannot hope to solve all the problems, for there are still too many gaps in our knowledge. I shall argue that attention to the origin of the codex forces us to reconsider several important issues. Even before Paul wrote his first 'canonical' letter c. AD 50, followers of Jesus were accustomed to use the predecessors of the codex-book format, various kinds of 'notebooks'. They used them for Scriptural excerpts and testimonies, for drafts and copies of letters, and probably also for collections of traditions of both the actions and the teaching of Jesus.

I owe the phrase 'addiction to the codex' to Sir Frederic G. Kenyon. His publication in 1933–7 of the Chester Beatty Biblical papyri sparked off interest in the emergence of the codex which continues to this day, for all twelve Chester Beatty manuscripts are in the codex format. For a decade or so the Chester Beatty manuscripts retained their standing among Biblical scholars as the sensation of the age. In the following decades, however, they were overshadowed somewhat by the even more dramatic discoveries of the Dead Sea Scrolls and the Nag Hammadi Library in the 1940s, and the Bodmer papyri in the 1950s.

The Chester Beatty papyri were published remarkably quickly by Kenyon in handsome editions which remain invaluable for specialists seventy years later.[1] Kenyon's comments on the collection as a whole and on the individual codices are astute, though he himself did not appreciate fully the importance of some of his observations.[2] Kenyon noted that the twelve Chester Beatty manuscripts revolutionize our knowledge of the early history of the codex form of book. He observed that the earlier part of the fourth century had been taken as the date of the supersession of the roll by the codex. The Chester Beatty papyri, however, not only 'confirm the belief that the Christian community was *addicted to the codex* rather than to the roll, but they carry back the use of the codex to an earlier date than there has hitherto been any good ground to assign to it'.[3] The Chester Beatty papyri seemed to confirm use of the codex in the second century, 'and even probably in the earlier part of it'.[4]

Kenyon noted that, so long as the roll was the form of book in use, no work of materially greater length than one of the gospels could be contained in a single roll. So, whereas five rolls would have been needed for the four gospels and Acts, among the Chester Beatty papyri *one* codex from the third century contained all these writings.[5] Kenyon was well aware of the significance of this new evidence for the physical existence of the fourfold Gospel. However, he seems not to have noted that this codex contains rare and important evidence for the joint circulation of Luke's Gospel and Acts, albeit almost certainly separated in this codex by Mark's Gospel.[6]

In at least one respect Kenyon's comments on the significance of the Chester Beatty papyri were truly prophetic. 'When, therefore, Irenaeus at the end of the second century writes of the four Gospels as the divinely provided evidence of Christianity, and the number four as almost axiomatic, it is now possible to believe that he may have been accustomed to the sight of volumes in which all four [Gospels] were contained.'[7] In 1933 those

---

[1] F. G. Kenyon, *The Chester Beatty Biblical Papyri: Descriptions and Texts of Twelve Manuscripts on Papyrus of the Greek Bible* (London: Emery Walker, 1933–7).

[2] Kenyon's textbooks were published in several editions and were widely influential. But neither he nor the later editors of his textbooks (Kenyon died in 1949) developed his comments on the origin of the codex format; hence his own contribution has not received the recognition it deserves. See, for example, *The Text of the Greek Bible*, 3rd edn, revised by A. W. Adams (London: Duckworth, 1975), p. 9, and *Our Bible and the Ancient Manuscripts* (London: Eyre and Spottiswoode), pp. 41–3.

[3] Kenyon, *Chester Beatty*, Vol. 1, p. 12. The italics are my own.

[4] This claim was based on Kenyon's proposed dating of the Numbers and Deuteronomy codex: 'written in a fine hand, of the second century, perhaps of the first half of it' (Vol. 1, p. 8). Although A. S. Hunt's more cautious late second- or early third-century dating has won the day, no one now doubts that Christians used the codex in the first half of the second century, if not even earlier.

[5] Kenyon, *Chester Beatty*, Vol. 1, p. 12.

[6] See T. C. Skeat, 'A Codicological Analysis of the Chester Beatty Papyrus Codex of Gospels and Acts (P45)', *Hermathena* 155 (1993) 27–43.

[7] Kenyon, *Chester Beatty*, Vol. 1, p. 13.

comments must have seemed to many Biblical scholars to be unduly speculative. For many decades little notice was taken of them. However, more
recent discoveries have enabled this insight to be placed on a much firmer
footing, for we now have almost certain evidence for the existence of two
earlier codices which originally contained all four canonical gospels.[8] The
theological case for acceptance of the fourfold Gospel and the availability
and pragmatic advantages of a single codex for four gospel writings did not
develop independently. Canon and codex are indeed inter-related.

8.1 'BIG BANG' THEORIES

Sir Frederic Kenyon did not discuss the reasons for early Christian addiction to the codex. Twenty years later, in 1954, C. H. Roberts took up
the challenge in 'The Codex', the published form of two lectures, which
remains a landmark in modern discussion.[9] Roberts suggested that it was
Mark's Gospel which provided the inspiration for the codex. The gospel,
he claimed, was written as a parchment notebook in Rome. When it (soon)
reached Egypt, it is likely that it would have been copied on papyrus, so
much more readily available there than parchment, and the papyrus codex
might thus have been created.

Roberts proposed a 'big bang' theory to account for the development
of the codex and for early Christian addiction to this format: the use of
the codex for Mark's Gospel by the church in Alexandria was the trigger
factor for early Christian use of the codex. In 1983 a completely revised and
extended version of 'The Codex' was published as a monograph by C. H.
Roberts and T. C. Skeat with the title *The Birth of the Codex*.[10] In spite
of more recent discoveries, this learned book remains the starting point
for serious discussion of our question: its presentation and assessment of
the Latin literary evidence and its statistics for the codex and roll in the
early Christian centuries are invaluable. However, in one important respect
the authors' approach was misguided, for they continued to search for one
major trigger factor to account for the birth of the codex.

Roberts and Skeat gave reasons for setting aside Roberts's own 1954
'big bang' theory and then proposed an alternative.[11] They drew on S.
Liebermann's claim that rabbinic sayings were written down on papyrus

---

[8] For full discussion, see Chapter 3 above.
[9] C. H. Roberts, 'The Codex', *Proceedings of the British Academy* 40 (1954) 169–204.
[10] C. H. Roberts and T. C. Skeat, *The Birth of the Codex* (London: Oxford University Press for the
British Academy, 1983).
[11] Ibid., pp. 54–61.

tablets (πίνακες), and proposed that sayings of Jesus may have been written down on papyrus tablets which were then developed into a primitive form of codex in Antioch, 'a Proto-Gospel'.[12]

In 1994 T. C. Skeat returned to the question yet again.[13] He noted that neither of the hypotheses advanced in *The Birth of the Codex* had won acceptance, and so he approached the problem from a different standpoint. 'We must assume', Skeat wrote, 'in the absence of any evidence to the contrary, that the Gospels originally circulated in the usual way, on papyrus rolls. What can have induced the Church so suddenly and totally to abandon rolls, and substitute not just codices but a single codex containing all four Gospels?'[14] Skeat's answer to his question is that the publication of John's Gospel (c. AD 100) may well have caused a crisis in the church. Believers must have been in a quandary: when would the production of gospels come to an end? So there must have been correspondence between the major churches, and perhaps conferences. The decision was reached to include all four Gospels in a codex, 'the new form of book recently developed in Rome' – and this would have been quite impossible in the universally used roll format. 'And once the Four-Gospel codex had been decided upon, every means must have been taken to spread the news throughout the Church.'[15]

Skeat's 1994 theory raises more questions than it answers. It is yet another 'big bang' theory, for it proposes one trigger event to account for the early church's initial acceptance of the codex format and its rapid addiction. In 1996 David Trobisch published a partly similar theory: early Christian use of the codex and of *nomina sacra* (the distinctive Christian method of abbreviation of 'sacred names' such as 'God' and 'Jesus') can be accounted for only by positing deliberate decisions concerning the appropriate format for canonical writings.[16]

In 1990 Harry Gamble published a very different 'big bang' theory.[17] Gamble accepted that 'there must have been a decisive, precedent-setting development in the publication and circulation of early Christian literature that rapidly established the codex in Christian use, and it is likely that this

[12] This hypothesis is discussed further below, pp. 186–8.
[13] T. C. Skeat, 'The Origin of the Christian Codex', *ZPE* 102 (1994) 263–8.
[14] Ibid., 266.   [15] Ibid., 267.
[16] D. Trobisch, *Die Endredaktion des Neuen Testaments: Eine Untersuchung zur Entstehung der christlichen Bibel* (Freiburg:Universitätsverlag; Göttingen: Vandenhoeck & Ruprecht, 1996).
[17] H. Y. Gamble, 'The Pauline Corpus and the Early Christian Book', in W. Babcock, ed., *Paul and the Legacies of Paul* (Dallas: Southern Methodist University Press, 1990), pp. 265–80. A summary of the theory was included in his *Books and Readers in the Early Church: A History of Early Christian Texts* (New Haven and London: Yale University Press, 1995), pp. 58–65.

development had to do with the religious authority accorded to whatever Christian document(s) first came to be known in codex form. There are good reasons to think that this distinction belonged to an early edition of the letters of Paul.'[18]

So there are at present a handful of 'big bang' theories 'on the table'. Alas, none of them is persuasive. Both Skeat and Trobisch envisage a much higher level of structure, centralized organization, and decision-making procedures within early second-century Christianity than I think likely. I do not think that we can posit the emergence of the four-gospel codex early enough to have been the trigger factor.[19] And Gamble has not convinced me that the collection of Paul's letters into a single codex is likely to have persuaded *all* strands of early Christianity to adopt the new codex format not only for Paul's writings, but also for gospels. E. J. Epp has recently shown that, among our fifty-four oldest codices of NT writings, 54 per cent are gospels, and only 22 per cent are Pauline, so the use of a single codex for Paul's letters seems to have been less influential than Gamble's theory envisages.[20]

The circulation of Paul's letters in a single codex and the four-gospel codex and a variety of other factors I shall mention below are likely to have helped to *sustain* early Christian addiction to the codex. But none of the 'big bang' hypotheses provides an adequate explanation for the initial adoption of the codex as the preferred format for early Christian writings.

8.2 THE ORIGIN OF THE CODEX: THREE STAGES

How is early Christian 'addiction' to the codex to be explained? Recent discoveries underline even more firmly the extent of the 'addiction'. Twelve further early fragmentary papyri of New Testament writings were published between 1997 and 1999.[21] All are in the codex format, not the roll which was still being used almost universally for literary texts.

I shall work backwards, so to speak, from the point at which scribes copying non-Christian literary writings began to prefer the codex format to the roll (my stage three). I shall then discuss the reasons why Christian scribes became obsessed with the new format at a much earlier period (stage two).

---

[18] Gamble, *Books and Readers*, p. 58.   [19] See Chapter 3 above.
[20] E. J. Epp, 'The Codex and Literacy in Early Christianity and at Oxyrhynchus: Issues Raised by Harry Y. Gamble's *Books and Readers in the Early Church*', *Critical Review of Books in Religion* 10 (1997) 15–37, esp. 35.
[21] *Oxyrhynchus Papyri*, Vols. LIV, LV, LVI. P. Oxy. 4403 and 4404 = 𝔓104–5, fragments of Matthew; P. Oxy. 4445–8 = 𝔓106–8, fragments of John; P. Oxy. 4494–4500 = 𝔓110–15, fragments of Matthew, Luke, Acts, Romans, Hebrews, and Revelation.

Finally, I shall turn to the key question (stage one): how are we to explain the *initial and precocious* use of the codex by Christian scribes? I shall argue that the answer to this key question forces us to reconsider several common assumptions concerning the transmission of early Christian traditions.

Before we proceed, a comment on the nature of the evidence and its interpretation is necessary. There are gaps in our knowledge at key points, and the limited evidence we have is often difficult to interpret. The evidence takes three forms. References to rolls and codices in writers such as Martial and Quintilian are often difficult to interpret. Iconographic depictions in portraits, on vases, and on reliefs on sarcophagi are invaluable, but they are often stylized and may have been influenced more strongly by iconographical conventions than by 'on the ground' practice. Extant examples of parchment and papyrus codices, and their predecessors, are difficult to date with precision, for palaeography is an art and not a science. So disciplined historical imagination and considerable caution are called for.

To complicate matters still further, there is varied use of terminology, both in our primary sources and in the secondary literature. For example, the Latin word *codex* is used both for a simple parchment or papyrus notebook intended primarily for personal use and also for a more substantial 'book' intended to be read by others. Although some modern writers use 'codex' for both, I shall refer to the former as 'notebook' and the latter as 'codex'.

Now back to my stage three. Up to about AD 300 very nearly all literary texts were 'published' or copied in the roll format. But, by the fourth century, only about 25 per cent still used the roll, and, by the fifth century, the percentage had dropped still lower, to around 10 per cent.[22] During these centuries almost all Christian copies of Biblical manuscripts were in the codex format; so too were most non-Biblical Christian manuscripts. On the other hand, Jewish scribes continued to prefer the roll.

Although early Christian use of the codex has attracted lively discussion, less attention has been given to the reasons why *non-Christian* scribes eventually adopted the codex format. That important transition can be pinpointed to the decades around AD 300. Fresh light on that major change has recently been shed by William V. Harris, well known for his work on levels of literacy in antiquity.[23]

[22] For the details, see Roberts and Skeat, *Birth*, pp. 36–7. More recent discoveries, or alternative datings for some of the papyri, do not alter the general picture.
[23] W. V. Harris, 'Why did the Codex Supplant the Book-Roll?', in J. Monfasani and R. G. Musto, eds, *Renaissance Society and Culture, FS E. F. Price Jr* (New York: Italica Press, 1991), pp. 71–85.

It is no coincidence, he argues, that the transition from roll to codex for literary writings took place c. AD 300, 'in a period when the numbers and the respectability of the Christians were strongly increasing'. By the end of the third century 'no simple contrast could be drawn between the culture of the Christians and the pagans. It was now possible to be both a Christian and an ardent lover of the classics without any great strain.'[24]

If Harris is correct, it was scribes' preference for the codex for *Christian* writings which provided a major impetus for the use of this format for 'secular' literary writings c. AD 300. In line with the views of earlier writers, Harris accepts that cost and ease of reference were vital advantages of the codex form, as was its increased capacity; he lays special emphasis on ease of reference as a key factor.

Only by about AD 300 is it plausible to postulate that Christian scribes' addiction to the codex may have influenced non-Christian scribes. That is inconceivable in the first and second centuries AD, when Christians were scattered minority groups, somewhat isolated from the literary intelligentsia of the day.

So much for stage three. We turn now to what I am calling stage two. In *The Birth of the Codex* (1983), C. H. Roberts and T. C. Skeat played down pragmatic reasons for acceptance of the codex format in order to leave room for their own 'big bang' theories. Along with William Harris, Joseph van Haelst,[25] and E. J. Epp,[26] I think that they were unwise to do so.

I am convinced that, once Christian scribes began to use the codex, their precocious devotion to the new format was sustained by a variety of pragmatic factors, some of which will have been more influential than others at particular times and in particular locations.[27] In Chapter 3, pp. 84–5, first published in 1997, I discussed briefly the various pragmatic explanations which have been offered and then set out my own. I noted that early Christian codices, whether Roman or Christian, were quite small in size and therefore much more portable than rolls. Christian scribes preparing writings to be carried by missionaries, messengers, and travellers over long distances would have readily appreciated the advantages of the codex. Their general counter-cultural stance would have made them more willing

---

[24] Ibid., pp. 74 and 84.

[25] J. van Haelst, 'Les Origines du codex', in Alain Blanchard, ed., *Les Débuts du codex*, Bibliologia 9 (Brepols: Turnhout, 1989), pp. 12–35. Van Haelst's article is an extended critical appraisal of Roberts and Skeat, *Birth*, with fresh evidence and discussion at many points.

[26] Epp, 'The Codex and Literacy', pp. 15–37. On p. 24 he notes that, in 1996, he and I both used the term 'big bang' theory within three months of one another, but quite independently.

[27] I owe the phrase 'precocious devotion' to Harris, 'Why did the Codex Supplant the Book-Roll?', p. 75.

than their non-Christian counterparts to break with the almost unanimous preference for the roll and experiment with the unfashionable codex. I also noted that copying and using the Old Testament Scriptures and their foundation writings in a new format was one of the ways Christians expressed their sense of 'newness'. Once the new format began to be adopted, its usefulness for collections of writings such as the four gospels and the Pauline corpus would have enhanced its value.

E. J. Epp has recently added a further important consideration. The likely content of the codices carried by early Christian missionaries and teachers (whether Mark, OT *testimonia*, the Pauline corpus, the four-gospel codex) is less important than the mere presence and use of the codex 'in the highly charged setting of evangelism and edification in pristine Christianity – especially when a respected visitor is present with this new mark [i.e. a codex] of his/her calling'.[28]

All these factors were instrumental in encouraging Christian scribes to use the new codex format. But they all relate to what I now call stage two: the rapid and almost universal acceptance of the new format by Christian communities. How are we to explain stage one: the *initial* use of the codex format by Christian scribes at a time when the papyrus or parchment roll was the norm in society at large?

The roll held sway for a very long time. The oldest papyrus roll yet discovered was found in an Egyptian tomb which dates from about 3000 BC. To the archaeologists' disappointment, it was blank, as it had been left ready for the dead man's use.[29] The longest roll, written about 1150 BC, is about 43 cm (17 in) high and 40.5 m (133 ft) long. Leather rolls could also be very large: the Temple Scroll, the largest of the Dead Sea Scrolls, is 8.2 m long (27ft).[30] A typical roll 18 cm (7 in) high and 6 m (20 ft) in length could hold a single gospel or Acts, and could be held comfortably between thumb and forefinger.[31] The demise of the roll was slow: only in about AD 300 did the codex reach parity with the roll for book production,[32] and the roll continued to be used for formal documents right up to medieval times and beyond.

---

[28] Epp, 'The Codex and Literacy', p. 21.
[29] Alan Millard, *Reading and Writing in the Time of Jesus* (Sheffield: Sheffield Academic Press, 2000), p. 24.
[30] Ibid., pp. 61–2.
[31] Roberts and Skeat, *Birth*, p. 47. For a good summary of the methods used to make papyrus and parchment rolls, see Gamble, *Books and Readers*, pp. 43–8.
[32] For details of the approximate percentages from the first to the fifth century, see Roberts and Skeat, *Birth*, p. 36.

When and why was the codex first used? Since 'nothing comes from nothing', the codex must have had predecessors. So, before we consider the origin of the codex, we must discuss its predecessors.

8.3 PREDECESSORS OF THE CODEX

The ubiquitous roll was obviously one of the predecessors of the parchment or papyrus codex, but there were others.[33]

(1) Wooden (or occasionally ivory) tablets had a rim around the edge, to hold wax in place.[34] They were incised with a stylus; they could be readily reused by smoothing over the wax. The wax tablets were used for notes and drafts of various kinds, including school exercises. Several wax tablets could be held together by a cord which passed through holes in the tablets. *Codex* or *caudex* were the Latin words for a set of tablets held together in this way; δέλτος or πίναξ the usual equivalent terms in Greek.[35]

Wooden wax-covered tablets are depicted in a number of portraits and sculptures, most notably in several wall paintings at Pompeii. Like the roll, they have a long history. From the second half of the second millennium BC wax-covered wooden tablets were widely used in the Near East. They have been discovered in places as far apart as Egypt and the north of England. A large number were found at Herculaneum and at Pompeii.[36] Up to ten tablets were sometimes tied together, but four would usually have been a handful. Writing in AD 85, the Roman poet Martial referred to a 'five-leaved wax tablet' (*quinquiplici cera*), a 'three leaved tablet', ivory tablets, and even waxed parchment which could be erased.[37] Wax tablets could be readily reused by smoothing over the wax (perhaps slightly warmed) with a spatula. Occasionally both sides were inscribed.

A particularly interesting example of a double-sided wax tablet was un-earthed in the 2001 archaeological season at Vindolanda, near Hadrian's

[33] An earlier version of parts of sections 8.3 and 8.4 was published in G. N. Stanton, 'The Early Reception of Matthew's Gospel', in D. E. Aune, ed., *The Gospel of Matthew in Current Study* (Grand Rapids: Eerdmans, 2001), pp. 53–60.

[34] For a wide-ranging, well-illustrated discussion of inorganic and organic materials used in antiquity for writing, see Horst Blanck, *Das Buch in der Antike* (Munich: C. H. Beck, 1992), pp. 40–63.

[35] On the difference between *codex* (referring to wooden tablets) and πίναξ, see M. Haran, 'Codex, Pinax and Writing Slat', *Scripta Classica Israelica* 15 (1996) 212–22. He claims that, whereas the former was Roman and not mentioned in the Talmud, the πίναξ had a Greek-Hellenistic background and a concertina-like form, and was occasionally used for other purposes such as serving food. The πίναξ is referred to in several Talmudic passages, but it was never made of papyrus.

[36] For details and full references see Millard, *Reading and Writing*, pp. 26–9. See also A. K. Bowman and J. D. Thomas, *Vindolanda: The Latin Writing-Tablets*, Britannia Monograph Series 4 (London: Society for the Promotion of Roman Studies, 1983), pp. 33–5.

[37] Martial, *Epigrams* XIV.4–7.

Wall in northern England. This tablet, which dates from c. AD 100, was inscribed not only with a stylus pen on the wax (which has long disappeared),
but also with pen and ink on the rim of the tablet, to assist filing.[38]

Like the roll, wax tablets remained in use long after the codex came into
general use. For example, they are listed as essential equipment for a monk
in the fifth-century Rule of St Benedict. A wax tablet is described in a riddle
written by Aldhelm, bishop of Sherborne in the latter part of the seventh
century:

Of honey-laden bees I first was born, but in the forest grew my outer coat; my
tough backs came from shoes (the leather thongs used to tie the tablets into a
notebook). An iron point in artful windings cuts a fair design, and leaves long
twisted furrows like a plough.[39]

From the same period we have an interesting example of the use of wax
tablets in the planning of a book. Adamnan, Abbot of Iona 679-704, wrote
an account of the Holy Places in Palestine. In his preface he tells us that
wax tablets were used to note down his pilgrim informer's experiences and
to make sketch plans of the places he had visited.[40]

(2) Until recently it was generally assumed that wooden wax-covered
tablets were the standard writing-material for letters and documents in
those parts of the Roman Empire where papyrus was not readily available.
However, the publication in 1983 and 1994 of the very large number of thin
leaf tablets from Vindolanda (Northumberland, England) which date from
c. AD 100 necessitates a reappraisal of this view. The Vindolanda discoveries
have not yet received the attention from New Testament scholars which
they deserve. They came too late for more than passing mention in Joseph
van Haelst's major study[41] and in Harry Gamble's survey.[42]

The Vindolanda tablets are 'thin slivers of smooth wood which are written with pen and ink', and may conveniently be referred to as 'leaf tablets'.[43]
Most were used for official documents, as well as for letters and drafts of
letters. However, at least one of the Vindolanda tablets contains a literary
text, a line of Virgil; three others may be literary or semi-literary.[44] In the

---

[38] This information comes from a display cabinet in the museum at Vindolanda. At the time of
writing, the Report of the 2001 excavations had not yet been published, nor had the promised full
publication of all the wax tablets discovered at Vindolanda taken place. For up-to-date information,
see the Vindolanda web site: www.vindolanda.com.
[39] Quoted by Janet Backhouse, *The Lindisfarne Gospels* (London: Phaidon, 1981), p. 31.
[40] Ibid., pp. 31–2.   [41] Van Haelst, 'Les Origines du codex' (above, n. 25), pp. 15–16.
[42] Gamble, *Books and Readers*, p. 268 n. 35.   [43] Bowman and Thomas, *Vindolanda*, p. 32.
[44] A. K. Bowman, *Life and Letters on the Roman Frontier: Vindolanda and its People* (London: British
Museum, 1994), p. 18.

light of their publication, it is probable that some of the many literary references in first- and second-century writings to notebooks (*pugillaria*) may be to leaf tablets rather than to wooden wax-covered tablets, also referred to as stylus tablets.

In 1983, the editors of the Vindolanda tablets accepted that for two reasons they could not be described as a primitive codex: some of them were linked together in 'concertina' format, and with only a couple of partial exceptions not both sides of the leaf had been written on. However, they also noted that the existence of this wooden notebook in this format at a period which was clearly an important one for the emergence of the codex may be of some significance for that development.[45]

In 1994 the tablets were re-edited, together with the considerable finds from the 1985–9 excavations. The editors noted that there was no standard format for documents, though a diptych format, with the address written on the back of the right-hand half of the diptych, is the norm for letters.[46] Somewhat surprisingly, the editors did not comment further on the relationship of the leaf tablets to the origins of the codex. But there can now be little doubt that, with the very thin Vindolanda leaf tablets from c. AD 100, inscribed with pen and ink, we have extant examples of notebooks with a strong a claim to be *one* of the forerunners of the codex.[47]

By 2001 a total of 1,400 or so leaf tablets had been discovered at Vindolanda, but only about 300 wax-covered stylus tablets. However, some 230 stylus pens have been found, so perhaps the numbers are misleading.[48] The 2001 excavations unearthed 35 leaf tablets and 17 stylus tablets.

A very small number of similar leaf tablets have been found in other parts of Britain, in Dacia, and in Vindonissa (Switzerland). One found among the Bar Kochba letters is especially important. It contains a letter from 'Shimo'on Bar Kosiba, the Prince of Israel, to Yehonatan and Masabalda' concerning three matters. The thin wooden slat, written in AD 134 or 135, has been incised down the middle, so that it could be folded. There are nine lines of writing on the right side, and eight on the left. The editor, Y. Yadin, notes that the practice of writing on wood was widespread throughout the

---

[45] Bowman and Thomas, *Vindolanda*, pp. 40–4.
[46] A. K. Bowman and J. D. Thomas, *The Vindolanda Writing-Tablets: Tabulae Vindolandenses* II (London: British Museum, 1994), pp. 40–6.
[47] Bowman, *Life and Letters*, p. 10 notes that, with writing-tablets still coming out of the ground in the 1990s, conclusions can only be tentative and provisional.
[48] In an oral presentation to an SNTS seminar in Durham in August 2002 Professor J. D. Thomas mentioned that, whereas wax tablets made excellent kindling, leaf tablets would not burn readily.

Orient, and is often mentioned even in rabbinical literature.[49] The signature does not correspond with the handwriting in the letter itself: as in one of the Vindolanda letters (the so-called Claudia Severa letter), and as Paul himself mentions at Gal. 6.11, the writer has dictated the letter and only then 'signed' it himself.

Unlike the wax-covered wooden tablets, the leaf tablet or slat could not be readily reused. They were too thin and too flimsy to allow ink to be scraped off. However, they were light and could be linked together, sometimes in concertina fashion. It was possible to write on both sides – and sometimes the reverse side was used, especially for the addressee of a letter. It is worth noting that there was a degree of overlap between the wax-covered tablet and the leaf tablet, and that the same Latin word, *pugillaria*, seems to have been used for both.[50] The rim of some of the Vindolanda wax tablets is marked with ink, either in order to give a summary of the contents, or to assist the process of filing. The wax was often incised so firmly that marks were left on the wood underneath. Although the wax has long since disappeared, some of the writing on these tablets can still be read; sometimes the writing comes from more than one document. Occasionally ink has been used on Vindolanda stylus or wax tablets.[51]

Although there are some lines of continuity from both the wax-covered stylus tablets and the leaf tablets or slats to the codex, there are also obvious differences. As with the codex, in both cases the materials used for writing were in a small 'page' format; occasionally the reverse side was also used. Although individual 'pages' were often linked together to form a 'booklet', the end result was clumsy and unsuitable for more than notes, drafts, and sketches.

(3) The third and much more direct predecessors of the codex were parchment or papyrus notebooks (*membranae*, μεμβράναι).[52] Although the earliest *extant* examples are from the end of the second or the third century AD, there is literary evidence which confirms that they were used much earlier.[53]

---

[49] Y. Yadin, 'Expedition D', *Israel Exploration Journal* 11 (1961) 41–2. See also Haran, 'Codex, *Pinax* and Writing Slat', 212–22.

[50] Bowman and Thomas, *Vindolanda*, p. 43.

[51] See Robin Birley, *Roman Records from Vindolanda on Hadrian's Wall*, Roman Army Museum Publications for the Vindolanda Trust, (Carvoran: Greenhead, 3rd edn, 1999), pp. 21–2.

[52] Cf. J. van Haelst: 'Le carnet de parchemin est une étape intermédiaire indispensable entre la tablette de cire et le codex. Ce sont ses feuillets qui, multipliés selon les besoins, pourront éventuellement contenir une œuvre littéraire de quelque étendue.' 'Les Origines du codex', p. 20.

[53] See Roberts and Skeat, *Birth*, pp. 15–23 and van Haelst, 'Les Origines du codex', p. 18 for details and bibliography. Part of a probable parchment notebook has been found at Dura-Europos and dated to the first century BC or AD. See Bowman and Thomas, *Vindolanda*, p. 43.

Quintilian's comments from about AD 90 are particularly important:

It is best to write on wax owing to the facility which it offers for erasure, though weak sight may make it desirable to employ parchment pages (*membranae*) by preference . . . But whichever we employ, we must leave blank pages that we may be free to make additions when we will. (*Inst. Or.* x.3.31–2)[54]

Wax tablets and parchment pages are quite clearly differentiated. The references to pages on the left side being left blank and to the better visibility of writing with ink on parchment confirms that Quintilian is well aware of the considerable advantages of the notebook. The use of parchment does not seem to be an innovation, yet one senses from this passage that the wax tablet is the norm in Quintilian's day.

There is only limited evidence for the existence of parchment or papyrus notebooks earlier in the first century. The words attributed to Paul in 2 Tim. 4:13 provide important support for their existence a decade or two before Quintilian wrote. 'When you come', 'Paul' writes to Timothy, 'bring the (traveller's) cloak I left with Carpus at Troas, and the books in roll format (τὰ βιβλία), particularly my parchment notebooks (μάλιστα τὰς μεμβράνας)'.[55] This sentence has elicited plenty of discussion.[56]

Are two groups of writings referred to, as in my translation, or only one? T. C. Skeat gained only minimal support for his view that one group of writings is referred to here, parchment notebooks: he took μάλιστα as 'to be precise, namely, I mean'.[57] However, most scholars accept that τὰ βιβλία is a general reference to writings, almost certainly in roll format, and that τὰς μεμβράνας refers to writings in a different format, about which the writer is especially anxious.

What does τὰς μεμβράνας refer to? Μεμβράνα is a Latin loan-word transliterated into Greek, for there was no Greek word available.[58] We

---

[54] 'Scribi optime ceris, in quibus facillima est ratio delendi, nisi forte visus infirmior membranarum potius usum exiget . . . Reliquendae autem in utrolibet genere contra erunt vacuae tabellae, in quibus libera adiciendi sit excursio.'

[55] See Michael McCormick, 'Typology, Codicology and Papyrology', *Scriptorium* 35 (1981) 331–4.

[56] See especially the discussion and references in I. H. Marshall, *The Pastoral Epistles*, ICC (Edinburgh: T. & T. Clark, 1999), pp. 818–21.

[57] T. C. Skeat, 'Especially the Parchments: A Note on 2 Timothy iv.13', *JTS* 30 (1979) 173–7. See also Roberts and Skeat, *Birth*, p. 22. This possible interpretation of μάλιστα is not even mentioned in BDAG. However, E. R. Richards, *The Secretary in the Letters of Paul* (Tübingen: Mohr, 1991), p. 164 n. 168 allows that Skeat may be correct, referring to Gal. 6.10; I Tim. 4.10; also Phil. 4.22; Philem. 16; I Tim. 5.8, 17; Titus 1.10.

[58] See further van Haelst, 'Les Origines du codex', p. 17. He notes that the term κῶδιξ, a transliteration of the Latin 'codex', is found in the Byzantine era, but it does not refer to a book containing literary works, whether ecclesiastical or secular; it refers to a register of taxes, or a collection of documents, inventories, or archives.

have just noted that Quintilian used *membrana* to refer to a parchment notebook, and this is clearly the meaning here.[59]

If only we knew what those parchment notebooks contained! The context gives us some clues, but not a clear answer. 'Paul' has just reminded Timothy of the importance of the Scriptures and has provided a list of the uses to which the Scriptures should be put (2 Tim. 3.14-17). So it is probable that τὰ βιβλία includes rolls of OT Scriptures. How many rolls could Timothy have been expected to carry, along with that traveller's cloak, and his own personal possessions? Surely not many. So, in order to supplement a small number of rolls, parchment notebooks may well have contained *excerpts* from Scripture, perhaps also some 'trustworthy sayings' (cf. II Tim. 2.11) and some drafts of letters. We shall return to this important point below.

It is not surprising that examples of parchment or papyrus notebooks from the first century have not survived. These notebooks were used for letters, and for ephemeral notes and documents of various kinds, but not for writings which might be treasured by a later generation, for which the carefully constructed roll was the norm. Although Quintilian and 2 Tim. 4.13 refer to parchment notebooks, it is probable that papyrus notebooks existed at the same time, particularly in Egypt and the East, where papyrus was readily available; we should not suppose that the one evolved out of the other.[60] The two types of notebook found at Vindolanda confirm that local availability dictated the material used. On the northern frontier of the Roman Empire, papyrus would not have been available, and parchment would have been difficult to prepare. The huge numbers of wax stylus tablets and ink leaf tablets (more than 1,700 in all by 2002) found in the sodden earth at Vindolanda call in question current assumptions about very limited levels of literacy in antiquity.

The evidence for the widespread use of the different types of notebooks confirms that, for many people in the Graeco-Roman world, notebooks were part of everyday life. Although we are still unable to reconstruct with confidence how, why, and when the more substantial papyrus and parchment codex evolved out of the various kinds of notebooks mentioned above, a gradual evolution is more probable than any one 'trigger' factor.[61]

[59] Pliny informs us that his uncle used to work with a slave standing by him holding a book and notebooks (*libro et pugillaribus*). *Ep.*III.5.15.
[60] See E. G. Turner, 'The Priority of Parchment or Papyrus?', in his *The Typology of the Early Codex* (Philadelphia: University of Pennsylvania Press, 1977), pp. 35–54. Turner challenges the older view that parchment codices preceded papyrus codices.
[61] Roberts and Skeat, *Birth*, p. 10 correctly note that the transition from papyrus to parchment was of an entirely different character from, and quite unconnected with, the transition from roll to codex.

8.4 THE FIRST CODICES FOR 'LITERARY' WRITINGS

By no later than the end of the first century AD the codex was being used by a small number of non-Christian writers for more substantial writings than notes, documents, drafts, and letters. As we shall see in a moment, some of these writings were literary: it is a mistake to assume from the origins of the codex that this format was reserved solely for utilitarian writings or handbooks.[62]

At present there are two rivals for the accolade of the earliest *extant* codex: P. Oxy. 30, a parchment codex in Latin from about AD 100 which is usually known as *De Bellis Macedonicis*,[63] and 𝔓52, the well-known papyrus fragment of John 18, which is generally dated to about AD 125. Although P. Oxy. 30 is fragmentary, it is clearly a historical writing. It is no mere set of ephemeral notes – and neither is John's Gospel!

Was the codex format first used by Christians, and only then adopted by non-Christian scribes? The earliest *extant* examples just noted do not settle the question. Their palaeographical dating is not certain, and in any case there is literary evidence for earlier non-Christian use of the codex which must be weighed carefully.

Writing in AD 85, the Roman poet Martial refers to the availability of parchment codices for travellers: 'pocket editions' of Homer, Virgil, Cicero, Livy, and Ovid which are referred with the words *in membranis* (in parchment page format) or *in pugillaribus membraneis* (hand-held parchment pages; *Epigrams* 1.2 and XIV.184–92). In Martial's terse two-line mottoes about these 'pocket editions' there is no hint that they are mere novelties, or a recent innovation. In their influential *The Birth of the Codex*, C. H. Roberts and T. C. Skeat claimed that Martial's 'experiment was still-born'.[64] In an equally memorable and in my judgement valid comment on that view, Joseph van Haelst is dismissive: 'C'est excessif.'[65]

We do have a sprinkling of codices of non-Christian writings from the second century. Although they make up only 2 per cent of the total (the remainder are on rolls), they should not be set aside as an insignificant aftermath of a still-born experiment. One of the second-century codices is a parchment in Latin (P. Oxy. 30, noted above). Three are parchment

---

They allow the possibility that the papyrus codex and the parchment codex may have developed in parallel (p. 29).

[62] Roberts and Skeat, *ibid.*, p. 5 n. 1 note that it is quite wrong to describe the papyrus codex as a 'bastard form'.

[63] Turner, *Typology*, pp. 38, 93 dates this to the early second century; J. Mallon (cited by Turner, p. 128), to the end of the first century.

[64] Roberts and Skeat, *Birth*, p. 29.   [65] Van Haelst, 'Les Origines du codex', p. 21.

codices in Greek; fourteen are papyrus codices in Greek. Many are literary writings.[66]

P. Petaus 30 (first published in 1969) is particularly important.[67] This letter in Greek, which can be dated confidently to the second century, but not more precisely, refers to eight parchment codices which were purchased, and six more which were not.

Julius Placidus to his father, Herclanus, greetings.
Deios has been with us and has shown us six parchment codices (τὰς μεμβράνας ἕξ). We didn't select any of them, but we did collate eight others, for which I paid on account a hundred drachmas . . . I wish you good health.

P. Petaus 30 'implies a touring book-seller offering literary *membranae*'.[68] As with Martial, there is no suggestion that these readily portable codices were an innovation. The social setting reflected in the letter is important: these codices were part of a *mobile* bookshop. Martial, it will be recalled, refers to pocket editions of literary codices (*membranae*) which *travellers* would find useful. The earliest non-Christian codices seem to have been used for a variety of writings, including literary writings in the 'classical canon' of the day. As far as we can judge, they first became popular with travellers.[69]

Taken together, the extant and the literary evidence suggest that codices for substantial writings were not unknown in non-Christian circles in the latter half of the first century, i.e. at the time of the composition of the New Testament writings. At this time it is most unlikely that invention of the codex format by Christian scribes would have been imitated and developed by non-Christian scribes, albeit in a limited way.[70] The reverse is possible: for their own reasons, Christian scribes may have imitated an innovation by a small minority of their secular counterparts. Or, Christian and non-Christian scribes may have begun to experiment with more substantial

---

[66] See the slightly different lists with full details in Roberts and Skeat, *Birth*, p. 71 and in van Haelst, 'Les Origines du codex', pp. 23–5.

[67] For the critical edition, see U. and D. Hagedorn and L. C. and H. C. Youtie, eds., *P. Petaus: Das Archiv des Petaus*, Pap. Colon., Vol. IV (Cologne and Opladen: Westdeutscher Verlag, 1969).

[68] E. G. Turner, *Greek Papyri*, 2nd edn (Oxford: Clarendon, 1980), p. 204.

[69] On the basis of his analysis of the second-century non-Christian codices, Michael McCormick suggests that the novel format appealed to some ancient doctors and teachers. As they were often on the move, they would have found the codex format handy. 'Typology, Codicology and Papyrology', pp. 331–4.

[70] Several more recent writers have been reluctant to accept the view of Roberts and Skeat, *Birth*, that Christians invented the codex. See, for example, Robin Lane Fox, 'Literacy and Power in Early Christianity', in A. K. Bowman and Greg Woolf, eds., *Literacy and Power in the Ancient World* (Cambridge: Cambridge University Press, 1994), p. 140; Epp, 'The Codex and Literacy' (above, n. 20), pp. 15–16, who states that he is now more hesitant than in some of his earlier publications.

notebooks, i.e. codices, at about the same time, but quite independently; only in Christian circles did an addiction to the new format take hold and become the norm rather than the exception. I think that the latter possibility is more likely.

At present the consensus view is that the autographs and the very earliest copies of Christian writings were on rolls, and that, at the end of the first century or thereabouts, Christian scribes switched to the codex under the influence of a hypothetical 'big bang'. We have seen that all the 'big bang' theories on offer fail to convince. Is there a more plausible reason why Christian scribes first turned to the codex? As noted above, several factors seem to have sustained and strengthened addiction to the codex (my stage two), but how did it take hold in the first place (my stage one)? And is it possible that the codex was used for the very first Christian writing?

8.5 EARLY CHRISTIAN NOTEBOOKS

We have seen that, in the first century, several kinds of notebooks were the predecessors of the codex. They were used for all manner of 'non-literary' writings all over the Roman Empire, from the Near East to Vindolanda in the far North-West. As we have seen, in the latter part of the first century, the same word *membranae* was used in Latin and in Greek both for a notebook (Quintilian; 2 Tim. 4.13) and for a 'literary' codex (Martial; P. Petaus 30). With hindsight, the use of codices for more permanent writings than ephemeral notes was a very natural development. However, preference for the roll for literary writings was so deeply entrenched that a change of format was anything but obvious to most in the first century.

In the post-Easter decades the followers of Jesus would almost certainly have made use of more than one kind of notebook: in some settings wax tablets, in others, wooden leaf tablets or slats, and, in others, papyrus or parchment notebooks – as well as, of course, single sheets. Their regular use for varied purposes may have encouraged Christians to make use of more substantial notebooks, i.e. codices, for their more permanent writings. And, since Christians formed minority, partly counter-cultural groups with limited literary pretensions, the use of the codex rather than the roll did not involve a major shift in mind-set. In short, a gradual evolution from 'notebook' to 'codex' is much more likely than a big bang development *ex nihilo*. This explanation for initial Christian use of the codex (my stage one) is more plausible than any of the alternatives which have been offered. The theory is both simple and elegant! But where is the evidence?

I must confess immediately that, with the exception of 2 Tim. 4.13, we do not have explicit evidence for use of notebooks by first- or even early second-century Christians. But surely Paul's first letter to the Thessalonians (c. AD 50) was not the very first time when writing was used by a Christian. By then some form of notebook may well have been used for a couple of decades for several different Christian purposes. I shall now refer to three possibilities.

8.5.1 *Scriptural excerpts and testimonies*

Luke records that Jesus read from the scroll of the prophet Isaiah in his home-town synagogue in Nazareth (Luke 4.16-20). Here NRSV and most modern translations correctly use the term 'scroll' or 'roll', abandoning the translation 'book' used in the 1611 AV/KJV, and even in the 1946 RSV. But what happened in the immediate post-Easter period?

We know very little about the 30s and 40s of the first century, but we have enough evidence to confirm that in those decades Christian missionaries or teachers did not always have ready access to local synagogues in order to consult rolls of the Scriptures. In any case, few of them could read. Making their own copies was time-consuming and expensive. And carrying handfuls of rolls of favourite Christian Scriptures such as the Psalms and Isaiah on their often arduous journeys was not easy. So in all probability some kind of notebook was used for Scriptural excerpts which were prominent in early Christian preaching and teaching.

Early Christian use of written collections of Scriptural excerpts and *testimonia*, i.e. proof-texts to support Christian claims concerning Jesus, is now attracting renewed scholarly interest. In 1889 Edwin Hatch suggested that the early Christians took over the Jewish practice of compiling extracts of Biblical passages, but his proposal attracted little attention.[71] In 1916 and 1920 J. Rendel Harris proposed that there existed in the early church a single *Testimony Book*, a compilation of Scriptural passages drawn on by several early Christian writers as 'testimonies' to underpin their convictions.[72] Although his work attracted plenty of attention, most scholars considered that the theory was unduly speculative. However, it is worth noting that Rendel Harris's views were less rigid than many of his critics

---

[71] E. Hatch, *Essays in Biblical Greek* (Oxford: Clarendon, 1889). I owe this reference to T. H. Lim, *Holy Scripture in the Qumran Communities and the Pauline Letters* (Oxford: Clarendon, 1997), pp. 151–2.

[72] J. Rendel Harris, *Testimonies* (2 vols., Cambridge: Cambridge University Press, 1916–20).

supposed: he allowed for editions, expansions, and changes in the content of the *Testimony Book*.[73]

The turn of the tide towards a more favourable view of the hypothesis came with the publication in 1956 of 4Q Testimonia (now known as 4Q175) and then of J. A. Fitzmyer's fine study, '"4Q Testimonia" and the New Testament' the following year.[74] On a single leather sheet probably compiled by an individual for his own reference, several OT passages are juxtaposed. 4Q175 is a small Jewish anthology of related Scriptural texts. George Brooke has shown convincingly that they refer to the eschatological figures of the prophet, royal Messiah, and priest.[75]

4Q176 (also known as 4Q *Tanhumim*) is also important for our present purposes. A large number of fragments of excerpts from Isaiah 40–55 have been found. The excerpts all relate to Yahweh's promises of 'comfort' for his afflicted people.[76] So we now have clear evidence that shortly before the first century AD excerpts of Scriptural passages were gathered together thematically.

There is an often-overlooked extant early Christian equivalent. The publication of 4Q175 has led to renewed interest in Papyrus Rylands Greek 460 (PRG 460), first published by C. H. Roberts in 1936, and recently examined in detail by Alessandro Falcetta.[77] Here we have a cluster of OT LXX-related passages, juxtaposed without comment on two leaves in simple codex format. The thematic linking of passages is strikingly reminiscent of 4Q175. Although this papyrus probably dates only from the early fourth century, PRG 460 provides clear evidence of early Christian use of written collections of related Scriptural texts. Falcetta has proposed that PRG 460 originally contained four sections of texts, each occupying one 'page' of the two leaves written on both sides. 'We may think that other leaves, similar in form to this one, were stitched together in order to make a book of testimonia. Each leaf may have dealt with a particular topic.' In the light of 4Q175, a single sheet which does deal with one topic, Falcetta's theory seems to me to be very plausible indeed.

---

[73] See Martin C. Albl, *"And Scripture Cannot be Broken": The Form and Function of the Early Christian Testimonia Collections* (Leiden: Brill, 1999), p. 20.

[74] J. A. Fitzmyer, *TS* 18 (1957) 513–37; reprinted in J. A. Fitzmyer, *Essays on the Semitic Background of the New Testament* (London: Chapman, 1971), pp. 59–89.

[75] G. Brooke, *Exegesis at Qumran: 4QFlorilegium in its Jewish Context* (Sheffield: JSOT, 1985).

[76] See C. D. Stanley, *Paul and the Language of Scripture* (Cambridge: Cambridge University Press, 1992), p. 76–7, and, more fully, his 'The Importance of 4Q Tanhumim (4Q176)', *RevQ* 15/60 (1992) 569–82.

[77] C. H. Roberts, 'Two Biblical Papyri in the John Rylands Library, Manchester', *BJRL* 20 (1936) 241–4; A. Falcetta, 'A Testimony Collection in Manchester: Papyrus Rylands Greek 460', *BJRL* 83 (2001) 3–19.

PRG 460 is most unlikely to have been the only early Christian written collection of Scriptural texts. Martin C. Albl has mounted an impressive cumulative argument for their existence in the early post-Easter period. He carefully distinguishes between *testimonia* collections 'which serve forensically to "prove" a certain point' and other collections of Scriptural passages used in the early church for a variety of purposes.[78] Albl provides plenty of Graeco-Roman and Jewish evidence for the popularity of written excerpts of valued writings,[79] and discusses at length the evidence for *testimonia* collections in the patristic era and in the NT writings themselves.

Two strands of Albl's argument are especially important for the present discussion. He sets out criteria which allow the detection of *written* collections of Scriptural passages as follows: '(1) quotations that deviate considerably from known scriptural texts (LXX or LXX recensions, MT), especially in a Christianizing direction; (2) composite quotations; (3) false attributions; (4) use of the same series of texts in independent authors; (5) editorial or interpretive comments indicative of a collection; (6) evident lack of awareness of the biblical context of a quotation; (7) use of the same exegetical comments in independent authors'.[80]

Timothy Lim has recently defended a similar view. He notes that, in the citation of Isaiah in Luke 4.18-19, parts of Isa. 61.1 and 58.6 are quoted *in that order*. 'It is possible that Jesus read the verses of Isa. 61 and 58 not from a biblical text of Isaiah, but from a collection of excerpts used in liturgy.'[81] Lim's main point stands even if one is less confident that Luke 4.18-19 goes back to Jesus.

If *written* collections of Scriptural excerpts existed among followers of Jesus even before Paul wrote I Thessalonians c. AD 50, they would have been in one of the forms of notebook referred to above. Since *testimonia* and Scriptural excerpts played such an important role in the very earliest Christian communities, the familiar notebook or 'page' format used is likely to have been retained and developed as a form of codex for more substantial writings *rather than the roll*.[82] So we have one ready explanation for the *initial* early Christian use of the codex format.

---

[78] Albl, *'And Scripture Cannot be Broken'*, p. 6.
[79] See also the examples noted by Stanley, *Paul and the Language of Scripture*, pp. 74–6.
[80] Albl, *'And Scripture cannot be Broken'*, p. 66.
[81] Lim, *Holy Scripture in the Qumran Communities*, p. 55.
[82] So too Albl, *'And Scripture Cannot be Broken'*, pp. 98–9. My own earlier comments along very similar lines published in 1997 are included above, p. 84. Albl and I seem to have reached the same conclusion independently. H. Y. Gamble also allows that the codex may first have been used by Christians for Scriptural *testimonia*, but claims that it was the collection of Paul's letters early in the second century (and probably earlier) which set the standard for use of the codex; *Books and Readers*, p. 65.

Interest in early Christian use of Scripture has intensified in recent decades in the wake of the publication of the Dead Sea Scrolls. But few scholars have paused to ask about the means by which the very earliest post-Easter followers of Jesus gained and retained their knowledge of the Scriptures, which they reinterpreted so creatively in the light of their new convictions.[83] Access to rolls of Scripture in synagogues was unlikely to have been granted readily to many. No doubt favourite passages of Scripture were eagerly memorized and transmitted orally, but a 'pan-oral' theory takes no account of the prevalence of written excerpts of 'classical' writings in the Graeco-Roman, Jewish, and early Christian worlds.

8.5.2 Drafts and copies of letters

In one of his letters to his friend Paetus, Cicero writes as follows (46 BC): 'I have just taken my place at table at three o'clock, and am scribbling a copy of this letter to you in my notebook' ('ad te harum exemplum in codicillis exeravi') (*Ad Fam.* 9.26.1).[84] The content of the letter is not especially noteworthy, yet Cicero keeps a copy in a notebook as a matter of course. This was by no means unusual.

If copies of Paul's letters were kept in notebook format, as were Cicero's, then there would have been a powerful incentive to use the developed form of the notebook, the codex, in the first collection of the letters, which was probably made by a co-worker shortly after Paul's death.[85] For a collection of the letters made in, say, AD 85, a codex would have been more suitable than a roll, for a standard-sized roll would not have held all the letters.[86]

Drafts of more formal 'literary' letters were usually transferred from notebooks to parchment or papyrus rolls. But this may not have happened with Paul's letters – perhaps not even with his more substantial letters. Paul and his colleagues were engaged in frenetic missionary work and may have had other priorities. I think that we have to consider the possibility that at least some of Paul's letters originally circulated in a notebook format rather

---

[83] Stanley, *Paul and the Language of Scripture*, pp. 74–5, is an exception. He suggests that, as Paul 'came across passages that promised to be useful later on, presumably he copied them down onto his handy wax tablet, or perhaps even directly onto a loose sheet of parchment'.

[84] I owe this reference to Richards, *The Secretary* (above, n. 57), p. 165 n. 169. His thorough examination of the primary evidence for the conventions of letter-writing shows that 'copies of letters were a desirable thing in the ancient world' (p. 6). See also David Trobisch, *Paul's Letter Collection: Tracing the Origins* (Minneapolis: Fortress, 1994), pp. 56–7.

[85] Trobisch, *Letter Collection*, argues that Paul himself collected together Romans, 1–2 Corinthians, and Galatians, edited them, and sent them as a unit to friends in Ephesus. Although many interesting points are made, the theory fails to convince.

[86] So too Gamble, *Books and Readers*, pp. 62–3.

than on rolls. Given the widespread use of notebooks referred to above, it is very probable that Paul and his co-workers and secretaries (and other early Christian letter-writers) used notebooks for preliminary notes and drafts and for copies of letters, as well as for collections of Scriptural texts.[87]

Although there is now greater willingness to allow that Paul's use of a secretary is relevant to authorship questions,[88] use of notebooks is rarely considered. I think that it is relevant to discussion of several of the complex problems thrown up by Paul's letters. For example, how are we to account for the juxtaposition in Ephesians of both Pauline and non-Pauline strands? John Muddiman has recently reopened this question by proposing that an authentic Pauline letter (to the Laodiceans) was subsequently edited and expanded, with the aim of adjusting the Pauline tradition to the situation prevailing at its time and place of composition.[89] Perhaps this attractive theory is made even more plausible if we bear in mind the possibility that the original, authentic letter only ever existed in draft form in a notebook – a draft which was expanded at a later point by one of Paul's co-workers or close followers.

8.5.3   *Jesus traditions?*

Were Jesus traditions also transmitted, at least in part, in some form of notebook? Even to pose the question is to court derision from scholars wedded to the view that, right up to the time Mark wrote his gospel, Jesus traditions were always transmitted orally, and only orally.[90] However, occasionally voices to the contrary have been raised; this is certainly a question which should be reopened.

In 1950 the respected Jewish specialist on the rabbinic writings, S. Lieberman, claimed that Jesus' disciples wrote down the sayings of Jesus:

Now the Jewish disciples of Jesus, in accordance with the general rabbinic practice, wrote the sayings of their master, pronounced not in the form of a book to be published, but as notes in their *pinakes*, codices, or in their note-books (or in

---

[87] So also Richards, *The Secretary*, pp. 161–5, 191, and K. P. Donfried, 'Paul as ΣΚΗΝΟΠΟΙΟΣ and the Use of the Codex', in his *Paul, Thessalonica and Early Christianity* (London: T. & T. Clark, 2002), pp. 293–304.

[88] See especially Richards, *The Secretary, passim.*

[89] John Muddiman, *The Epistle to the Ephesians*, Black's NT Commentaries (London and New York: Continuum, 2001). A translation of the tentatively reconstructed authentic letter is printed as Appendix B, pp. 302–5.

[90] For a vigorous rejection of Werner Kelber's claim that Mark's first written gospel was intended to supersede oral tradition by the creation of a literary 'counterform' see J. Halverson, 'Oral and Written Gospel: A Critique of Werner Kelber', *NTS* 40 (1994) 180–95.

private small rolls). They did this because otherwise they would have transgressed the law.[91]

In making this suggestion Lieberman set a cat among the form-critical pigeons – but the pigeons simply looked the other way. There were, however, two notable exceptions. In 1964 Birger Gerhardsson re-examined the rabbinic evidence in the light of Lieberman's comments. He confirmed that in rabbinic circles written notes were used to facilitate the private repetition and the maintenance of knowledge of the oral Torah. Teachers and pupils used writing tablets and notebooks – and this may have been more usual in Palestine than in Babylon, perhaps under the influence of Hellenistic schools of rhetoric and philosophy.[92] Gerhardsson's book was misread and criticized strongly in some circles, but a rehabilitation is now under way, with the strong support of Jacob Neusner's extended Preface to the 1998 second edition.[93] His general point concerning the use of notebooks in some rabbinic circles is based on solid textual evidence, especially the reference in m. Kelim 24.7 to three kinds of writing tablets.[94]

C. H. Roberts and T. C. Skeat also drew on Lieberman's comments and appealed to m. Kelim 24.7: 'three kinds of writings tablets, wax, ivory, "and those of papyrus"'. 'It is possible, therefore, that papyrus tablets were used to record the Oral Law as pronounced by Jesus, and that these tablets might have developed into the primitive form of codex.'[95] This supposed reference to papyrus notebooks became a linchpin in their preferred explanation for the Christian adoption of the codex. However, Colette Sirat has undermined their theory by showing that Lieberman misinterpreted the rabbinic references to *pinkasim*: they were not made of papyrus, but of wood.[96]

M. Kelim 24.7 suggests that it is highly likely that the first followers of Jesus were familiar with notebooks made from wood, both wax stylus tablets

---

[91] S. Lieberman, *Hellenism in Jewish Palestine*, 2nd edn (New York: Jewish Theological Seminary, 1962), p. 203.

[92] B. Gerhardsson, *Memory and Manuscript: Oral Tradition and Written Transmission in Rabbinic Judaism and Early Christianity* (Lund: Gleerup, 1964), pp. 29, 157–63.

[93] B. Gerhardsson, *Memory and Manuscript*, 2nd edn (Grand Rapids: Eerdmans, 1998), pp. xxv–xlvi.

[94] Herbert Danby's translation of m. Kelim 24.7 is as follows: 'There are three kinds of writing-tablet: that of papyrus, which is susceptible to *midras*-uncleannness; that which has a receptacle for wax, which is susceptible to corpse-uncleanness; and that which is polished, which is not susceptible to any uncleanness.' *The Mishnah* (Oxford: Oxford University Press, 1933).

[95] Roberts and Skeat, *Birth*, p. 59.

[96] Colette Sirat, 'Le Livre hébreu dans les premiers siècles de notre ère: le témoinage des textes', in J. Lemaire and E. van Balberghe, eds., *Calames et cahiers: mélanges de codicologie et de paléographie offerts à Léon Gilissen* (Brussels: Centre d'étude des manuscrits, 1985), pp. 169–76; reprinted in *Les Débuts du codex*, pp. 115–24.

and ink leaf tablets, and perhaps ivory as well. As noted above, an example of an ink leaf tablet has been found in a cave near the Dead Sea, and dated to AD 134-5. I am not for a moment suggesting that Jesus traditions did not circulate orally, but those traditions were first transmitted in Herodian Palestine, and we now have a mountain of evidence gathered together by A. R. Millard, which shows that writing was widespread at all levels of society.[97] Millard's conclusion, based on extensive knowledge of writing in the Near East generally, is surely sound: 'far more weight than has been allowed should be given to the role of writing in preserving information about Jesus of Nazareth from his lifetime onwards and so in forming the Gospel tradition'.[98]

There are important implications for the Q hypothesis which I accept as the most plausible explanation of the extensive non-Marcan agreements between Matthew and Luke. The consensus view at present is that Q was a written document drawn on by both Matthew and Luke. But supporters of this version of the Q hypothesis always shuffle when confronted with the very considerable *variation* in the level of agreement between Matthew and Luke in alleged Q passages. In some passages the level of agreement is as high as 90 per cent, and even almost 100 per cent in shorter sections (compare, for example, Matt. 11.2-27 and Luke 7.18-35; 10.12-15, 21-2). But in other passages agreement is as low as 10 per cent (e.g. Matt. 25.14-30 and Luke 19.12-27).[99] If we take seriously the possibility that Jesus traditions were transmitted both orally and in written form, then an explanation is to hand. Q passages where there is close agreement may come from a written document or from more than one set of notes; where the level of agreement is low, oral traditions may have been used.[100]

Ulrich Luz and his pupil Migaku Sato have made a similar proposal. Luz suggests that Q traditions may have been collected in a rather large notebook 'bound together with strings on the margin. It permitted an insertion of new leaves at any time. The Gospel of Mark, however, was a solidly bound codex and therefore a literary work which for this reason continued to be handed down even after its expansion by Matthew.'[101]

The widely held view that the followers of Jesus were either illiterate or deliberately spurned the use of notes and notebooks for recording and

[97] Millard, *Reading and Writing* (above, n. 29), pp. 84–131.   [98] Ibid., pp. 228–9.
[99] See S. Hultgren, *Narrative Elements in the Double Tradition* (Berlin: de Gruyter, 2002), pp. 325–30 for a fresh discussion.
[100] See now ibid., p. 328.
[101] U. Luz, *Matthew 1–7* (Edinburgh: T. & T. Clark, 1989), pp. 46–7. See also Migaku Sato, *Q und Prophetie. Studien zur Gattungs- und Traditionsgeschichte der Quelle Q*, WUNT 2. Reihe, Vol. 29 (Tübingen: Mohr, 1988), pp. 72–7.

transmitting Jesus traditions needs to be abandoned. Oral and written traditions were not like oil and water.[102] They could exist side by side; orally transmitted traditions could be written down by the recipients – and written traditions could be memorized and passed on orally.

8.6 CONCLUSIONS

The first followers of Jesus will have been familiar with several forms of notebooks, whether they were in Judaea, in Galilee, or in eastern Mediterranean cities. So it is natural to suppose that notebooks will have been used for *testimonia* and for other collections of excerpts of Scriptural passages, for drafts and copies of letters, and for short collections of sayings of Jesus, perhaps grouped thematically. A given Christian community may have been familiar with all these forms of written traditions in notebook format. But, once Christian scribes discovered how useful the 'page' format was, it very quickly became the norm for copies of Paul's letters and of the gospels, and for Christian copies of the Scriptures.

When did Christian addiction to the codex format *first* begin to take hold (my stage one)? In the past I have assumed, along with most scholars, that this happened at the end of the first or early in the second century. The corollary would then be that in the first post-Easter decades Christians made considerable use of notebooks as sketched above, then rolls for both letters and gospels written between, say, AD 50 and 90, before switching to the codex early in the second century.

For two main reasons this scenario has seemed plausible to many. (1) The first strong evidence for the use of the codex for writings more substantial than notes or drafts emerges only towards the end of the first century (Martial; P. Petaus 30), some decades after the first Christian writings began to circulate. Christian scribes are more likely to have borrowed the new format from their non-Christian counterparts than vice versa. (2) At least some New Testament writings seem to have been designed for rolls. Luke's Gospel and his Acts would have fitted neatly into two 'standard-sized' rolls, and the prefaces to both writings strongly suggest that this was Luke's intention. Hebrews is a sophisticated writing, well suited to the roll format.

However, I am now much less confident about the consensus view. Once big bang theories are abandoned, as I have argued above, a gradual transition

---

[102] See J. Halverson's vigorous protest against W. Kelber's 'almost metaphysical split between speech and writing'. 'Oral and Written Gospel', 180–95.

from notebook to codex is easier to envisage than the alternative, i.e. notebook to roll, and then to codex very shortly afterwards.

Martial and the writers of P. Petaus 30 may well have had predecessors;
in neither case is there even a hint that the codex is a recent invention.
So use of the codex in the middle of the first century is perfectly possible.
Christian and non-Christian scribes may have begun to experiment with
the codex quite independently.

Perhaps the evangelist Mark did write his gospel in an early form of codex.
We would then have to reconsider the possibility that both the opening and
the ending of Mark's Gospel have been lost, for this is much more likely
to have happened to an early version of the codex than to a roll.[103] The
autograph of Luke's more sophisticated 'literary' gospel may have been in
the roll format, but, by the time the first copies of Luke's Gospel were made,
Christian addiction to the codex may have begun to take hold in earnest.

The speed with which the new format was adopted universally within
early Christianity is astonishing: I have noted above a set of factors which
encouraged and strengthened precocious use of the codex. The deployment
and development of *nomina sacra*, the method of abbreviation used for
'God', 'Jesus', and other related terms, is a related question which cannot
be discussed here.[104] Taken together, addiction to the codex and addiction
to the use of *nomina sacra* suggest that Christian communities around the
eastern Mediterranean were in closer touch with one another than is usually
supposed to have been the case.

---

[103] J. K. Elliott claims that Mark 1.1–3 contains too many non-Marcan features to stem from the
hand of the evangelist. He suggests that both the original opening and ending of Mark were lost
shortly after this gospel circulated in codex form at the beginning of the second century. The
present opening, Mark 1.1–3, and the present conclusion, Mark 16.9–20, were added in the second
century. Elliott notes that the outer leaves of a codex are particularly vulnerable to damage or loss.
He implies that Mark was written on a roll before being transferred to a codex. 'Mark 1.1–3 – A
Later Addition to the Gospel', *NTS* 46 (2000) 584–8. N. Clayton Croy's stimulating book, *The
Mutilation of Mark's Gospel* (Nashville: Abingdon, 2003), reached me while my typescript was in
the press. Croy argues that Mark may have existed in single-quire codex form 'at a very early stage,
perhaps even in the autograph, and that damage to the autograph (or *perhaps* to an early copy
from which all manuscripts derive) resulted in simultaneous loss of the first and last leaves. It is
possible (although I think it less likely) that Mark was originally composed on a scroll and that it
lost both beginning and ending in separate accidents' (p. 168; see also pp. 149–52). Croy's cautious
conclusion is broadly in line with my own comments above; he implies that Martial's codices may
have encouraged Christian scribes to use the codex format for the autograph and/or earliest copies
of Mark's Gospel (p. 150).

[104] See now C. M. Tuckett's thorough discussion with full bibliographical references, '"Nomina Sacra":
Yes and No?', in J.-M. Auwers and H. J. de Jonge, eds., *The Biblical Canons* (Leuven: Peeters, 2003),
pp. 431–58. See also A. R. Millard, 'Ancient Abbreviations and the *Nomina Sacra*', in C. Eyre, A.
Leahy, and L. M. Leahy, eds., *The Unbroken Reed: Studies in the Culture and Heritage of Ancient
Egypt* (London: The Egypt Exploration Society, 1994), pp. 221–6; L. W. Hurtado, 'The Origin of
the *Nomina Sacra*: A Proposal', *JBL* 117 (1998) 655–73.

There is a further consideration which has a direct bearing on the early reception of the gospels. We need not suppose that, once the codex began to be used for early Christian writings, notebooks with Jesus traditions (or with *testimonia* or collections of Scriptural passages) immediately ceased to be used. Quintilian speaks of seeing Cicero's own notes for some of his speeches, which were still in circulation more than a century after the author's death![105] So why should we not suppose that notebooks with Jesus traditions continued to be used even after copies of individual gospels began to circulate? Christian communities which did not have a copy of a full Gospel may have had to make do with parchment or papyrus notebooks for some time. So Christian missionaries and teachers may well have continued to use parchment or papyrus notebooks with Jesus traditions (and OT passages) *alongside* copies of the gospels and, of course, oral traditions. If so, we should not be surprised at the varied ways OT and Jesus traditions are cited or alluded to in the apostolic fathers and in the writings of Justin Martyr.[106]

This chapter opened with Sir Frederic Kenyon's observation that the Chester Beatty Biblical papyri revolutionize our knowledge of the early history of the codex form of book. Perhaps we may dare to hope that further discoveries of manuscripts as important as the Chester Beatty Biblical papyri will extend our knowledge of the transition from the roll to the codex-book format, and in particular of the reasons why Christian scribes were the first to become addicted to the codex. For the time being we do have enough new evidence to suggest that several widely held assumptions concerning the transmission of traditions in early Christianity need to be reconsidered.

---

[105] Quintilian, *Inst. Or.* x.7.30–1.
[106] For further discussion, see section 2.9 of Chapter 2 and Chapter 4 above.

CHAPTER 9

What are the gospels? New evidence from papyri?

In recent decades the question, 'What are the gospels?' has been discussed from three perspectives. I shall refer to two briefly, before concentrating on the third.

In discussion of this question, pride of place must always go the literary genre of the gospels. What kind of writings are we dealing with? Histories, religious novels, biographies, early Christian sermons in narrative dress, or catechetical handbooks? The very first step in the interpretation of any writing, whether ancient or modern, is to establish its literary genre.[1] If we make a mistake about the literary genre of the gospels, interpretation will be skewed or even misguided. A decision about the genre of a work and the discovery of its meaning are inextricably inter-related; different types of text require different types of interpretation.[2]

In this chapter I do not propose to consider yet again whether or not the gospels are biographies. I have had my say on that topic more than once.[3] Following intensive recent discussion, broad agreement has been reached. The gospels are now widely considered to be a sub-set of the broad ancient literary genre of βίοι, biographies. Even if the evangelists were largely ignorant of the tradition of Greek and Roman βίοι, that is how the gospels were received and listened to in the first decades after their composition.[4]

The question, 'What are the gospels?' has recently been given an unexpected answer: they were intended to be writings *for all Christians*. For

---

[1] Cf. E. D. Hirsch, *Validity in Interpretation* (New Haven: Yale, 1967), p. 76: 'All understanding of verbal meaning is necessarily genre-bound.'

[2] On this see A. Fowler, *Kinds of Literature* (Oxford: Oxford University Press, 1982), p. 38; Hirsch, *Validity*, p. 113.

[3] I first tackled this topic when it was right out of fashion. See G. N. Stanton, *Jesus of Nazareth in New Testament Preaching* (Cambridge: Cambridge University Press, 1974), pp. 117–36; more recently, *The Gospels and Jesus*, 2nd edn (Oxford: Oxford University Press, 2002), pp. 13–18.

[4] See especially R. A. Burridge, *What are the Gospels? A Comparison with Graeco-Roman Biography* (Cambridge: Cambridge University Press, 1992; 2nd edn Grand Rapids: Eerdmans, 2004); D. Frickenschmidt, *Evangelium als Biographie. Die vier Evangelien im Rahmen antiker Erzählungskunst* (Tübingen and Basle: A. Francke, 1997).

decades now most writers on the gospels have accepted as axiomatic that the four evangelists all wrote for their own particular Christian communities. However, Richard Bauckham and a number of British scholars have offered a 'new paradigm':[5] the evangelists did not write for one Christian community, or even for a cluster of Christian communities, but for *all* Christians everywhere. Widely held assumptions concerning the intentions of the evangelists and the audiences they envisaged have been confronted head on.

I welcome some of the essayists' concerns, but not quite unreservedly.[6] I have protested more than once against the failure to appreciate that the gospels are not letters directed to the problems of a particular early Christian community: the primary intention of the evangelists is to set out the story of Jesus of Nazareth. In recent years I have become increasingly uneasy about the constructs, '*the* Q community', '*the* Matthean community', '*the* Johannine community', and so on.[7] However, firm new evidence for the actual circulation of the first copies of the gospels is not set out in any of the essays edited by Bauckham. Equally conspicuous by its absence is the evidence of the earliest surviving copies of the gospels, evidence which will concern us in this chapter.

I intend to take up the question, 'What are the gospels?' from a third angle, which deserves more attention than it has received. I am convinced that the early papyri of the gospels can make a contribution to this question. I concede immediately that the contribution is likely to be limited, for the earliest papyri have survived by chance in only one geographical area, and thus they may not be representative of all the early copies of the gospels. Nonetheless, here we have evidence which has grown significantly in the last few years, and which has been overlooked all too often. In the impressive array of major commentaries, as well as in the continuing flood of monographs, next to nothing is said about the earliest surviving papyri, even though their importance for the textual traditions of the gospels can hardly be overestimated.

In this chapter I shall discuss the earliest papyri fragments of the gospels, with special reference to the Oxyrhynchus papyri published between 1997

---

[5] R. J. Bauckham, ed., *The Gospels for All Christians: Rethinking the Gospel Audiences* (Grand Rapids: Eerdmans, 1998).

[6] See P. F. Esler, 'Community and Gospel in Early Christianity: A Response to Richard Bauckham', *SJT* (1998) 235–48 and R. Bauckham's reply in the same issue (pp. 249–53); David Sim, 'The Gospels for all Christians? A Response to Richard Bauckham', *JSNT* 84 (2001) 3–27.

[7] See G. N. Stanton, 'Revisiting Matthew's Communities,' in *SBL Seminar Papers 1994*, ed. E. H. Lovering Jr. (Atlanta: Scholars Press, 1994), pp. 9–23.

and 1999.[8] These papyri force us to reconsider an influential answer to the question: what are the gospels? On this view, a sharp contrast is drawn between the carefully produced contemporary copies of Jewish writings on rolls and early copies of the gospels in codices. Whereas Jewish rolls are said to have been written with care in a formal hand, the gospels are said to be the 'workaday', 'utilitarian', 'downmarket' handbooks of an inward-looking sect. I hope to show that this differentiation is unwarranted.

9.1   THE GOSPELS AS UTILITARIAN HANDBOOKS

Several Greek palaeographers have been more astute than New Testament specialists in their use of the evidence of the earliest copies of the gospels.[9] In his important Schweich lectures, *Manuscript, Society and Belief in Early Christian Egypt*, C. H. Roberts broke new ground.[10] As his title implies, Roberts shows how early Christian manuscripts shed light on the social and religious setting of early Christianity in Egypt. I am convinced that Roberts was asking the right questions, but the recently published papyri force us to modify several of his conclusions – conclusions which have influenced a number of New Testament scholars.

   First I must sketch the consensus view, of which the palaeographers C. H. Roberts and Sir Eric Turner[11] are the most distinguished proponents.[12] In their view, manuscripts written in Greek in the early centuries of Christian era can be divided into two groups: 'bookhands' and 'documentary hands'. Bookhands were usually used for literary works, but occasionally for other

---

[8] E. W. Handley, U. Wartenberg, et al., eds., *The Oxyrhynchus Papyri*, Vol. LXIV (London: Egypt Exploration Society for the British Academy, 1997); M. W. Haslam et al., eds., *The Oxyrhynchus Papyri*, Vol. LXV (1998); N. Gomis et al., eds., *The Oxyrhynchus Papyri*, Vol. LXVI (1999). For discussion of the textual evidence of these papyri, see J. K. Elliott, 'Five New Papyri of the New Testament', *NovT* 41 (1999) 209–13, and 'Seven Recently Published New Testament Fragments from Oxyrhynchus', *NovT* 42 (2000) 209–13; P. M. Head, 'Some Recently Published NT Papyri from Oxyrhynchus: An Overview and Preliminary Assessment', *TB* 51 (2000) 1–16.

[9] This section and the following one have been adapted and revised from part of my 'The Early Reception of Matthew's Gospel', in D. E. Aune, ed., *The Gospel of Matthew in Current Study* (Grand Rapids: Eerdmans, 2001), pp. 42–52.

[10] C. H. Roberts, *Manuscript, Society and Belief in Early Christian Egypt* (London: Oxford University Press for the British Academy, 1979).

[11] E. G. Turner, *The Typology of the Early Codex* (Philadelphia: University of Pennsylvania Press, 1977). See also E. G. Turner, *Greek Manuscripts of the Ancient World* (Oxford: Oxford University Press, 1971; 2nd edn, 1987); G. Cavallo and H. Maehler, *Greek Bookhands of the Early Byzantine Period, AD 300–800*, Bulletin Supplement 47 (London: University of London Institute of Classical Studies, 1987).

[12] I cannot claim to be a palaeographer myself, and stand in awe of the specialists whose publications I have consulted. I have looked carefully at the plates of the papyri discussed below: the general characteristics of the styles of handwriting used seem to me to be clear. However, on palaeographical questions, I have quoted the judgements of the specialists, not my own.

kinds of writings. The manuscripts were carefully written by very skilled scribes, often by slaves. Bookhands use upright, independent letters (not ligatures), often with serifs; they are usually bilinear, i.e. individual letters rarely protrude beyond two imaginary horizontal lines on the papyrus or parchment. Cursive forms are not used. Manuscripts prepared carefully in this way were more expensive; they were used by the more educated elite. The 'classic' examples of Christian manuscripts in this style are Codex Sinaiticus and Codex Vaticanus from the fourth century. Sinaiticus is a splendid 'pulpit edition' of the whole Greek Bible; Vaticanus is a 'pulpit edition' of the gospels, Acts, and most of the Pauline corpus.[13]

Documentary hands were used for workaday documents of all kinds. They were written rapidly, usually with long lines, and with little concern for bilinearity. Some individual letters were joined together (i.e. ligatures were often used). Manuscripts written in this way were often used in a business setting, or for private use. In comparison with 'bookhands', they were 'downmarket'.

However, it is important to note that there are literary texts which are written 'cursively' in documentary hands, and there are documents in which the letters are generally formed separately, with bilinearity. A copy of Aristotle's Ἀθηναίων Πολιτεία (*On the Constitution of Athens*) on a roll from the end of the first century is a good example of the former. It has obviously been written very quickly, with little regard for the appearance of the text. In places, up to five letters are joined together in a single sequence. It is written on the back of four rolls, the rectos of which have agricultural accounts dated A D 78/9. Presumably this was a private rather than a library copy of Aristotle. A private letter dated to c. A D 170, P. Oxy. 2192, is a good example of a document written in a bookhand in a competent professional manner by a skilled scribe. A hastily written postscript in documentary cursive style has been added by the author, who had presumably dictated the letter.[14]

In his Schweich lectures, C. H. Roberts contrasted sharply the 'hieratic elegance of the Graeco-Jewish rolls of the Law' with the 'workaday appearance of the first Christian codices (whether of OT or Christian writings)' (p. 19). With a few exceptions, Christian manuscripts are 'based on . . . the model of documents, not that of the Greek classical manuscripts nor on that of the Graeco-Jewish tradition' (p. 20). Roberts concluded that, if Christian

---

[13] For an important fresh discussion of the origin of Sinaiticus and Vaticanus, see T. C. Skeat, 'The Codex Sinaiticus, the Codex Vaticanus, and Constantine', *JTS* 50 (2000) 583–625.

[14] For the two examples, compare Plates 60 and 68 in E. G. Turner, *Greek Manuscripts*, 2nd edn, pp. 102 and 114.

communities are faintly mirrored in their books, they would seem 'to have been composed not so much of intellectuals or the wealthy as of ordinary men of middle or lower classes' (p. 25).

In 1977 Sir Eric Turner made similar observations in his now classic study of papyrus codices of the second or third centuries. He noted that it is not easy to find examples of calligraphy among papyrus codices of this period. 'Their handwriting is in fact often of an informal and workaday type, fairly quickly written, serviceable rather than beautiful, of value to a man interested in the content of what he is reading rather than its presentation.' Turner then lists some examples, including the majority of the Chester Beatty codices. 'These give the impression of being "utility" books; margins are small, lines usually long'; their status is second-class in comparison with the contemporary papyrus roll.[15]

The views of these two giants among palaeographers have been echoed by several New Testament scholars. In 1997 Harry Gamble noted that a bookhand is rarely found in Christian texts before the fourth century; with Sinaiticus and Vaticanus 'a barrier was broken': 'never before had Christian books been so fine'.[16] Until that time, Christians had little aesthetic regard for their literature, and they do not seem to have had a cultic attitude towards their books. In contrast, Jewish Greek manuscripts are better written: they 'usually display an even, formal script with tendencies not only towards a bookhand but toward a somewhat decorated style with footed and serifed letters'.[17]

Similar comments have been made recently by Loveday Alexander[18] and by Bart Ehrman.[19] Hence it is not an exaggeration to claim that the C. H. Roberts–E. G. Turner view has become the consensus. It will be apparent that it undermines, at least in part, the contention that the gospels are a subset of Graeco-Roman biography, for the latter was not normally second-class and downmarket. And it places an even firmer question mark against various literary approaches to the gospels which have become fashionable in recent decades. Are the evangelists likely to have been rather sophisticated writers who used a whole gamut of literary techniques, if the earliest copies

---

[15] Turner, *Typology*, p. 37.
[16] Harry Y. Gamble, *Books and Readers in the Early Church: A History of Early Christian Texts* (New Haven and London: Yale University Press, 1995), p. 80.
[17] Ibid., pp. 78–9.
[18] Loveday Alexander, 'Ancient Book Production and the Circulation of the Gospels', in Bauckham, *The Gospels for All Christians*, pp. 71–111.
[19] Bart Ehrman, 'The Text as Window: New Testament Manuscripts and the Social History of Early Christianity', in B. D. Ehrman and M. W. Holmes, eds., *The Text of the New Testament in Contemporary Research* (Grand Rapids: Eerdmans, 1995), pp. 372–5.

of their work were decidedly workaday and utilitarian? Were the evangelists' literary skills not appreciated by early copyists? Or were early Christian communities not able to afford to produce copies of their writings at the level of sophistication they deserved?

We do not need to trouble ourselves with such questions, for the recently published papyri force us to modify the consensus view. I shall set out below basic details of what are almost certainly the earliest surviving papyri of the four gospels.[20] The papyri are all from no later than the middle of the third century, though papyrologists are always rightly wary about dating precisely what are often very fragmentary writings. I shall set out the papyri according to their 𝔓 number (as used in modern editions of the Greek text); this corresponds closely to the order in which the papyri were first published.[21]

9.2 EARLY PAPYRI OF MATTHEW

We now have seven papyri of Matthew which were probably written before the middle of the third century.

(1) 𝔓1 (= P. Oxy. 2; 1907). This small fragment of Matthew's genealogy (Matt. 1:1-9; 14-20) is usually dated to the early third century. The hand is generally bilinear, with only a few ligatures. It is at least as close to a book-hand as to a documentary hand. When this fragment was first published in 1898, it was considered to be 'the oldest known manuscript of any part of the NT'.[22]

(2) 𝔓45 (= P. Chester Beatty I; 1933). This codex, which is usually dated to the first half of the third century, contains parts of the final chapters of Matthew (Matt. 20:24-32; 21:13-19; 25:41-26:39), as well as parts of Mark, Luke, John, and Acts. The first editor noted that the codex is written by a competent scribe, but without calligraphic pretensions, in a small and very clear hand; the letters have a decided slope to the right, as opposed to the uprightness generally found in Roman hands of the first two centuries.[23]

---

[20] For full details of the original publication of the fragments, photographic plates, and bibliography, see J. K. Elliott, *A Bibliography of Greek New Testament Manuscripts* (Cambridge: Cambridge University Press, 1989; 2nd edn, 2000). See also K. Aland, ed., *Kurzgefasste Liste der griechischen Handschriften des Neuen Testaments*, 2nd edn (Berlin: de Gruyter, 1994).

[21] For fuller details of (1)–(5) in my list, see K. Aland, *Repertorium der griechischen christlichen Papyri*, Vol. I: *Biblische Papyri* (Berlin and New York: De Gruyter, 1976).

[22] *Oxyrhynchus Papyri*, ed. Bernard P. Grenfell and Arthur S. Hunt, Vol. I (London: Egypt Exploration Fund, 1898), p. 4. There is a good reproduction of this fragment as the frontispiece to this edition.

[23] F. G. Kenyon, ed., *The Chester Beatty Biblical Papyri*, Vol. II (London: Emery Walker, 1933), pp. viii–ix.

T. C. Skeat, the doyen of contemporary papyrologists, has recently observed that, in contrast to 𝔓64 + 𝔓67 + 𝔓4 ((4) below in this list of early Matthean papyri), 𝔓45 was 'not intended for liturgical use'.²⁴ In the opening pages of Chapter 8 above, attention was drawn to the significance of the publication of the Chester Beatty Biblical papyri by Sir Frederic Kenyon for the origin of the codex. However, it also has to be said that 𝔓45 has exercised too great an influence on studies of the handwriting of the early papyri. As we shall see, the hand of 𝔓45 is not the norm.

(3) 𝔓53 (Ann Arbor, University of Michigan, Inv. 6652; 1937). This small fragment of parts of Matt. 26:29-40 may date from the middle of the third century. The hand is described as 'semi-uncial', with upright symmetrical letters.²⁵

(4) 𝔓64 (Magdalen College, Oxford, Gr. 18; 1957) + 𝔓67 (P. Barcelona I; 1961). These fragments of Matthew 3, 5, and 26 are from the same codex as the more extensive fragments of Luke 1, 3, and 5 known as 𝔓4 (Paris, Bibliothèque nationale, Suppl. Gr. 1120, 1892). 𝔓64 was considered by its first editor, C. H. Roberts, to date from the end of the second century. In spite of the attempt of C. P. Thiede to date 𝔓64 and 𝔓67 to the first century, Roberts's dating is still generally accepted.²⁶ T. C. Skeat's theory that 𝔓64 + 𝔓67 + 𝔓4 are from the same four-gospel codex is winning wide support.²⁷

C. H. Roberts recognized that 𝔓64 was an early example of a Biblical uncial hand: 'a thorough-going literary production', i.e. in effect a predecessor of Codex Sinaiticus and Codex Vaticanus.²⁸ In a letter to me dated 30 March 1996 Skeat echoed Roberts's comment, and noted that the hand of 𝔓64 + 𝔓67 + 𝔓4 is quite clearly a literary one.

The significance of one of the codex's most striking features, its double columns, has not received adequate attention. The format of two columns to the page is rare in papyrus codices. This is the only example of a two-column Greek New Testament papyrus manuscript, though there are four

²⁴ T. C. Skeat, 'The Oldest Manuscript of the Four Gospels?', *NTS* 43 (1997) 1–34. See also pp. 71–5 above.
²⁵ See Aland, *Reportorium*, p. 283. A separate sheet, probably not from the same codex, contains parts of Acts 9.33–10.1.
²⁶ For full discussion and references, see G. N. Stanton, *Gospel Truth? New Light on Jesus and the Gospels* (London: HarperCollins, 1995), pp. 1–10. The 1997 paperback edition includes an Afterword with further references. For discussion of Thiede's rash theory, see the references given above on p. 73 n. 37.
²⁷ Skeat, 'The Oldest Manuscript', pp. 1–34.
²⁸ Roberts, *Manuscript*, p. 13. Skeat noted that in this codex 'organised text-division is now carried back well into the second century'. 'The Oldest Manuscript', p. 7.

examples in early fragments of OT papyri.²⁹ The narrow columns, with
only about fifteen letters in each column, would have assisted reading aloud
in the context of worship. So the use of two columns in 𝔓64 + 𝔓67 + 𝔓4
is almost certainly an indication of a high-class codex, a splendid 'pulpit
edition' intended for liturgical use.³⁰

There are several other indications that this codex was an *édition de luxe.*³¹
The codex was planned and executed meticulously: the skill of the scribe
in constructing it is most impressive. All these features indicate a most
handsome edition of the four gospels, which would have been expensive to
produce.

(5) 𝔓77 (= P. Oxy. 2683; 1968). This small fragment contains parts of
Matt. 23.30-9. Another fragment from the same page of Matthew 23 has
recently been published (P. Oxy. LXIV 4405 (1997)). The first editor of
P. Oxy. 2683, Peter Parsons, noted that 𝔓77 is 'delicately executed with a
fine pen', to be dated to the late second century, and hence among the
oldest New Testament texts.³² C. H. Roberts noted its elegant hand, and
its use of 'what was or became a standard system of chapter division as well
as punctuation and breathings'.³³

(6) 𝔓103 (= P. Oxy. 4403; 1997). This small fragment of Matthew 13 and
14 is dated by its editor, J. D. Thomas, to the late second or the early third
century.³⁴ In Thomas's opinion 'the hand is quite elegant, with noticeable
hooks at the top of most hastas, and occasional serifs elsewhere'. The hand
is so similar to P. Oxy. 4405 = 𝔓77 ((5) above) that Thomas allows the
possibility that they may be from the same codex, though he concludes
that it is 'safest to treat the papyri as from two different codices'.

(7) 𝔓104 (= P. Oxy. 4404; 1997). J. D. Thomas considers that we may
assign this fragment of Matthew 21 'with some confidence to the second half
of the second century, while not wishing to exclude altogether a slightly
earlier or a slightly later date'.³⁵ This cautious judgement is a mark not
of indecisiveness, but of the difficulty papyrologists have in dating small
fragments. Thomas notes that the hand is very carefully written, with

²⁹ See E. G. Turner's list of papyrus codices written in two columns, *Typology*, p. 36.
³⁰ Cf. ibid., pp. 36–7. J. van Haelst, *Catalogue des papyrus littéraires juifs et chrétiens*, Papyrologie I (Paris: Publications de la Sorbonne, 1976), no. 336, even says that this is the oldest example of a codex with two columns; presumably he means the oldest *Biblical* codex, though, in the light of Turner's list, this is a doubtful claim.
³¹ This is T. C. Skeat's phrase, 'The Oldest Manuscript', p. 26.
³² P. J. Parsons, in *The Oxyrhynchus Papyri*, Vol. XXXIV (1968).
³³ Roberts, *Manuscript*, p. 23.
³⁴ J. D. Thomas, in Handley et al., *The Oxyrhynchus Papyri*, Vol. LXIV, pp. 5–6.
³⁵ J. D. Thomas, in *The Oxyrhynchus Papyri*, Vol. LXIV, p. 8.

extensive use of serifs; bilinearity is strictly observed. Once again Thomas refers to the hand as 'elegant'.

In formulating what I have dubbed above 'the consensus view', C. H. Roberts drew on a list of what he considered in 1970 to be the ten earliest Christian Biblical papyri and the four earliest Christian non-Biblical papyri.[36] Roberts emphasized that, with three exceptions, 'there is no calligraphic hand in the group'.[37] In ten cases out of fourteen, Roberts detected 'basically a documentary hand'; these earliest papyri might be described as 'reformed documentary'.[38] The three exceptions were (4) and (5) in my list above, along with P. Oxy. I, 1, one of the three Greek fragments of the Gospel of Thomas.

In the list above of the seven earliest papyri of Matthew's Gospel, (4) and (5) are not, as C. H. Roberts supposed, exceptions to the general pattern of 'reformed documentary' hands: they are the rule! The recent publication of (6) and (7) has altered the picture very considerably: four of the earliest seven papyri of Matthew are at least as close to 'bookhands' as they are to 'reformed documentary' hands. It is worth noting that, even though dating papyri is a skilled art rather than a science, the more literary hands among the seven (my (4), (5), (6), and (7)) have the strongest claims to be the earliest of the group.

The fact that four of the seven earliest surviving papyri of Matthew are carefully written in an elegant hand is significant, but it is of course possible that future publication of further papyri may spring further surprises. My main point is that the consensus view now needs to be modified: the earliest surviving copies of the gospels present a much more diverse picture than recent scholarship has allowed. The seven earliest papyri of Matthew suggest that this gospel was used both in private and in public settings. Matthew's Gospel was not considered by some of those who copied it and used it in the second half of the second century to be of 'second-class' status, quite without literary pretensions.

9.3 EARLY PAPYRI OF JOHN

The provisional conclusions set out in the preceding three paragraphs now need to be tested against the evidence of the early papyri of John's Gospel.

---

[36] C. H. Roberts, 'Books in the Graeco-Roman World', in *The Cambridge History of the Bible*, ed. P. R. Ackroyd and C. F. Evans (Cambridge: Cambridge University Press, 1970), pp. 12–23.

[37] Roberts, *Manuscript*, pp. 12–13.

[38] Ibid., p. 14.

At present there are ten papyri of John's Gospel which seem to date from no later than the middle of the third century. Four of the ten were published as recently as 1998.[39] This time there is no need to comment on the papyri one by one: all the papyri of John's Gospel published up to 1995 have been edited carefully and republished with full transcriptions and extensive plates.[40]

Of the ten early papyri of John, four may be said to have been written in a bookhand or a 'near' bookhand: 𝔓66, 𝔓90, 𝔓95, and 𝔓108. Three are perhaps closer to a bookhand than to a documentary hand: 𝔓52, 𝔓75, and 𝔓109. The three remaining early papyri are probably closer to a documentary hand than to a bookhand, though none is a classic example of a documentary hand: 𝔓45, 𝔓106, 𝔓107. In short, the early papyri of John are written in a *range* of hands from 'near' bookhands to 'reformed' documentary hands. As we noted above, the latter term was used by C. H. Roberts to categorize the style of handwriting used as the norm in early Christian papyri.

I shall now comment briefly on the four at the upper end of the spectrum, for they most clearly undermine what I have called the current consensus, i.e. the view that the gospels were at first considered to be utilitarian, 'second-class' writings using a 'reformed documentary' hand.

(1) 𝔓66 (= P. Bodmer II; c. AD 200; 1956). In his initial edition of this manuscript Victor Martin included extended comments on the fine hand used. He described it as a strongly stylized hand, which could even be described as 'literary'. He noted that the letters are strictly independent and largely bilinear, and even noted some similarities with the classic bookhand of Codex Sinaiticus.[41]

(2) 𝔓90 (= P. Oxy. 3523; 1983). These fragments of John 18 and 19 are dated confidently to the end of the second century.[42] The well-formed, decorated style with some small serifs is basically bilinear. It is considered to be similar to 𝔓104, (7) in the preceding list of early Matthean papyri, which is described as an 'elegant hand'.[43] The editor of 𝔓90, T. C. Skeat, noted

---

[39] See Vol. LXV of *The Oxyrhynchus Papyri*. All four papyri, P. Oxy. 4445–8 (= 𝔓106–9), have been edited by W. E. H. Cockle.

[40] See W. J. Elliott and D. C. Parker, eds., *The New Testament in Greek*, Vol. IV, *The Gospel According to St John: The Papyri* (Leiden: Brill, 1995). Four further papyri are listed in Nestle–Aland, 27th edn, as third century: 𝔓5, 𝔓22, 𝔓28, 𝔓39. But, as the specialists whose views are noted by Elliott and Parker suggest late third century or even early fourth century, I have not included them here.

[41] See V. Martin, *Papyrus Bodmer II, évangile de Jean*, chs. 1–14 (Cologne and Geneva: Bibliotheca Bodmeriana, 1956), pp. 14–17.

[42] See Elliott and Parker, *The New Testament in Greek*, Vol. IV, for details and plates (47a and b). T. C. Skeat, in *The Oxyrhynchus Papyri*, Vol. L, ed. A. K. Bowman (1983), pp. 3–8, notes that the codex may possibly have contained two gospels.

[43] J. D. Thomas, in *The Oxyrhynchus Papyri*, Vol. LXIV (1997), p. 8.

that the manuscript had been prepared carefully with blank space before a change of speaker and that the original codex may well have contained two gospels.

(3) $\mathfrak{P}$95 (= Florence, P. Laur. Inv. II/31; 1985), an early third-century small fragment of parts of nine lines of John 5, is in the Biblical uncial or majuscule style, i.e. not unlike (4) in my list of Matthean papyri.[44] This similarity can be seen clearly even by an untrained eye.

(4) $\mathfrak{P}$108 (= P. Oxy. 4447; 1998). Two joining fragments of the end of John 17 and the beginning of John 18 are written in independently formed letters, i.e. without ligatures. The editor, W. E. H. Cockle, notes that this is a practised hand, a 'handsome, medium-sized, upright, capital hand', 'firmly bilinear'.[45] As metallic ink is used, the piece is unlikely to be earlier than the first decades of the third century.

9.4 EARLY PAPYRI OF MARK'S AND LUKE'S GOSPELS

We have only three copies of Mark's Gospel on papyrus. $\mathfrak{P}$84, with parts of Mark 2 and 6 (and John 5 and 17) dates from the sixth century. $\mathfrak{P}$88, from the fourth century, contains almost the whole of Mark 2. Only $\mathfrak{P}$45 is probably from before the mid third century. This is the Chester Beatty codex with parts of all four gospels and Acts, which was discussed above. Alas, there are no fragments of Mark's Gospel among the papyri published in recent years.

If, as claimed by José O'Callaghan in 1972 and Carsten Thiede in several publications since 1992, a fragment of a roll discovered in Cave 7 at Qumran does contain parts of Mark 6:52-3, our knowledge of the text of this gospel would be taken back 200 years.[46] Several further questions concerning the early reception of Mark would arise. Since the roll was probably placed in Cave 7 shortly before the Romans arrived in AD 68, Mark must have been written earlier than is generally accepted. If Mark was written in Rome (as most scholars hold), how did it arrive at Qumran very shortly after its composition? Is it conceivable that Mark would have been of interest to members of the Qumran community? And if not, are we to suppose that someone else placed the roll in Cave 7? The questions multiply. Much is at

---

[44] S. R. Pickering, *Recently Published New Testament Papyri: P89–P95, Papyrology and Historical Perspectives 2* (Sydney: The Ancient History Documentary Research Centre, Macquarie University, 1991), p. 49. See Elliott and Parker, *The New Testament in Greek*, Vol. IV, for details and plates (48b and c).

[45] P. Oxy. 4447 is edited by Cockle in *The Oxyrhynchus Papyri*, Vol. LXV, pp. 16–20.

[46] See Carsten Thiede, *The Earliest Gospel Manuscript?* (Exeter, Paternoster, 1992); Carsten Thiede and Matthew d'Ancona, *The Jesus Papyrus* (London: Weidenfeld & Nicolson, 1996). The latter book was published in New York by Doubleday under the title *Eyewitness to Jesus*.

stake, so it is not surprising that discussion of this theory has been vigorous over the last decade.

However, one implication of the theory that 7Q5 is a fragment of Mark's Gospel has received barely a mention in the literature. 7Q5, like all the other Qumran writings, is written on only one side, so it is from a *roll* – not a *codex*. If the fragment is from Mark, then this gospel was probably first written on a roll, and only later were copies made in codices. Parts of Chapter 8 of this book would have to be rewritten!

The claim that 7Q5 is a fragment of Mark 6 has been subjected to close cross-examination.[47] The jury has now returned. The verdict is unanimous. 7Q5 is not part of Mark's Gospel! I shall be surprised if we hear anything more of this theory.

At present we have only five papyri of Luke's Gospel from before the middle of the third century. (1) 𝔓4, from the end of the second century, is from the same codex as 𝔓64 and 𝔓67, fragments of Matthew's Gospel. I noted above (pp. 198–9) C. H. Roberts's view that it is 'a thorough-going literary production'. (2) 𝔓45, the Chester Beatty codex discussed above (pp. 197–8), contains substantial parts of the central chapters of Luke: it is said to be 'without calligraphic pretensions'. (3) 𝔓69 (= P. Oxy. 2383; 1957) contains fragments of Luke 22 from a mid-third-century codex. Its handwriting is said by the editor, E. G. Turner, to be 'of the type found in a good documentary rather than a literary hand'.[48] (4) 𝔓75, the Bodmer papyrus of Luke and John from early in the third century, was noted above as probably closer to a bookhand than to a documentary hand. (5) 𝔓111 (= P. Oxy. 4495). These tiny fragments of five verses in Luke 17 were published as recently as 1999 and dated to the first half of the third century. The hand is said by the editor, W. E. H. Cockle, to be 'semi-documentary'.[49]

Although it would be rash to draw far-reaching conclusions on the basis of very limited evidence, the five early papyri of Luke turn out to have been written in quite a wide spectrum of hands, as is more clearly the case with the early papyri of both Matthew and John.

9.5 EARLY PAPYRI AND THE RECEPTION OF THE GOSPELS

We have far fewer early papyri of Mark and Luke than of Matthew and John. And, if we were to consider *all* the papyri of the gospels, this would

[47] See especially R. Gundry, 'No *NU* in Line 2 of 7Q5: A Final Disidentification of 7Q5 with Mark 6:52-3', *JBL* 118 (1999) 698–707.
[48] E. Lobel et al., eds., *The Oxyrhynchus Papyri*, Vol. xxiv (1957), p. 1.
[49] *The Oxyrhynchus Papyri*, Vol. lxvi.

also be the case. While the sheer chance of discovery cannot be ignored, the numbers are almost certainly significant: we may reasonably conclude that Matthew's and John's Gospels were copied far more frequently than Mark's and Luke's. This is very much in keeping with the evidence we have of early quotations from, and allusions to, the gospels. The main reason for the greater popularity of Matthew and John is not hard to find: they were considered to have been written by the apostles themselves, and not, as with Mark and Luke, by associates or later followers of apostles.

The recently published early Oxyrhynchus papyri fragments of Matthew and John strongly suggest that these gospels were particularly popular in Egypt, so local factors may have been at work. However, taken as a whole, the Oxyrhynchus papyri do not simply reflect the preferences of one geographical area, for they were not all written in Egypt. Some are in Latin, which would have been known by few in the town of Oxyrhynchus, where the papyri were discovered. For example, P. Oxy. 30, a codex in Latin now usually entitled *De Bellis Macedonicis*, probably originated in Rome.[50] A fragment of Irenaeus, P. Oxy. 405 (a roll), travelled all the way from Lyons to Oxyrhynchus within twenty years of its production, 'not long after the ink was dry on the author's manuscript', to quote again Roberts's memorable comment.[51]

Several further points need to be made. We have noted that in the latter half of the second century some copies of Matthew and John were made with great skill and at some expense. The communities for which they were made must have been reasonably wealthy, perhaps with a higher degree of literacy than has usually been supposed.[52] The carefully made copies, some with signs of punctuation, strongly suggest that they were used for liturgical reading in public rather than for private reading. They confirm Justin Martyr's comment from the middle of the second century that 'the memoirs of the apostles', i.e. the gospels, were read in the context of worship 'as long as time allows' (I Apol. 67).

In Chapter 4 above, I noted that Justin's phrase 'the memoirs of the apostles' suggested that Justin considered the gospels to be literary writings of some sophistication. So it should not surprise us that some of the earliest papyri of the gospels, perhaps copied soon after Justin wrote, are 'upmarket'.

[50] Joseph van Haelst, 'Les Origines du codex', in *Les Débuts du codex*, ed. Alain Blanchard, Bibliologia 9 (Brepols: Turnhout, 1989), p. 27.

[51] Roberts, *Manuscript*, p. 53. See also Chapter 3, p. 74 and n. 45.

[52] E. J. Epp, 'The Codex and Literacy in Early Christianity and at Oxyrhynchus: Issues Raised by Harry Y. Gamble's *Books and Readers in the Early Church*,' *Critical Review of Books in Religion* 10 (1997) 29–32 suggests that the papyri from Oxyrhynchus encourage at least a questioning of the 10–20 per cent average literacy rate for the entire Graeco-Roman world proposed by W. Harris.

They provide general support for my insistence in Chapter 4 that Justin comes within a whisker of regarding sayings of Jesus and the gospels as Scripture.

At the beginning of this chapter, I noted that both C. H. Roberts and Harry Gamble have drawn a sharp contrast between the 'hieratic elegance' of Graeco-Jewish writings 'with their even, formal script with tendencies not only towards a bookhand but toward a somewhat decorated style with footed and serifed letters' and the 'workaday appearance' of first Christian codices.[53] The recently published evidence suggests that Roberts and Gamble were incorrect to differentiate Christian and Jewish attitudes to authoritative texts on the basis of the handwriting styles used. The most striking difference is the marked preference of early Christian scribes for the codex format and their use of *nomina sacra*, the distinctive Christian way of abbreviating 'divine names'.[54]

This conclusion is strongly supported by two of the Oxyrhynchus papyri published in 1998. P. Oxy. 4442 is a fragment of an early third-century *codex* of a Septuagintal text of parts of Exodus 20; it has a good-sized formal Biblical majuscule hand, basically bilinear, and much closer to a bookhand than to a documentary hand. It is broadly comparable with $\mathfrak{P}64 + \mathfrak{P}67$ (Matthew) and $\mathfrak{P}4$ (Luke), (4) above in my list of early Matthean papyri. There are two examples of the *nomen sacrum* θϹ in lines 11 and 16. The use of the codex format and the standard Christian abbreviation of θεός, 'God', confirms that this is a Christian copy of Exodus. Unless Christian scribes were reusing a roll by writing on the reverse side (and we have only four examples), in copying Biblical writings they always used the codex format.

In contrast, P. Oxy. 4443 is a late first- or early-second century *roll* with a Septuagintal text of parts of Esther 8 and 9, and of the fifth of the so-called 'Additions to Esther'. It has frequent ligatures and cursive forms. Its editor, K. Luchner, notes that it perhaps owes more to official documentary styles than to bookhands. In line 12 there is no abbreviation of θεοῦ, confirmation, along with the roll format, that it is Jewish rather than Christian.

There is no reason to doubt that the gospels were often used also as 'workaday', 'utilitarian' handbooks, or even as 'school handbooks' or 'manuals of the teaching traditions of this pragmatically oriented group'.[55] But

---

[53] Roberts, *Manuscript*, pp. 19–20; Gamble, *Books and Readers*, p. 79.
[54] On the latter, see especially C. M. Tuckett's thorough discussion with full bibliographical references, '"Nomina Sacra": Yes and No?', in J.-M. Auwers and H. J. de Jonge, eds., *The Biblical Canons* (Leuven: Peeters, 2003), pp. 431–58; and L. W. Hurtado, 'The Origin of the *Nomina Sacra*: A Proposal', *JBL* 117 (1998) 655–73.
[55] Alexander, 'Ancient Book Production' (above, n. 18), p. 105.

the recently published papyri suggest that, by the second half of the second century, much earlier than has usually been assumed, their literary qualities and their authoritative status for the life and faith of the church were widely recognized. By then, if not even earlier, some copies of the gospels were prepared most carefully, probably for use in worship. The often-repeated claim that the gospels were considered at first to be utilitarian handbooks needs to be modified.

Early Christian obsession with the codex does not call these conclusions · into question. As we saw in Chapter 8, the codex was a natural development from the widespread use of papyrus, parchment, and wooden notebooks. But we should not suppose that the contents of the codex were necessarily considered to be 'second-class'. Martial confirms that towards the end of first century the codex was used by travellers for the writings of Homer, Virgil, Cicero and others; our earliest non-Christian papyrus codex is a historical work, and we do have a handful of second-century codices with literary texts.

Christians had their own good reasons for preferring the codex. What continues to surprise is the almost universal adoption of this format by Christian scribes, as well as their use of *nomina sacra*. That both 'fashions' caught on so quickly and so universally suggests that Christian communities were in much closer touch with one another than we have usually supposed.

At the beginning of this chapter I welcomed C. H. Roberts's insight in 1979 that early Christian papyri shed light on the social and religious setting of early Christianity in Egypt. However, my conclusions differ. The more recently published papyri suggest greater diversity than Roberts allowed. In particular, some of the very earliest papyri of the gospels are far from being fragments from 'utilitarian handbooks'. $\mathfrak{P}52$, still considered to be the very earliest papyrus fragment and thus the earliest material evidence of Christianity, may have been copied only three or four decades after John's Gospel was written. The handwriting style in this justifiably famous fragment is closer to a literary bookhand than to reformed documentary. And this is also true of $\mathfrak{P}64 + \mathfrak{P}67 + \mathfrak{P}4$ (from a four-gospel codex), $\mathfrak{P}77$, $\mathfrak{P}90$ and $\mathfrak{P}104$ (Matthew), and $\mathfrak{P}66$ and $\mathfrak{P}90$ (John). These are the papyri with the strongest claims to dating from the latter decades of the second century, the very time when Irenaeus was underlining the authority of the gospels for the life of the church and their status as Scripture. No wonder these papyri were copied carefully, in stylish handwriting.

Bibliography

PRIMARY SOURCES

(Editions and translations of the main non-canonical writings discussed. For Philo, Josephus, Cicero, and Martial, I have used the Loeb Classical Library editions.)

THE DEAD SEA SCROLLS

The Dead Sea Scrolls: English and Hebrew, ed. and trans. Florentino García Martínez and Eibert J. C. Tigchelaar, Vols. I and II (Leiden: Brill, 1997–8)

PAPYRI AND INSCRIPTIONS

The Oxyrhynchus Papyri (London: Egypt Exploration Fund, 1898–[2003])

Brunt, P. A. and Moore, J. M., eds., *Res Gestae Divi Augusti* (Oxford: Oxford University Press, 1967)

Hagedorn, U. and D. and Youtie, L. C. and H. C., eds., *P. Petaus: Das Archiv des Petaus*, Pap. Colon., Vol. IV (Cologne and Opladen, 1969)

Kenyon, F. G., *The Chester Beatty Biblical Papyri: Descriptions and Texts of Twelve Manuscripts on Papyrus of the Greek Bible*, Vols. I and II (London: Emery Walker, 1933)

Laffi, U., 'Le iscrizioni relative all'introduzione nel 9 a.C. del nuovo calendario della Provincia d'Asia', *Studi Classici e Orientali* 16 (1968) 5–98

Sherk, R. K., *Roman Documents from the Greek East: Senatus Consulta and Epistula to the Age of Augustus* (Baltimore: Johns Hopkins, 1969)

APOSTOLIC FATHERS

Holmes, M. W., ed., *The Apostolic Fathers: Greek Texts and English Translations*, 2nd edn (Grand Rapids: Baker, 1992)

JUSTIN MARTYR

Marcovich, M., *Iustini Martyris Apologiae Pro Christianis*, Patristische Texte und Studien 38 (Berlin: de Gruyter, 1994)

    Iustini Martyris Dialogus cum Tryphone, Patristische Texte und Studien 47 (Berlin: de Gruyter, 1997)

208 *Bibliography*

IRENAEUS

Rousseau, A. and Doutreleau, L., eds., *Irénée de Lyon. Contre les hérésies*, III, Sources Chrétiennes 211 (Paris: Cerf, 1974)

MURATORIAN FRAGMENT

Lietzmann, H., *Das Muratorische Fragment und die monarchianischen Prologue zu den Evangelien*, Kleine Texte, i (Bonn, 1902)
Tregelles, S. P., *Canon Muratorianus* (Oxford: Clarendon, 1867)

ACTS OF THOMAS

Bonnet, M., ed., *Acta Apostolorum Apocrypha* II/2 (Hildesheim, 1903, repr. 1959) for the Greek text.

ORIGEN

Chadwick, H., *Origen: Contra Celsum* (Cambridge: Cambridge University Press, 1953)

SECONDARY LITERATURE

Abramowski, L., 'Die "Erinnerungen der Apostel" bei Justin', in P. Stuhlmacher, ed., *Das Evangelium und die Evangelien* (Tübingen: Mohr, 1983), pp. 341–54
Aland, K., *Repertorium der griechischen christlichen Papyri*, Vol. I: *Biblische Papyri* (Berlin and New York: de Gruyter, 1976)
Aland, K., ed., *Kurzgefasste Liste der griechischen Handschriften des Neuen Testaments*, 2nd edn (Berlin: de Gruyter, 1994)
Albl, M. C., *'And Scripture Cannot be Broken': The Form and Function of the Early Christian Testimonia Collections* (Leiden: Brill, 1999)
Alexander, L. A., 'Ancient Book Production and the Circulation of the Gospels', in R. J. Bauckham, ed., *The Gospels for All Christians: Rethinking the Gospel Audiences* (Grand Rapids: Eerdmans, 1998), pp. 71–111
  'The Living Voice: Scepticism towards the Written Word in Early Christian and in Graeco-Roman Texts', in D. J. A. Clines, S. E. Fowl, and S. E. Porter, eds., *The Bible in Three Dimensions* (Sheffield: JSOT, 1990)
Alexander, P. S., 'Incantations and Books of Magic', in E. Schürer, *The History of the Jewish People in the Age of Jesus Christ* III.1, ed. G. Vermes, F. Millar, and M. Goodman (Edinburgh: T. & T. Clark, 1986), §32.VII, pp. 342–79
Alföldy, G., 'Subject and Ruler, Subjects and Methods: An Attempt at a Conclusion', in A. Small, ed., *Subject and Ruler: The Cult of the Ruling Power in Classical Antiquity*. Papers presented at a conference held in the University of Alberta on April 13–15th, 1994, to celebrate the 65th anniversary of Duncan Fishwick (*Journal of Roman Archaeology* Supplementary Series 17 (1996))

Aune, D. E., 'Magic in Early Christianity', *ANRW* 11.23.2, ed. W. Haase (Berlin: de Gruyter, 1980)

 Prophecy in Early Christianity and the Ancient Mediterranean World (Grand Rapids: Eerdmans, 1983), pp. 153–89

Baarda, T., *Essays on the Diatessaron* (Kampen: Kok Pharos, 1994)

Babcock, W., ed., *Paul and the Legacies of Paul* (Dallas: Southern Methodist University Press, 1990)

Backhouse, J., *The Lindisfarne Gospels* (London: Phaidon, 1981)

Bammel, E., 'Der Jude des Celsus', in his *Judaica: Kleine Schriften I* (Tübingen: Mohr, 1986), pp. 265–83

Barclay, J. M. G., *Jews in the Mediterranean Diaspora* (Edinburgh: T. & T. Clark, 1996)

 'Mirror-Reading a Polemical Letter: Galatians as a Test Case', *JSNT* 31 (1987) 73–93

 Obeying the Truth (Edinburgh: T. & T. Clark, 1988)

Barton, J., *The Spirit and the Letter: Studies in the Biblical Canon* (London, SPCK, 1997)

Bauckham, R. J., ed., *The Gospels for All Christians: Rethinking the Gospel Audiences* (Grand Rapids: Eerdmans, 1998)

Bellinzoni, A. J., 'The Gospel of Matthew in the Second Century', *SC* 9 (1992) 197–258

 The Sayings of Jesus in the Writings of Justin Martyr (Leiden: Brill, 1967)

Benko, S., 'Pagan Criticism of Christianity during the First Two Centuries', *ANRW* 11.23.2, ed. W. Haase (Berlin: de Gruyter, 1980), pp. 1055–1118

Benoit, A., *Saint Irénée. Introduction à l'étude de sa théologie* (Paris: Presses Universitaires de France, 1960)

Betz, H. D., *Galatians*, Hermeneia Commentary (Philadelphia: Fortress, 1979)

Bingham, D. J., *Irenaeus's Use of Matthew's Gospel in Adversus Haereses* (Leuven: Peeters, 1998)

Birley, R., *Roman Records from Vindolanda on Hadrian's Wall*, 3rd edn, Roman Army Museum Publications for the Vindolanda Trust (Carvoran: Greenhead, 1999)

Blanchard, Alain, ed., *Les Débuts du codex*, Bibliologia 9 (Brepols: Turnhout, 1989)

Blanchard, Y.-M., *Aux sources du canon, le témoinage d'Irénée*, Cogitatio Fidei 174 (Paris: Cerf, 1993)

Blanck, Horst, *Das Buch in der Antike* (Munich: C. H. Beck, 1992)

Borg, M. et al., eds., *The Lost Gospel Q: The Original Sayings of Jesus* (Berkeley, Calif.: Ulysses, 1996)

Bovon, F., 'La Structure canonique de l'Evangile et de l'Apôtre', *Cristianesimo nella Storia* 15 (1994) 559–76

Bowman, A. K., *Life and Letters on the Roman Frontier: Vindolanda and its People* (London: British Museum, 1994)

Bowman, A. K. and Thomas, J. D., *Vindolanda: The Latin Writing-Tablets*, Britannia Monograph Series 4 (London: Society for the Promotion of Roman Studies, 1983)

The Vindolanda Writing-Tablets: Tabulae Vindolandansenses II (London: British Museum, 1994)

Brent, A., *The Imperial Cult and the Development of Church Order* (Leiden: Brill, 1999)

Breytenbach, C., *Paulus und Barnabas in der Provinz Galatien. Studien zu Apostelgeschichte 13f.; 16, 6; 18, 23 und den Adressaten des Galaterbriefes* (Leiden: Brill, 1996)

Brooke, G., *Exegesis at Qumran: 4QFlorilegium in its Jewish Context* (Sheffield: JSOT, 1985)

Brown, R. E., *The Epistles of John*, Anchor Bible (Garden City: Doubleday, 1982)

Burridge, R. A., *Four Gospels, One Jesus?* (London: SPCK, 1994)

What are the Gospels? A Comparison with Graeco-Roman Biography (Cambridge: Cambridge University Press, 1992; 2nd edn Grand Rapids: Eerdmans, 2004)

Campenhausen, H. von, *Die Entstehung der christlichen Bibel* (Tübingen: Mohr, 1968); E. tr. *The Formation of the Christian Bible* (Philadelphia: Fortress; London: Black, 1972)

Carleton Paget, James, 'Some Observations on Josephus and Christianity', *JTS* 52 (2001) 539–624

Carroll, K. L., 'The Creation of the Fourfold Gospel', *BJRL* 37 (1954–5) 68–77

Cavallo, G., and Maehler, H., *Greek Bookhands of the Early Byzantine Period, AD 300–88*, Bulletin Supplement 47 (London: University of London Institute of Classical Studies, 1987)

Chilton, B. D. 'Jésus, le *mamzer* (Mt 1.18)', *NTS* 46 (2000) 222–7

Collins, J. J., 'Jesus, Messianism and the Dead Sea Scrolls', in J. H. Charlesworth, H. Lichtenberger, and G. S. Oegema, eds., *Qumran–Messianism: Studies on the Messianic Expectations in the Dead Sea Scrolls* (Tübingen: Mohr–Siebeck, 1998), pp. 100–19

The Scepter and the Star (New York: Doubleday, 1995)

Cosgrove, C. H., 'Justin Martyr and the Emerging Christian Canon: Observations on the Purpose and Destination of the Dialogue with Trypho', *Vig. Chr.* 36 (1982) 209–32

Coulmas, Florian, ed., *The Handbook of Sociolinguistics* (Oxford: Blackwell, 1997)

Crossan, J. D., *The Historical Jesus: The Life of a Mediterranean Jewish Peasant* (Edinburgh: T. & T. Clark, 1991)

Croy, N. Clayton, *The Mutilation of Mark's Gospel* (Nashville: Abingdon, 2003)

Cullmann, O., 'Die Pluralität der Evangelien als theologisches Problem im Altertum', *Theologische Zeitschrift* 1 (1945), 23–42; E. tr. in Cullmann's *The Early Church*, ed. A. J. B. Higgins (London: SCM, 1956)

Danker, F. W., *Benefactor* (St Louis, Miss.: Clayton, 1982)

Davies, W. D., *The Setting of the Sermon on the Mount* (Cambridge: Cambridge University Press, 1963)

Deissmann, A., *Light from the Ancient East* (London: Hodder and Stoughton, E. tr. 1910)

Denney, J., *Jesus and the Gospels: Christianity Justified in the Mind of Christ* (London: Hodder & Stoughton, 1908)

Dibelius, M., *From Tradition to Gospels* (London: Ivor Nicholson and Watson, E. tr. 1934)

Dodd, C. H., *More New Testament Studies* (Manchester: Manchester University Press, 1968)

Dohmen, C. and Oeming, M., *Biblischer Kanon, warum und wozu?: eine Kanontheologie* (Freiburg: Herder, 1992)

Donfried, K. P., *Paul, Thessalonica and Early Christianity* (London: T. & T. Clark, 2002)

Ehrhardt, A. T., *The Framework of the New Testament Stories* (Manchester: Manchester University Press, 1964)

Ehrman, B. D. and Holmes, M. W., *The Text of the New Testament in Contemporary Research* (Grand Rapids: Eerdmans, 1995)

Elliott, J. K., *The Apocryphal New Testament* (Oxford: Clarendon Press, 1993)

   A Bibliography of Greek New Testament Manuscripts (Cambridge: Cambridge University Press, 1989; 2nd edn, 2000)

   'Five New Papyri of the New Testament', *NovT* 41 (1999) 209–13

   'Manuscripts, the Codex and the Canon', *JSNT* 63 (1996) 105–23

   'Seven Recently Published New Testament Fragments from Oxyrhynchus', *NovT* 42 (2000) 209–13

Elliott, W. J. and Parker, D. C., eds., *The New Testament in Greek*, Vol. IV, *The Gospel According to St John: The Papyri* (Leiden: Brill, 1995)

Epp, E. J., 'The Codex and Literacy in Early Christianity and at Oxyrhynchus: Issues Raised by Harry Y. Gamble's *Books and Readers in the Early Church*', *Critical Review of Books in Religion* 10 (1997) 15–37

   'New Testament Papyrus Manuscripts and Letter Carrying in Greco-Roman Times', in B. A. Pearson, ed., *The Future of Early Christianity*, FS H. Koester (Minneapolis: Fortress, 1991), pp. 35–56

   'The Papyrus Manuscripts of the New Testament', in B. D. Ehrman and M. W. Holmes, eds., *The Text of the New Testament in Contemporary Research*, FS B. M. Metzger (Grand Rapids: Eerdmans, 1995), pp. 3–21

Evans, C. A., 'Jesus and the Dead Sea Scrolls', in P. W. Flint and J. C. Vanderkam, eds., *The Dead Sea Scrolls after Fifty Years* (Leiden: Brill, 1999)

Falcetta, A., 'A Testimony Collection in Manchester: Papyrus Rylands Greek 460' *BJRL* 83 (2002) 3–19

Farmer, W. R. and Farkasfalvy, D. M., *The Formation of the New Testament Canon* (New York, 1983)

Ferguson, E., 'Canon Muratori: Date and Provenance', *Studia Patristica* 18 (1982) 677–83

Fitzmyer, J. A., *Essays on the Semitic Background of the New Testament* (London: Chapman, 1971)

Ford, D. F. and Stanton, G. N., *Scripture and Theology: Reading Texts, Seeking Wisdom* (London: SCM, 2003)

Frankemölle, H., *Evangelium. Begriff und Gattung*, 2nd edn (Stuttgart: Katholisches Bibelwerk, 1994)
    Jahwebund und Kirche Christi (Münster: Aschendorff, 1974)
French, D., 'Acts and the Roman Roads of Asia Minor', in D. W. J. Gill and C. Gempf, eds., *The Book of Acts in its Graeco-Roman Setting* (Grand Rapids: Eerdmans, 1994), pp. 49–58
Frickenschmidt, D., *Evangelium als Biographie. Die vier Evangelien im Rahmen antiker Erzählungskunst* (Tübingen and Basle: A. Francke, 1997)
Friedrich G., art. εὐαγγέλιον in *Theological Dictionary of the New Testament*, ed. G. Kittel, Vol. II (Grand Rapids: Eerdmans, E. tr. 1964), pp. 707–37
Friesen, S. J., *Twice Neokoros. Ephesus, Asia and the Cult of the Flavian Imperial Family* (Leiden: Brill, 1993)
Funk, R. W., ed., *The Gospel of Jesus according to the Jesus Seminar* (Sonoma, Calif.: Polebridge, 1999)
Gamble, H. Y., *Books and Readers in the Early Church: A History of Early Christian Texts* (New Haven and London: Yale University Press, 1995)
Gerhardsson, B., *Memory and Manuscript: Oral Tradition and Written Transmission in Rabbinic Judaism and Early Christianity*, 2nd edn (Grand Rapids: Eerdmans, 1998)
Goodspeed, E. J., *The Formation of the New Testament* (Chicago: University of Chicago Press, 1937)
Gradel, I., *Emperor Worship and Roman Religion* (Oxford: Clarendon, 2002)
Grant, R. M., *The Earliest Lives of Jesus* (London: SPCK, 1961)
Guelich, R., *Mark*, Word Biblical Commentary (Dallas: Word, 1989)
Gundry, R., 'No *NU* in Line 2 of 7Q5: A Final Disidentification of 7Q5 with Mark 6:52-3', *JBL* (1999) 698–702
Haacker, K., 'Das Bekenntnis des Paulus zur Hoffnung Israels nach der Apostelgeschichte des Lukas', *NTS* 31 (1985) 437–51
Haelst, J. van, *Catalogue des papyrus littéraires juifs et chrétiens*, Papyrologie I (Paris: Publications de la Sorbonne, 1976)
    'Les Origines du codex', in A. Blanchard, ed., *Les Débuts du codex*, Bibliologia 9 (Brepols: Turnhout, 1989), pp. 12–35
Hahneman, G. M., *The Muratorian Fragment and the Development of the Canon* (Oxford: Clarendon, 1992)
Halverson, J., 'Oral and Written Gospel: A Critique of Werner Kelber', *NTS* 40 (1994) 180–95
Haran, M., 'Codex, *Pinax* and Writing Slat', *Scripta Classica Israelica* 15 (1996) 212–22
Harnack, A., *Judentum und Judenchristentum in Justins Dialog mit Tryphon* (Leipzig, 1930)
    Marcion: Das Evangelium vom fremden Gott (Leipzig: J. C. Hinrichs, 1921)
    The Origin of the New Testament and the Most Important Consequences of the New Creation (London and New York, 1925)

Harris, W. F., 'Why did the Codex Supplant the Book-Roll?', in J. Monfasani and R. G. Musto, eds., *Renaissance Society and Culture, FS E. F. Price Jr.* (New York: Italica Press, 1991), pp. 71–85

Harrison, J. R., 'Paul and the Imperial Gospel at Thessaloniki', *JSNT* 25 (2002) 71–96

'Paul, Eschatology and the Augustan Age of Grace', *TB* 50 (1999) 79–91

'Paul's Language of Grace (Χάρις) in its Graeco-Roman Context', Macquarie University Ph.D. 1996, to be published in the WUNT series by J. C. B. Mohr, Tübingen

Hays, R. B., 'Christology and Ethics in Galatians: The Law of Christ', *CBQ* 49 (1987) 268–90

Head, P. M., 'Some Recently Published NT Papyri from Oxyrhynchus: An Overview and Preliminary Assessment', *TB* 51 (2000) 1–16

Heckel, T. K., *Vom Evangelium des Markus zum viergestaltigen Evangelium* (Tübingen: Mohr, 1999)

Hengel, M., *The Four Gospels and the One Gospel of Jesus Christ* (London: SCM, 2000)

'The Titles of the Gospels and the Gospel of Mark', in *Studies in the Gospel of Mark* (London: SCM, 1985)

Hengel, M. and Schwemer, A. M., *Paul between Damascus and Antioch* (London: SCM, 1997)

Henne, P., 'La Datation du *Canon de Muratori*', *RB* 100 (1993) 54–75

Hill, C. E., 'Justin and the New Testament Writings', in E. A. Livingstone, ed., *Studia Patristica* 30 (Leuven: Peeters, 1997)

Horbury, W., 'The Wisdom of Solomon in the Muratorian Fragment', *JTS* 45 (1994) 149–59

Horsley, G. H. R., 'The "Good News" of a Wedding', *New Documents Illustrating Early Christianity*, Vol. III (Sydney: The Ancient History Documentary Research Centre, Macquarie University, 1983), pp. 10–15

Horsley, R. A., *Paul and Politics: Ekklesia, Imperium, Interpretation* (Harrisburg, Pa.: Trinity Press International, 2000)

Hultgren, S., *Narrative Elements in the Double Tradition* (Berlin: de Gruyter, 2002)

Hurtado, L. W., 'The Origin of the *Nomina Sacra*: A Proposal', *JBL* 117 (1998) 655–73

Hyldahl, N., 'Hesesipps Hypomnemata', *ST* 14 (1960) 70–113

Kaestli, J.-D., 'La Place du *Fragment de Muratori* dans l'histoire du canon. A propos de la thèse de Sundberg et Hahneman', *Cristianesimo nella Storia* 15 (1994) 609–34

Kingsbury, J. D., *Matthew: Structure, Christology, Kingdom* (London: SPCK, 1975)

Knoch, O., 'Kenntnis und Verwendung des Matthäus-Evangeliums bei den Apostolischen Vätern', in L. Schenke, ed., *Studien zum Matthäusevangeliums, FS W. Pesch* (Stuttgart: Katholisches Bibelwerk, 1988)

Knox J., *Marcion and the New Testament* (Chicago: University of Chicago Press, 1942)

Koch, D.-A., *Die Schrift als Zeuge des Evangeliums* (Tübingen: Mohr, 1986)

Koester, H., *Ancient Christian Gospels: Their History and Development* (London: SCM and Philadelphia: Trinity, 1990)

  'From the Kerygma-Gospel to Written Gospels', *NTS* 35 (1989) 361–81

  History and Literature of Early Christianity (Philadelphia: Fortress, 1982)

  'The Text of the Synoptic Gospels in the Second Century', in W. L. Petersen, ed., *Gospel Traditions in the Second Century* (Notre Dame and London: University of Notre Dame Press, 1989), pp. 28–33

Köhler, W., *Die Rezeption des Matthäusevangeliums in der Zeit vor Irenäus*, WUNT 24 (Tübingen: Mohr, 1987)

Lane Fox, R., 'Literacy and Power in Early Christianity', in A. K. Bowman and G. Woolf, eds., *Literacy and Power in the Ancient World* (Cambridge: Cambridge University Press, 1994), pp. 126–48

Lapide, Pinchas, *The Resurrection of Jesus* (London: SPCK, 1984)

Layton, B., ed., *Nag Hammadi Codex II, 2–7* (Leiden: Brill, 1989)

Levick, B., *Roman Colonies in Southern Asia Minor* (Oxford: Oxford University Press, 1967)

Lieberman, S., *Hellenism in Jewish Palestine*, 2nd edn (New York: Jewish Theological Seminary, 1962)

Lim, T. H., *Holy Scripture in the Qumran Communities and the Pauline Letters* (Oxford: Clarendon, 1997)

Llewelyn, S. R., *New Documents Illustrating Early Christianity*, Vol. VII (Sydney: The Ancient History Documentary Research Centre, Macquarie University, 1994)

Longenecker, B. W., ed., *Narrative Dynamics in Paul* (Louisville: Westminster John Knox, 2002)

Luz, U., *Das Evangelium nach Matthäus*, EKK I/1, 5th edn (Düsseldorf and Zurich: Benziger, 2002); *Matthew* (Edinburgh: T. & T. Clark, E. tr. of 1st edn, 1989)

McCormick, M., 'The Birth of the Codex and the Apostolic Life-Style', *Scriptorium* 39 (1985) 150–8

  'Typology, Codicology and Papyrology', *Scriptorium* 35 (1981) 331–4

McDonald, J. I. H., 'Questioning and Discernment in Gospel Discourse: Communicative Strategy in Matthew 11.2-9', in B. Chilton and C. A. Evans, eds., *Authenticating the Words of Jesus* (Leiden: Brill, 1999)

McKnight, S., 'Calling Jesus *Mamzer*', *Journal for the Study of the Historical Jesus* 1 (2003) 73–103

Maier, J., *Jesus von Nazareth in der talmudischen Überlieferung* (Darmstadt: Wissenschaftliche Buchgesellschaft, 1978)

Malina, Bruce J. and Neyrey, Jerome H., *Calling Jesus Names: The Social Value of Labels in Matthew* (Sonoma, Calif.: Polebridge, 1988)

Marcus, J., 'Mark – Interpreter of Paul', *NTS* 46 (2000) 473–87

  Mark 1–8, Anchor Bible 27 (New York: Doubleday, 2000)

Marshall, I. H., *The Pastoral Epistles*, ICC (Edinburgh, T. & T. Clark, 1999)

Martin, V., *Papyrus Bodmer II, Evangile de Jean*, chs. 1–14 (Cologne and Geneva: Bibliotheca Bodmeriana, 1956), pp. 14–17

Marxsen, W., *Mark the Evangelist* (E. tr. Nashville: Abingdon, 1969)

Meeks, W., *The First Urban Christians: The Social World of the Apostle Paul* (New Haven: Yale, 1983)

Meggitt, J., 'Taking the Emperor's Clothes Seriously: The New Testament and the Roman Emperor', in Christine E. Joynes, ed., *The Quest for Wisdom: Essays in Honour of Philip Budd* (Cambridge: Orchard Academic, 2002)

Meier, J. P., 'Jesus in Josephus: A Modest Proposal', *CBQ* 52 (1990) 76–103

Merkel, H., *Die Pluralität der Evangelien als theologisches und exegetisches Problem in der alten Kirche* (Bern: Peter Lang, 1978)

Die Widersprüche zwischen den Evangelien. Ihre polemische und apologetische Behandlung in der alten Kirche bis zu Augustin (Tübingen: Mohr, 1971)

Metzger, B. M., *The Canon of the New Testament: Its Origin, Development, and Significance* (Oxford: Clarendon, 1987)

Millar, F., 'The Impact of Monarchy', in F. Millar and E. Segal, eds., *Caesar Augustus: Seven Aspects* (Oxford: Clarendon, 1984)

Millard, A. R., *Reading and Writing in the Time of Jesus* (Sheffield: Sheffield Academic Press, 2000)

Mitchell, M. M., 'Rhetorical Shorthand in Pauline Argumentation: The Functions of "the Gospel" in the Corinthian Correspondence', in L. A. Jervis and P. Richardson, eds., *Gospel in Paul, FS R. N. Longenecker* (Sheffield: JSOT Press, 1994), pp. 63–88

Mitchell, S., *Anatolia: Land, Men and Gods in Asia Minor*, Vols. I and II (Oxford: Oxford University Press, 1993)

Mitchell, S. and Waelkens, M., eds., *Pisidian Antioch: The Site and its Monuments* (London, Duckworth, 1998)

Morgan, R. C., 'The Hermeneutical Significance of Four Gospels', *Interpretation* 33 (1979) 376–88

Muddiman, J., *The Epistle to the Ephesians*, Black's NT Commentaries (London and New York: Continuum, 2001)

Oakes, Peter, *Philippians: From People to Letter* (Cambridge: Cambridge University Press, 2001)

Osborn, E., *Justin Martyr* (Tübingen: Mohr, 1973)

Parsons, M. C. and Pervo, R. I., *Rethinking the Unity of Luke and Acts* (Minneapolis: Augsburg Fortress, 1993)

Petersen, W. L., *Gospel Traditions in the Second Century* (Notre Dame and London: University of Notre Dame Press, 1989)

Tatian's Diatessaron: Its Creation, Dissemination, Significance, and History in Scholarship (Leiden: Brill, 1994)

Pickering, S. R., *Recently Published New Testament Papyri: P89–P95*, Papyrology and Historical Perspectives 2 (Sydney: The Ancient History Documentary Research Centre, Macquarie University, 1991)

Pilhofer, P., 'Luke's Knowledge of Antioch', in T. Drew Bear, M. Tashalan, and C. M. Thomas, eds., *Actes du Ier Congrès International sur Antioche de Pisidie* (Lyons and Paris: Université Lumière-Lyon 2 and Diffusion de Boccard, 2000)

Price, S. R. F., *Rituals and Power: The Roman Imperial Cult in Asia Minor* (Cambridge: Cambridge University Press, 1984)

Pryor, J. W., 'Justin Martyr and the Fourth Gospel', *The Second Century* 9 (1992) 153–69

Reeve, Anne, *Erasmus's Annotations on the New Testament. Galatians to the Apocalypse: Facsimile of the Final Latin Text with All Earlier Variants* (Leiden: Brill, 1993)

Rendel Harris, J., *Testimonies* (2 vols., Cambridge: Cambridge University Press, 1916–20)

Richards, E. R., *The Secretary in the Letters of Paul* (Tübingen: Mohr, 1991)

Riesner, R., *Paul's Early Period: Chronology, Mission Strategy, Theology* (Grand Rapids: Eerdmans, 1998)

Robbins, G. A., 'Muratorian Fragment', in D. N. Freedman, ed., *The Anchor Bible Dictionary* (New York: Doubleday 1992)

Roberts, C. H., 'Books in the Graeco-Roman World', in *The Cambridge History of the Bible*, ed. P. R. Ackroyd and C. F. Evans (Cambridge: Cambridge University Press, 1970), pp. 12–23

    'The Codex', *Proceedings of the British Academy* 40 (1954) 169–204

    Manuscript, Society and Belief in Early Christian Egypt (London: Oxford University Press for the British Academy, 1979)

    An Unpublished Fragment of the Fourth Gospel in the John Rylands Library (Manchester: Manchester University Press, 1935)

Roberts, C. H. and Skeat, T. C., *The Birth of the Codex* (London: Oxford University Press for the British Academy, 1983)

Sanders, J. N., *The Fourth Gospel in the Early Church* (Cambridge: Cambridge University Press, 1943)

Sato, M., *Q und Prophetie. Studien zur Gattungs- und Traditionsgeschichte der Quelle Q*, WUNT 2. Reihe, Vol. 29 (Tübingen: Mohr, 1988)

Schenk, W., *Die Sprache des Matthäus* (Göttingen: Vandenhoeck & Ruprecht, 1987)

Schnackenburg, R., *Jesus in the Gospels: A Biblical Christology* (Louisville: Westminster John Knox, E. tr. 1995)

Schneemelcher, W., ed., *New Testament Apocrypha*, Vol. II (Cambridge: Clarke, 1992)

Schniewind, J., *Euangelion. Ursprung und erste Gestalt des Begriffs Evangelium*, Vols. I–II (Gütersloh, 1927–31)

Schoedel, W. R., *Ignatius of Antioch*, Hermeneia (Philadelphia: Fortress, 1985)

Shum, S.-L., *Paul's Use of Isaiah in Romans* (Tübingen: Mohr Siebeck, 2002)

Sirat, C., 'Le Livre hébreu dans les premiers siècles de nôtre ère: le témoinage des textes', in A. Blanchard, ed., *Les Débuts du codex* (Brepols: Turnhout, 1989)

Skarsaune, O., *The Proof from Prophecy. A Study in Justin Martyr's Proof-Text Tradition: Text-Type, Provenance, Theological Profile* (Leiden: Brill, 1987)

Skeat, T. C., 'The Codex Sinaiticus, the Codex Vaticanus, and Constantine', *JTS* 50 (2000) 583–625

    'A Codicological Analysis of the Chester Beatty Papyrus Codex of Gospels and Acts (P45)', *Hermathena* 155 (1993) 27–43

'Irenaeus and the Four-Gospel Canon', *NovT* 34 (1992) 193–9

'The Oldest Manuscript of the Four Gospels?', *NTS* 43 (1997) 1–34

'The Origin of the Christian Codex', *ZPE* 102 (1994) 263–8

Small, A., ed., *Subject and Ruler: The Cult of the Ruling Power in Classical Antiquity* (*Journal of Roman Archaeology* Supplementary Series 17 (1996))

Smith, M., *Jesus the Magician* (London: Victor Gollancz, 1978)

Spallek, A. J., 'The Origin and Meaning of Εὐαγγέλιον in the Pauline Corpus', *CTQ* 57 (1993) 177–90

Stanley, C. D., *Paul and the Language of Scripture* (Cambridge: Cambridge University Press, 1992)

Stanton, G. N., 'Form Criticism Revisited', in M. Hooker and C. J. A. Hickling, eds., *What about the New Testament? FS C. F. Evans* (London: SCM, 1975), pp. 13–27

A Gospel for a New People: Studies in Matthew (Edinburgh: T. & T. Clark, 1992)

Gospel Truth? New Light on Jesus and the Gospels (London: HarperCollins, 1995)

The Gospels and Jesus, 2nd edn (Oxford: Oxford University Press, 2002)

Jesus of Nazareth in New Testament Preaching (Cambridge: Cambridge University Press, 1974).

'Matthew: βίβλος, εὐαγγέλιον, or βίος?', in F. Van Segbroeck et al., eds., *The Four Gospels 1992, FS Franz Neirynck*, Vol. II (Leuven: Leuven University Press, 1992), pp. 1187–1202

'On the Christology of Q', in B. Lindars and S. S. Smalley, eds., *Christ and Spirit in the New Testament* (Cambridge: Cambridge University Press, 1973), pp. 27–42

'Revisiting Matthew's Communities', in *SBL Seminar Papers 1994*, ed. E. H. Lovering Jr. (Atlanta: Scholars Press, 1994), pp. 9–23

'Stephen in Lucan Perspective', in E. A. Livingstone, ed., *Studia Biblica III* (Sheffield: JSOT Press, 1980), pp. 345–60

'The Two Parousias of Christ: Justin Martyr and Matthew', in M. C. de Boer, ed., *From Jesus to John*, FS *M. de Jonge* (Sheffield: JSOT Press, 1993), pp. 183–96

Strange, W. A., *The Problem of the Text of Acts* (Cambridge: Cambridge University Press, 1992)

Strecker, G., 'Das Evangelium Jesu Christi', in G. Strecker, ed., *Jesus Christus in Historie und Theologie, FS H. Conzelmann* (Tübingen: Mohr, 1975), pp. 503–48

Stuhlmacher, P., *Das paulinische Evangelium* (Göttingen: Vandenhoeck & Ruprecht, 1968)

Stuhlmacher, P., ed., *Das Evangelium und die Evangelien* (Tübingen: Mohr, 1983)

The Gospel and the Gospels (Grand Rapids: Eerdmans, 1991)

Sundberg, A. C., 'Canon Muratori: A Fourth Century List', *HTR* 66 (1973) 1–41

'Towards a Revised History of the New Testament Canon', *Studia Evangelica* 4/1 (1968), pp. 452–61

Thiede, C. and d'Ancona, M., *The Jesus Papyrus* (London: Weidenfeld & Nicolson, 1996)

Thompson, M. B., *Clothed with Christ: The Example and Teaching of Jesus in Romans 12.1–15.3* (Sheffield: Sheffield Academic Press, 1991)

Trebilco, Paul, *Jewish Communities in Asia Minor* (Cambridge: Cambridge University Press, 1991)

Trobisch, D., *Die Endredaktion des Neuen Testaments. Eine Untersuchung zur Entstehung der christlichen Bibel* (Freiburg: Universitätsverlag; Göttingen: Vandenhoeck & Ruprecht, 1996)

Paul's Letter Collection: Tracing the Origins (Minneapolis: Fortress, 1994)

Tuckett, C. M., '"Nomina Sacra": Yes and No?', in J.-M. Auwers and H. J. de Jonge, eds., *The Biblical Canons* (Leuven: Peeters, 2003), pp. 431–58

'Scripture and Q', in C. M. Tuckett, ed., *The Scriptures in the Gospels* (Leuven: University Press, 1997), pp. 20–6

Turner, E. G., *Greek Manuscripts of the Ancient World* (Oxford: Oxford University Press, 1971; 2nd edn, 1987)

Greek Papyri, 2nd edn (Oxford: Clarendon, 1980)

The Typology of the Early Codex (Philadelphia: University of Pennsylvania Press, 1977)

Unnik, W. C. van, 'De la règle Μήτε προσθεῖναι μήτε ἀφελεῖν', *Vig. Chr.* 3 (1949) 1–36

Verheyden, J., 'The Canon Muratori: A Matter of Dispute', in J.-M. Auwers and H. J. de Jonge, eds., *The Biblical Canons* (Leuven: Peeters, 2003), pp. 487–586

Vocke, H., 'Papyrus Magdalen 17 – Weitere Argumente gegen die Frühdatierung des angeblichen Jesus-Papyrus', *ZPE* 113 (1996) 153–7

Wachtel, K., 'П64/67: Fragmente des Matthäusevangeliums aus dem 1. Jahrhundert?', *ZPE* 107 (1995) 73–80

Wengst, K., *Schriften des Urchristentums*, Vol. II (Darmstadt: Wissenschaftliche Buchgesellschaft, 1984)

Whittaker, Molly, *Jews and Christians: Graeco-Roman Views* (Cambridge: Cambridge University Press, 1984)

Wilken, R. L., *The Christians as the Romans Saw Them* (New Haven and London: Yale University Press, 1984)

Williams, A. Lukyn, *Justin Martyr: The Dialogue with Trypho* (London: SPCK, 1930)

Winger, M., 'Act One: Paul Arrives in Galatia', *NTS* 48 (2002) 548–67

'The Law of Christ', *NTS* 46 (2000) 537–46

Winter, B. W., 'The Imperial Cult and Early Christians in Roman Galatia (Acts XIII 13-50 and Galatians VI 11-18', in T. Drew-Bear, M. Tashalan, and C. M. Thomas, eds., *Actes du Ier Congrès International sur Antioche de Pisidie* (Université Lumière-Lyon 2 and Diffusion de Boccard, 2002)

Witulski, T., *Die Adressaten des Galaterbriefes. Untersuchungen zur Gemeinde von Antiochia ad Pisidiam* (Göttingen: Vandenhoeck & Ruprecht, 2000)

Wright, N. T., 'Five Gospels but No Gospel', in B. Chilton and C. A. Evans, eds., *Authenticating the Activities of Jesus* (Leiden: Brill, 1999)

Yadin, Y., 'Expedition D', *Israel Exploration Journal* 11 (1961) 41–2

Zahn, Th., *Geschichte des neutestamentlichen Kanons* (Erlangen: Deichert, 1888)

    Grundriss der Geschichte des neutestamentlichen Kanons, 2nd edn (Leipzig: Deichert, 1904)

Zanker, P., *The Power of Images in the Age of Augustus* (Ann Arbor: University of Michigan Press, 1990)

Index of passages cited

Old Testament

Isaiah
1.3   97
1.16–20   97
3.9–11   98
5.18–20   98
9.1   116
29.18   15
35.1–7   129
35.5–6   15
40.9   13
52.5   98
52.7   13, 17, 21
58.6   184
60.6   13
61   14–15, 17–18, 99
61.1   184
61.1–2   11, 13, 15, 16, 17, 20, 22

Jeremiah
7.11   98

Ezekiel
1   65

Micah
5.2   98

Old Testament apocrypha

Sirach
29.1   116

Testament of Levi
16.3   135

Tobit
14.9   116

New Testament

Matthew
1.23   116
2.5   98
4.16   116
4.17   116
4.22   116
4.23   57, 58, 60
5.17–19   116
5.21–48   116
6.9–11   55
7.12   116
7.15   105

General index